Business Traveler's Atlas

By Christine Miles, Janet Bamford, and Alice Huston

Produced by Spade & Archer, Inc.
New York

CONTENTS

J.C. Suarés, Dominique Bluhdorn, and Stephen D. Kaplan.

Editing: Christine Miles *Reporting:* Janet Bamford and Alice Huston *Factchecking:* Mary Makarushka
Copyediting: Catherine Schurdak *Production:* Gates Studio

H.M. Gousha
A Division of Simon & Schuster Inc.
A Paramount Communications Company

ISBN 0-13-092115-7

Problem-Solving in Thirty-Five Cities

Your plane roars into Houston at 4:30pm, one hour late, and you need to know who can still have your business documents typeset by the following morning. Or your rented Ford Taurus runs out of steam on the Massachusetts Turnpike, and you need to know how to get towing help. Or maybe you just want to avoid the notorious traffic jams in downtown Chicago on your way to that 5:30pm seminar.

The *Business Travelers Atlas* was designed with the frustrations of being on the road in mind. It will give you all the pertinent information about local business services, city convention centers, airport transportation, getting around town, fitness clubs, sports, entertainment, and shopping areas. But this atlas avoids the "just the facts, ma'am" attitude of other business travelers guides. Here, you will find keys to unlocking almost any problem you may encounter in an unfamiliar city—or even in a familiar one—and that's what a successful business trip is all about.

All this practical information is accompanied by maps and text designed to ease stress and worry during your trip.

Maps: Regional maps, city street maps, downtown maps, and airport diagrams help you telescope in on exactly what you need to know. They show routes from airports to downtown areas, visitors centers, convention facilities, major shopping areas, and sports arenas, as well as outlying business communities.

City-By-City Guides: Each entry begins with a business brief about the city and the major information phone numbers. Airline flying times are realistic and may include allowances for changing planes en route. Detailed explanations about travel to the city and then into the city-center are followed by tips for those on "Overland Adventures"—traveling by car, train, or limo. A special section called "Bottleneck Busters" tells which areas to avoid during rush hour, or those under construction.

International Travelers: This section isolates the specific needs of travelers from other countries. You'll find currency exchange locations, consulates, foreign business association offices, translation services, and newsstands with publications from around the world. In Boston, you'll even find a limo service with drivers who speak Japanese.

Business Visitor's Needs: You'll find many 'round-the-clock services like messengers, couriers, copying and faxing companies, printers and secretarial firms, and, in many cases, extended hours to accommodate the business traveler. Twenty-four hour pharmacy phone numbers are included, as are those for major hospitals,

and dental referral numbers for those 2:30am toothaches.

Descriptions of each city's convention centers are supplemented with information numbers for meetings and special transportation. Sports facilities get the same value-added coverage: facts about a city's sports teams, information numbers, and playing arenas let every sports fan devise his own game plan. Same-day ticket numbers are included for cultural events and a taste of what the city has to offer in the way of music, theater, and dance.

Home Away From Home: The atlas's list of toll-free numbers for hotel chains is complemented by mention of special places to stay that may appeal to the traveler with the desire to diversify. These selections are usually one-of-a-kind, quaint, or top-quality.

If you have specific requirements or business needs (like faxing or copying), check with your hotel ahead of time. In the war to get occupants, many hotels will exaggerate the ease with which you can get business services. But major business hotels now have machines available to guests in their lobby or in meeting rooms. At the very least, the manager should be able to help you find a solution to your problem, even if it involves an outside service. This kind of convenience is what really distinguishes business hotels from budget hotels. (By the way, a recent survey found that business travelers using budget hotels did so by choice, and that their average household income, education levels, and likelihood of having a profession were just as high as those using luxury hotels.)

Dining: The restaurants listed are selected for the "accidental diner" who'd rather be in his or her favorite little place at home. The section's title, "Four Stars and Our Stars," reflects the choice of world-class restaurants and the lesser-known, dependable, and less pricey places to break bread. These were gleaned from recommendations by local business people.

Tone Away From Home: Being on the road doesn't have to mean being away from a fitness routine. Many health clubs offer traveler's privileges. Most cities have jogging trails and almost any major hotel will have its own exercise room and possibly a pool. Many have also struck cooperative arrangements with local sport operators and workout clubs. Bikers will find rentals listed, and golfers, bring your clubs: public golf courses are included for each city.

Shopping: The shopping guide was designed with the business shopper in mind. You'll find the best places to buy clothes for corporate meetings and dinners, where to get that last-minute professional thank-you, and how to steer clear of the areas catering only to the tourist crowd.

CROSSING THE BORDER

Canada:
U.S. citizens do not need passports, but should carry proof of citizenship. Persons under 18, not traveling with an adult, should submit a letter permitting them to travel in Canada.

Canada admits vehicles and trailers for touring up to 12 months without fee. U.S. licensed amateur radio operators may operate their stations (not exceeding 100 milli-watts in power) in Canada but must comply with both U.S. and Canadian regulations. For more information, contact DOS-F Radio Regulatory Branch, Dept. of Communications, Ottawa, Ontario, K1A 0C8, Canada. Transportation of firearms into Canada is rigidly controlled. For information governing hunting and fishing in Canada, contact the Fish and Game Department in the

province you plan to visit.

Each U.S. resident who has been in Canada 48 hours may bring in to the U.S., duty free, articles purchased for personal use, and not intended for resale, to a retail value of $400, if he/she has not claimed the exemption during the preceding 30 days. Ask Customs officials about regulations governing the importation of alcoholic beverages and tobacco.

For more information, write: Canadian Government Office of Tourism, 235 Queen Street, Ottawa, Ontario, K1A 0H6, Canada.

Mexico:
U.S. citizens do not need passports, but must have proof of citizenship. All persons must carry the free Tourist Card, which is available

at the border. Persons under 18, not traveling with both parents, require additional documents. Consult nearest Mexican Consulate or Mexican Tourist Office for further information.

Car permits are obtainable at the border upon presentation of driver's license and proof of ownership. It's advisable to arrange for Mexican insurance; U.S. automobile insurance is not valid in Mexico. Contact your agent for more information. Border town visits of less than 72 hours do not require the Tourist Card, passport or car permit. Gasoline is readily available on main highways. On other roads fill tank often.

Citizens band radios may be used in Mexico. Inquire locally for usable channels. Firearms may not be taken into Mexico except for hunting trips. Contact the nearest Mexican Consulate in advance for details.

Each U.S. resident may bring back into the U.S., duty free, articles purchased in Mexico for personal or household use, and not intended for resale, to a retail value of $300, if he/she has not claimed the exemption during the preceding 30 days.

It is recommended that dollars be exchanged for pesos only at airport exchange booths or banks in the U.S. or Mexico. Be sure credit card charges are in pesos, not dollars.

For more information, contact the Mexican Consulate nearest you.

R O A D   C O N D I T I O N   N U M B E R S

AL 205-353-0631	IN NORTH 317-232-8300	800-332-6171	OR 503-238-8400
AK 907-243-7675	SOUTH 317-232-8298	(In-State MT only)	PA 717-939-9871
AZ 602-256-7706	IA 515-288-1047	NE 402-471-4533	RI 401-647-3311
AR 501-371-2157	KS 913-296-3102	NV NORTH 1-702-793-1313	SC 803-737-1030
CA 916-445-7623	KY 502-564-3579	SOUTH 1-702-385-0181	SD 605-773-3536
CO EAST 303-639-1234	LA 504-925-6325	(Winter only)	TN 615-741-2060
WEST 303-639-1111	ME 207-289-3427	NH 603-485-5767	TX 512-463-8588
CT 203-566-4880	MD 301-768-7000	NJ 609-530-3718	UT 801-964-6000
DE 302-736-5851	MA 617-566-4500	NM 505-827-5594	VA 804-786-3181
DC 202-936-1212	MI 800-543-2937 (Winter only)	NY 518-457-6811	VT 802-828-2648
(Weather only)	MN 612-296-3076	518-449-1293	WA 206-976-ROAD
FL 904-385-5175	MS 601-987-1212	(Thruway Report)	WV 304-348-3758
GA 404-656-5267	MO 314-636-5171	NC 919-733-3861	WI 608-266-7040
ID 208-334-3665	(Central MO only)	ND 800-472-2686	WY 307-635-9966
IL 217-782-5730	MT 406-444-6339	OH 614-466-2660	(October 1-April 30)
(November 15-April 1)	(November 1-April 15)	OK 405-425-2385	

T O L L - F R E E   E X T R A S   (D I A L   1 - 8 0 0   P L U S   T H E   N U M B E R)

Money
Cirrus 424-7787
Plus 843-7587
Overnight and
Worldwide Delivery
Federal Express 238-5355
Emery & Purolator 645-3333

DHL Worldwide 225-5345
Credit Cards
American Express:
Travelers Cheque Refunds and
   Lost or Stolen Credit Cards
   528-4800
   (from NYC: 212-477-5700)

Express Cash 227-4669
Global Assistance Hotline
   554-2639
AT&T 222-0400
Diners Club/Carte Blanche
   525-9135
Citicorp Card 638-4767

Discover Card 322-4566
Communications
Western Union:
Credit Card 325-4176
Mailgram/Cable 325-6000
Se Habla Español 325-4045

H O T E L / M O T E L   8 0 0   D I R E C T O R Y

Best Western Incorporated
800-528-1234
Clarion Hotels and Resorts
800-252-7466
Comfort Inn
800-228-5150
Days Inn of America
800-325-2525
Downtowner Motor Inn
800-238-6161
800-582-6173
(Tennessee only)
Econo-Travel Lodges
800-446-6900
Embassy Suites

800-EMBASSY
Friendship Inns
International
800-453-4511
Hilton Inns
800-445-8667
Holiday Inns Incorporated
800-465-4329
Howard Johnson
800-654-2000
Hyatt Hotels
800-228-9000
La Quinta Motor Inns
800-531-5900
Marriott Hotels

800-228-9290
Master Host/Red Carpet/
Scottish Inns of America
800-251-1962
Motel 6 Incorporated
505-891-6161
National 9 Inns
800-521-9999
Quality Inns
800-228-5151
Ramada Inns
800-228-2828
Red Roof Inns
800-848-7878
Rodeway Inns of America

800-228-2000
Sheraton Hotels and Motor Inns
800-325-3535
Sonesta Hotels
800-343-7170
Super 8 Motels
800-343-7170
TraveLodge
800-255-3050
Treadway Inns and Resorts
800-631-0182
201-368-9624 (New Jersey
residents, call collect)
Western International Hotels
800-228-3000

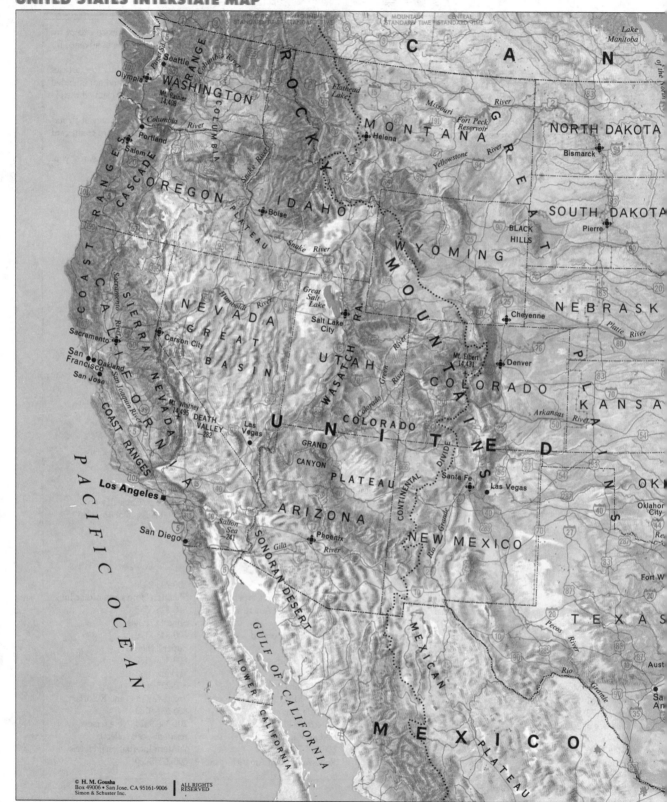

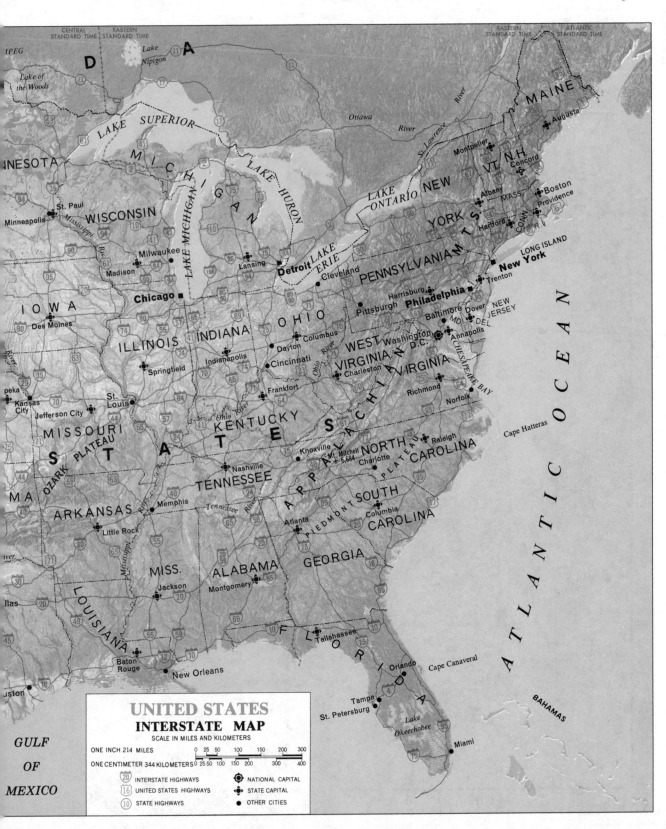

UNITED STATES
INTERSTATE MAP
SCALE IN MILES AND KILOMETERS

ONE INCH 214 MILES

ONE CENTIMETER 344 KILOMETERS

0 25 50 100 150 200 300

0 25 50 100 150 200 300 400

20 INTERSTATE HIGHWAYS

16 UNITED STATES HIGHWAYS

10 STATE HIGHWAYS

◉ NATIONAL CAPITAL

◆ STATE CAPITAL

● OTHER CITIES

PACIFIC STATES

Alaska - California - Hawaii - Oregon - Washington

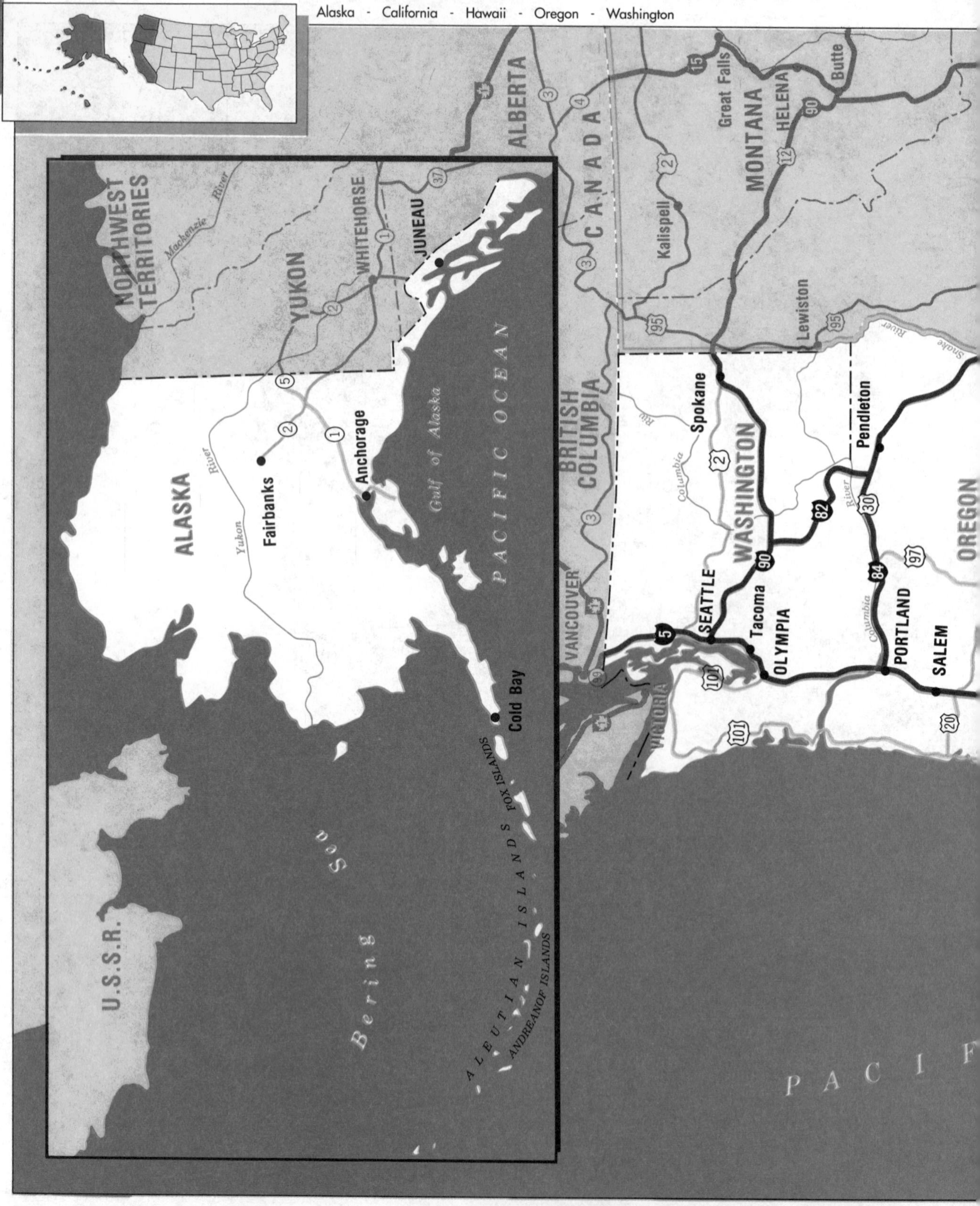

ALBERTA

CANADA

Great Falls

15

Butte

HELENA

MONTANA

90

3

4

12

2

Kalispell

NORTHWEST
TERRITORIES

Mackenzie River

YUKON

37

1

WHITEHORSE

JUNEAU

2

95

Lewiston

95

Snake River

BRITISH
COLUMBIA

3

3

Columbia River

Spokane

2

WASHINGTON

Pendleton

5

Yukon River

Fairbanks

2

1

Anchorage

ALASKA

Gulf of Alaska

PACIFIC OCEAN

82

90

30

River

OREGON

SEATLE

Tacoma

84

97

VANCOUVER

5

OLYMPIA

PORTLAND

SALEM

Columbia

101

VICTORIA

101

20

Cold Bay

FOX ISLANDS

Bering Sea

U.S.S.R.

ALEUTIAN ISLANDS

ANDREANOF ISLANDS

PACIFI

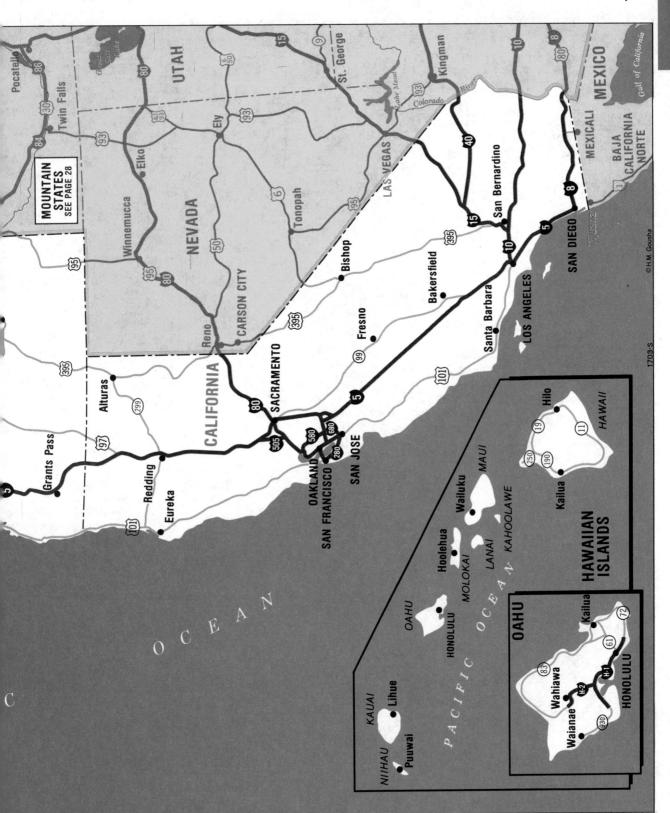

©H.M. Gousha

7-IV-428-S

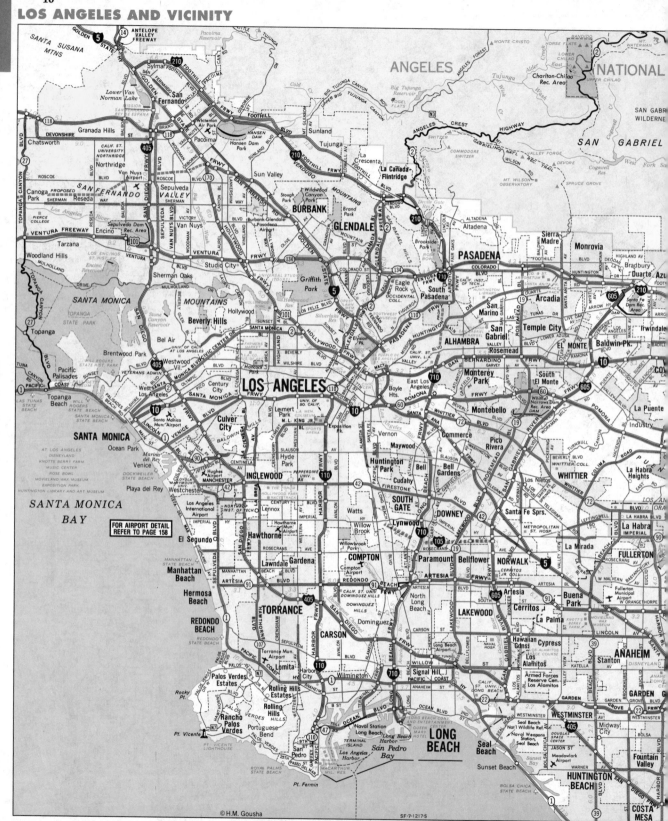

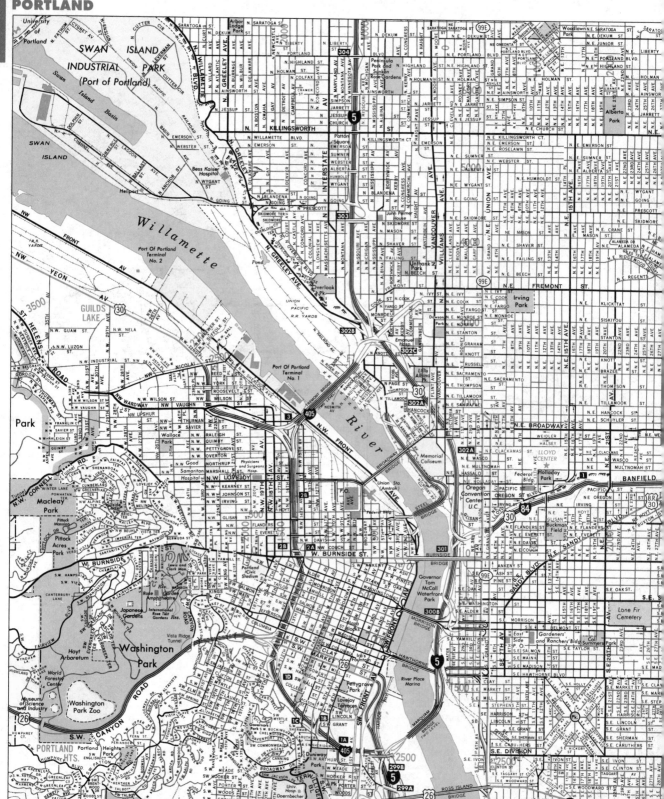

© H.M. Gousha

PORTLAND AND VICINITY

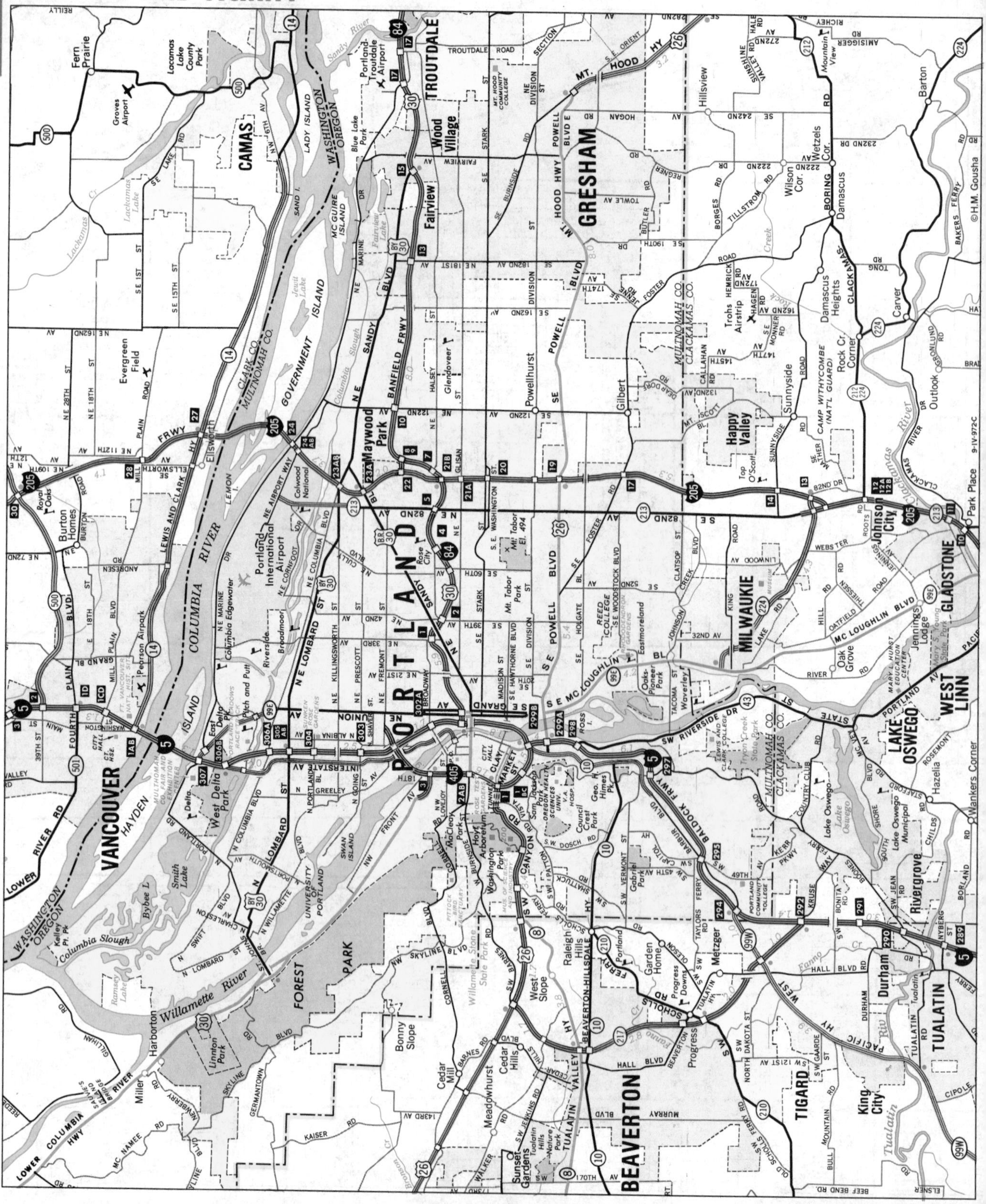

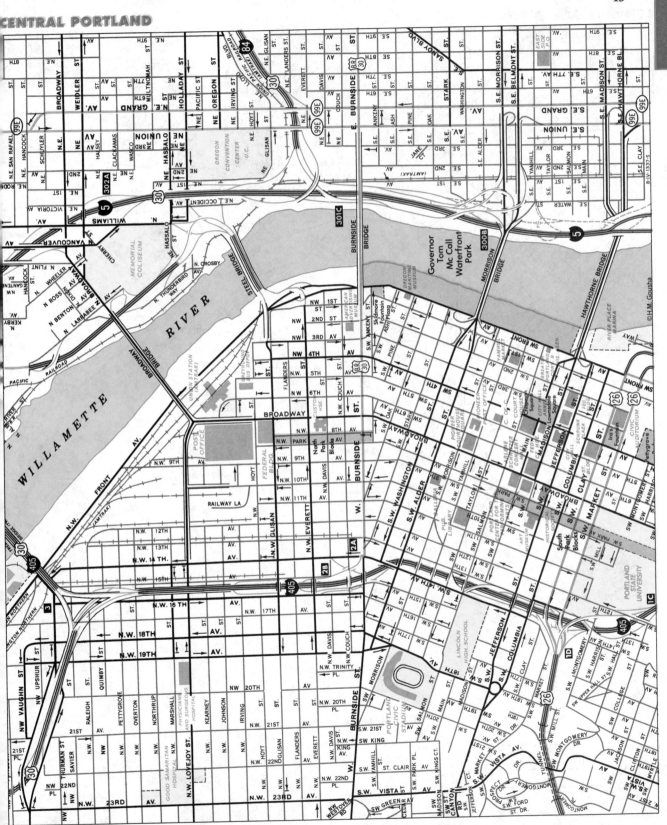

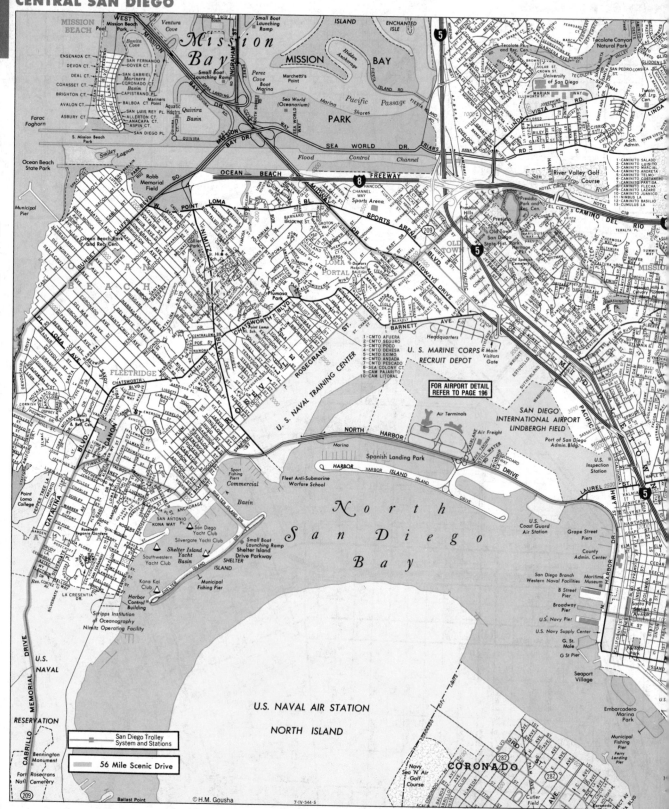

San Diego Trolley System and Stations

56 Mile Scenic Drive

© H.M. Gousha   7-IV-544-5

SAN DIEGO AND VICINITY

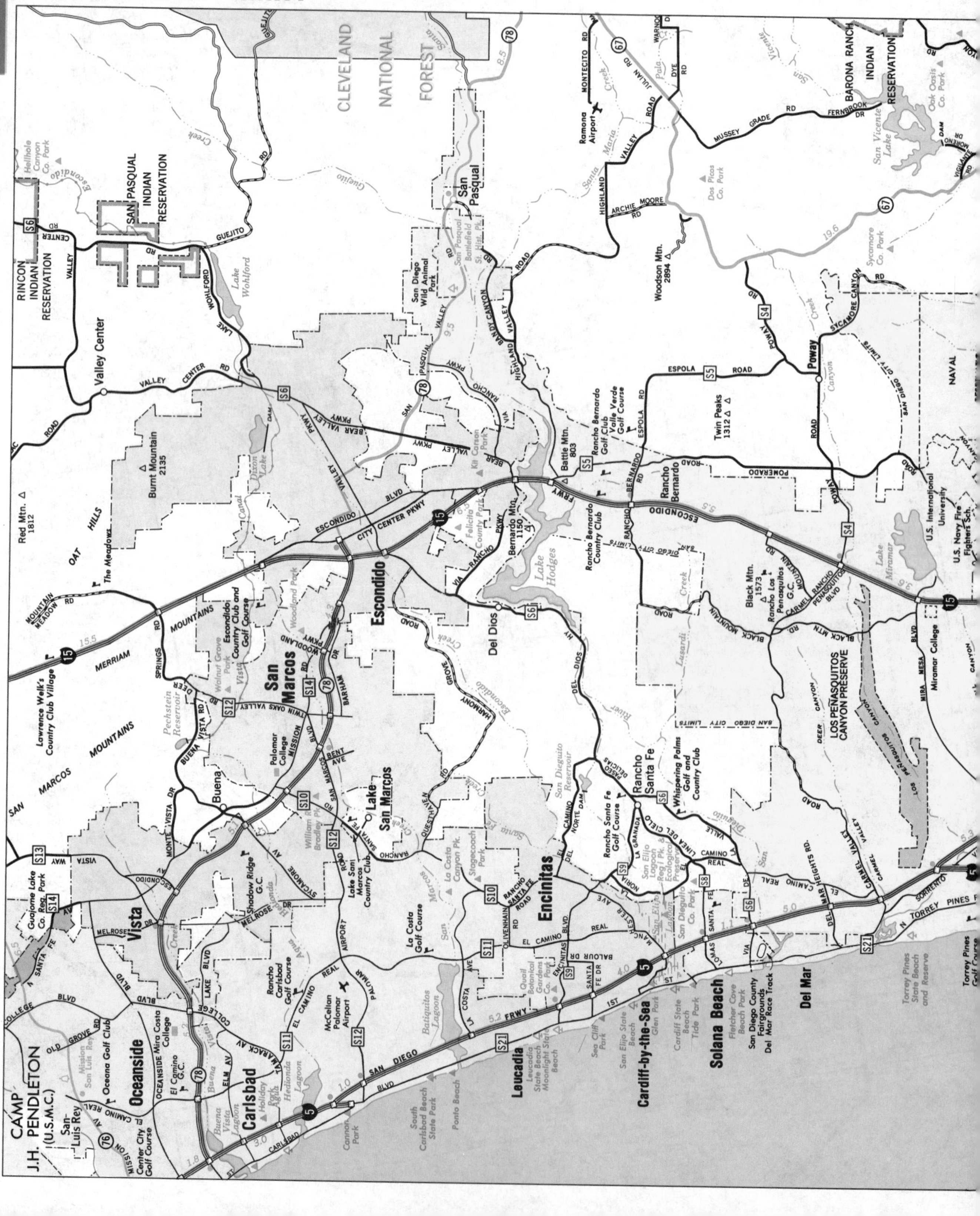

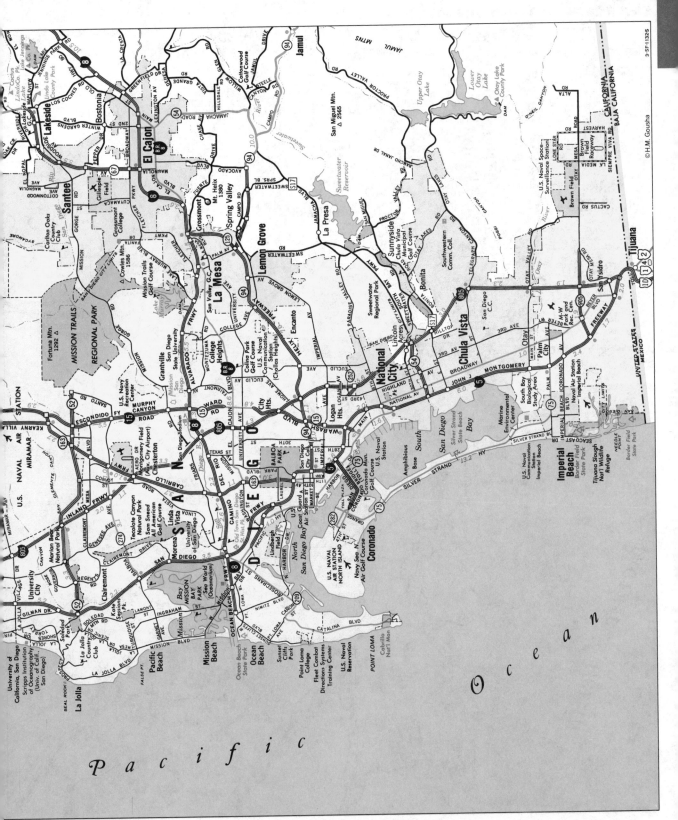

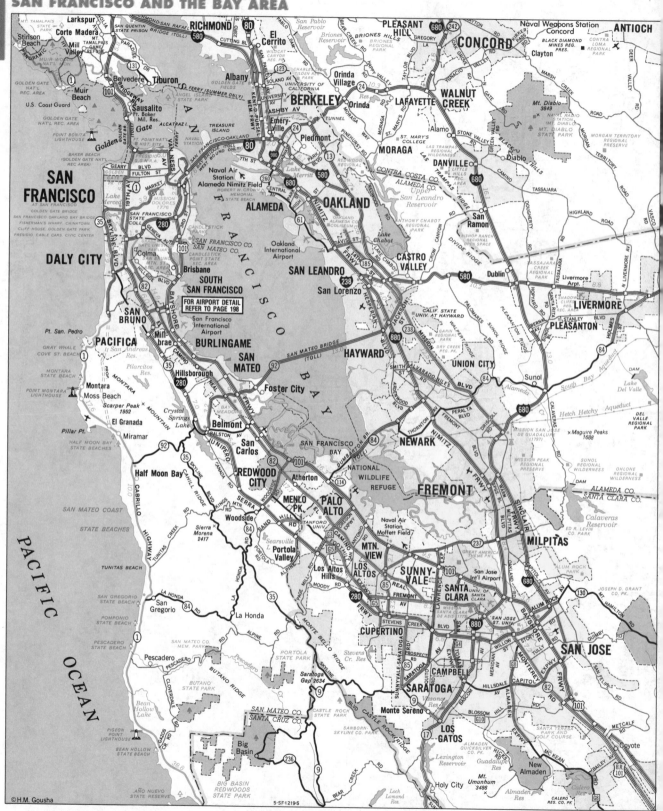

FOR AIRPORT DETAIL
REFER TO PAGE 198

© H.M. Gousha

5-SF-1219-S

SAN FRANCISCO

Bay Area Rapid Transit System and Stations

49 Mile Scenic Drive

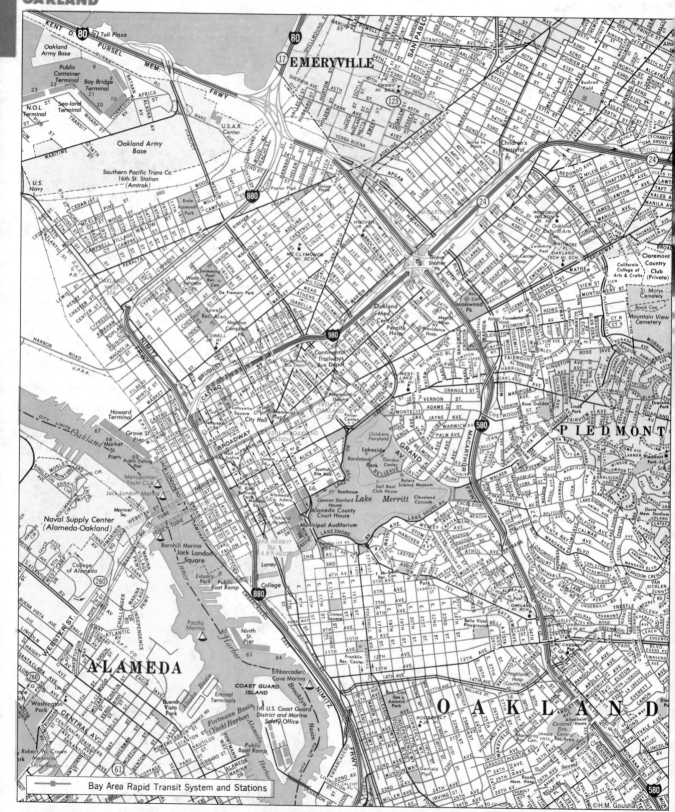

Bay Area Rapid Transit System and Stations

©H.M. Gousha

SAN JOSE

Guadalupe Corridor Light
Rail System and Stations.

©H.M. Gousha

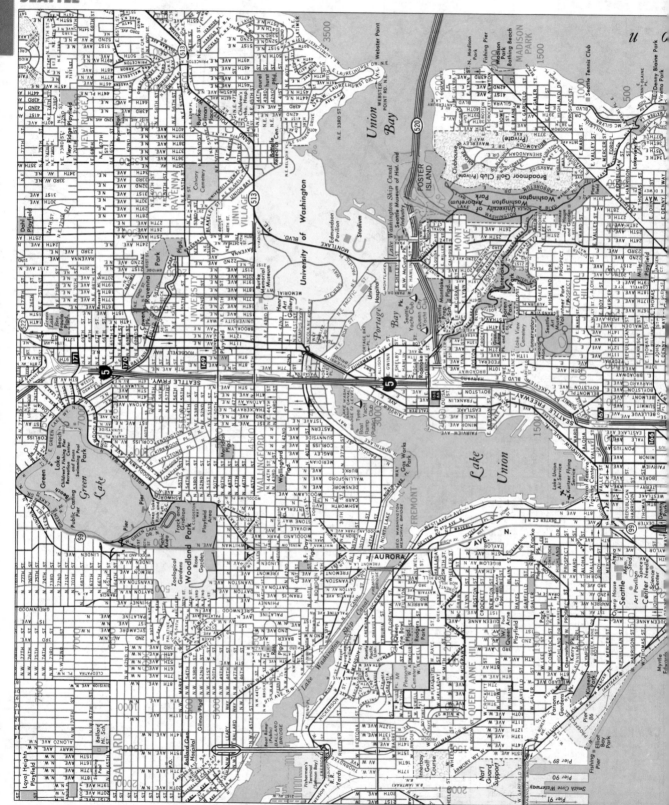

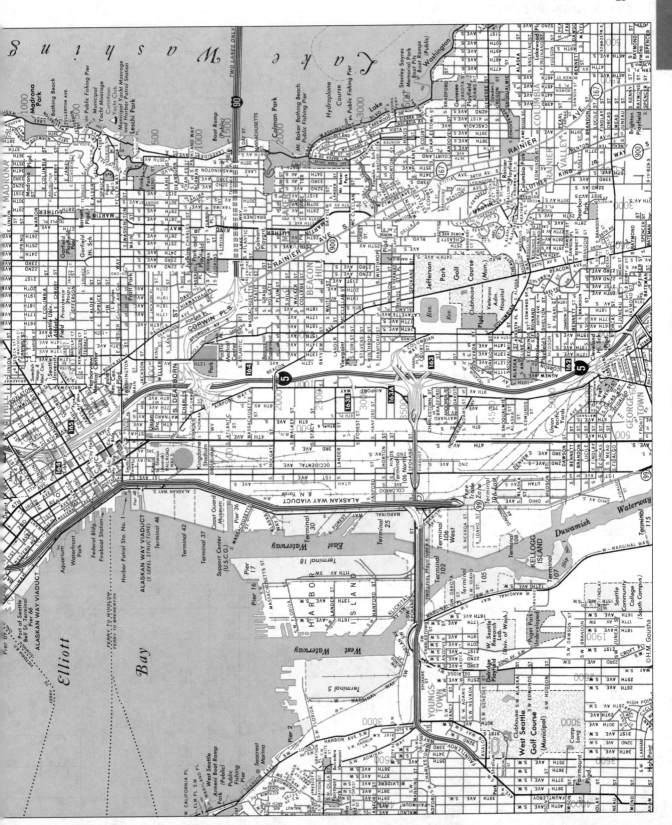

SEATTLE AND VICINITY

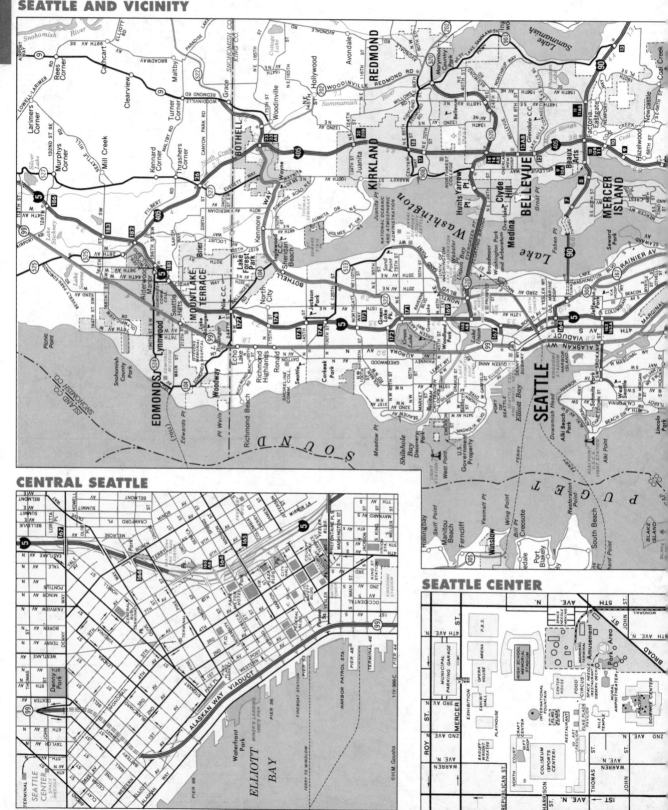

CENTRAL SEATTLE

SEATTLE CENTER

MOUNTAIN STATES

Arizona - Colorado - Idaho - Montana - Nevada - New Mexico - Utah - Wyoming

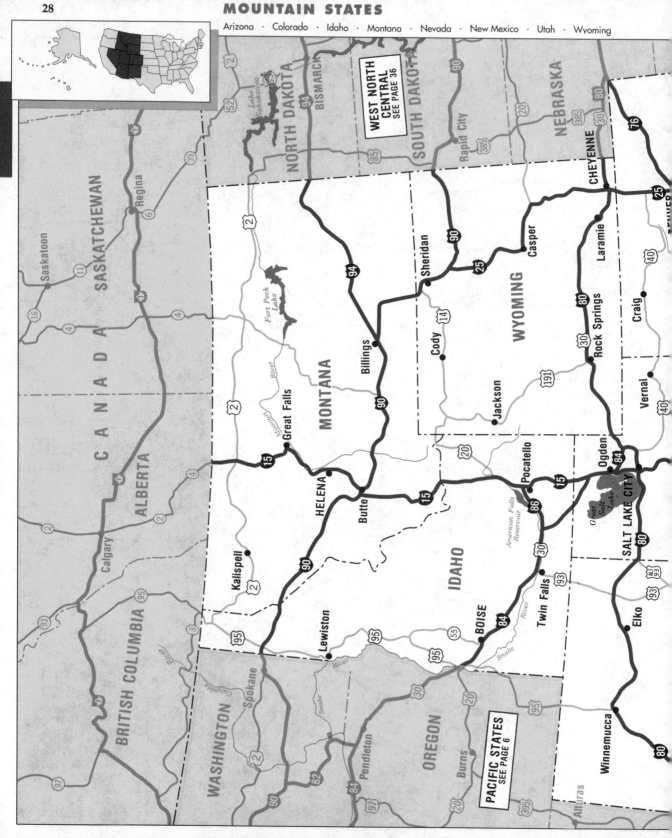

WEST NORTH CENTRAL SEE PAGE 36

PACIFIC STATES SEE PAGE 6

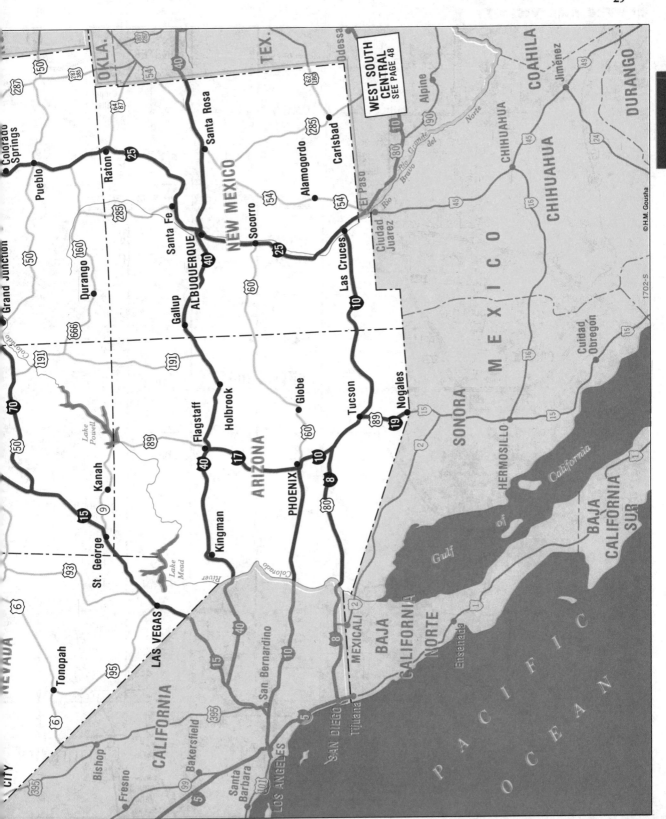

WEST SOUTH
CENTRAL
SEE PAGE 48

PACIFIC OCEAN

NEVADA

CALIFORNIA

ARIZONA

NEW MEXICO

TEX.

OKLA.

MEXICO

SONORA

CHIHUAHUA

COAHILA

DURANGO

BAJA CALIFORNIA NORTE

BAJA CALIFORNIA SUR

Colorado Springs
Pueblo
Grand Junction
Raton
Santa Rosa
Santa Fe
ALBUQUERQUE
Socorro
Alamogordo
Carlsbad
El Paso
Las Cruces
Ciudad Juarez
Durango
Gallup
Holbrook
Globe
Tucson
Nogales
Flagstaff
PHOENIX
Kingman
Kanab
St. George
LAS VEGAS
Tonopah
Bishop
Fresno
Bakersfield
Santa Barbara
LOS ANGELES
San Bernardino
SAN DIEGO
Tijuana
MEXICALI
Ensenada
HERMOSILLO
Cuidad Obregón
CHIHUAHUA
Jiménez
Alpine
Odessa

©H.M. Gousha

1702-S

©H.M. Gousha

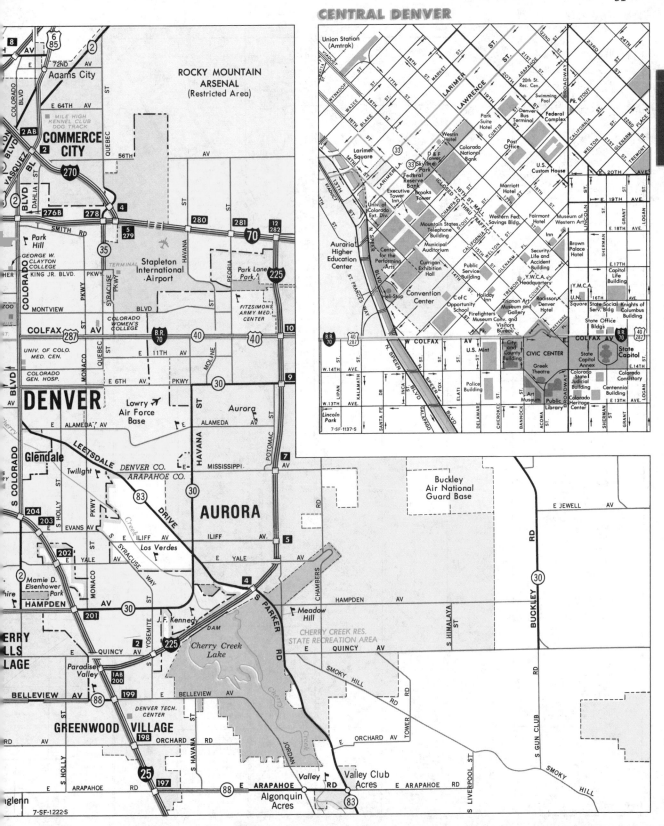

CENTRAL DENVER

ROCKY MOUNTAIN
ARSENAL
(Restricted Area)

Aaams City

Adams City

COMMERCE
CITY

Park
Hill

MILE HIGH
KENNEL CLUB
DOG TRACK

GEORGE W.
CLAYTON
COLLEGE

KING JR. BLVD.

Stapleton
International
Airport

Park Lane
Park

FITZSIMONS
ARMY MED.
CENTER

COLORADO
WOMEN'S
COLLEGE

MONTVIEW

COLFAX AV

UNIV. OF COLO.
MED. CEN.

COLORADO
GEN. HOSP.

DENVER

Lowry
Air Force
Base

Aurora

Glendale

Twilight

DENVER CO.
ARAPAHOE CO.

Creek

AURORA

Los Verdes

Mamie D.
Eisenhower
Park

HAMPDEN

J.F. Kennedy

DAM

Cherry Creek
Lake

CHERRY
HILLS
VILLAGE

Paradise
Valley

Meadow
Hill

CHERRY CREEK RES.
STATE RECREATION AREA

BELLEVIEW AV

DENVER TECH.
CENTER

GREENWOOD VILLAGE

ORCHARD

Valley

Valley Club
Acres

Algonquin
Acres

inglenn

7-SF-1222-S

Buckley
Air National
Guard Base

E JEWELL AV

SMOKY HILL

Central Denver detail

Union Station
(Amtrak)

20th St.
Rec. Cen.

Swimming
Pool

LARIMER ST.

LAWRENCE

Denver Bus
Terminal

Federal
Complex

Park
Suite
Hotel

Westin
Hotel

Larimer Square

Colorado
National
Bank

Post
Office

D & F
Tower

Skyline
Park

U.S.
Custom House

Federal
Reserve
Bank

Brooks
Tower

Executive
Tower Inn

Univ. of
Colorado
Ext. Div.

Marriott
Hotel

Western Fed.
Savings Bldg.

Fairmont
Hotel

Museum of
Western Art

Brown
Palace
Hotel

Capitol
Life
Building

Auraria
Higher
Education
Center

Center
for the
Performing
Arts

Mountain States
Telephone
Building

Municipal
Auditorium

Security
Life and
Accident
Building

Y.W.C.A.
Headquarters

Public
Service
Building

Curigan
Exhibition
Hall

Y.M.C.A.

Heli-Stop

Convention
Center

C of C
Opportunity
School

Holiday
Inn

Radisson
Denver
Hotel

Trianon Art
Museum and
Gallery

U.N.
Square

State Social
Serv. Bldg

Knights of
Columbus
Building

Firefighters
Museum Conv. and
Visitors Bureau

State Office
Bldgs

W COLFAX AV

COLFAX AV

U.S. Mint

City
and County
Building

CIVIC CENTER

Greek
Theatre

State
Capitol
Annex

State
Capitol

Police
Building

Art
Museum

Public
Library

Colorado
State
Judicial
Building

Colorado
Heritage
Center

Colorado
Consistory

State
Office
Bldgs

Centennial
Building

Lincoln
Park

7-SF-1137-S

PHOENIX AND VICINITY

© H.M. Gousha

CENTRAL PHOENIX

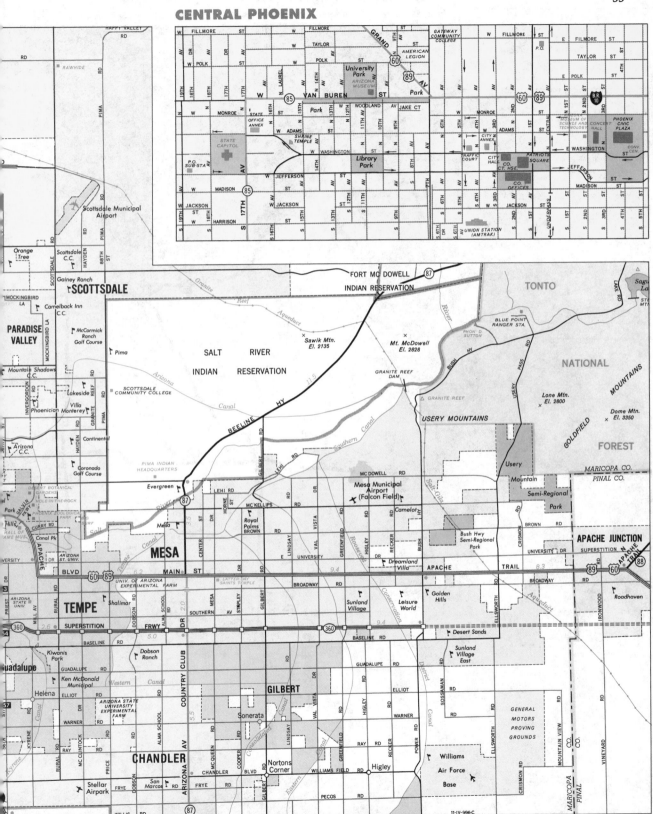

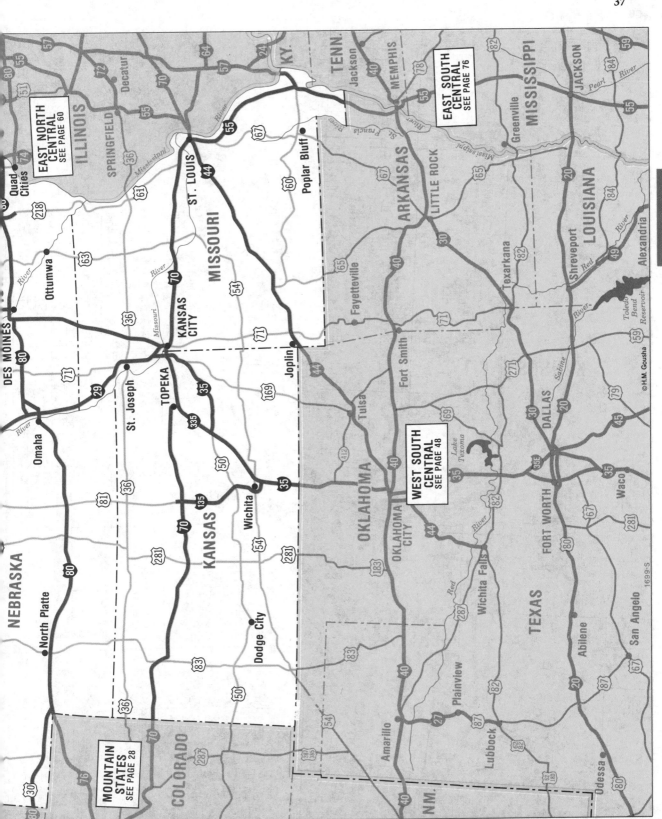

37

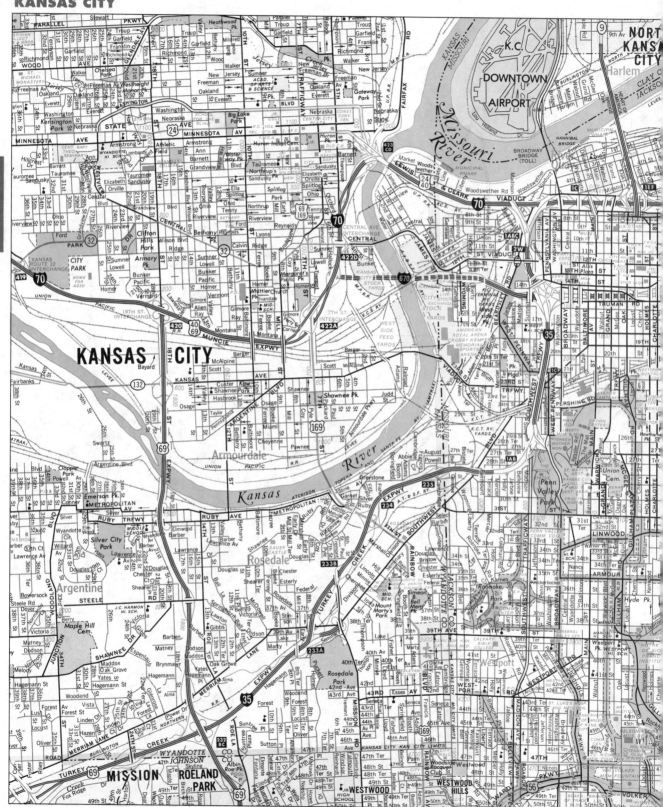

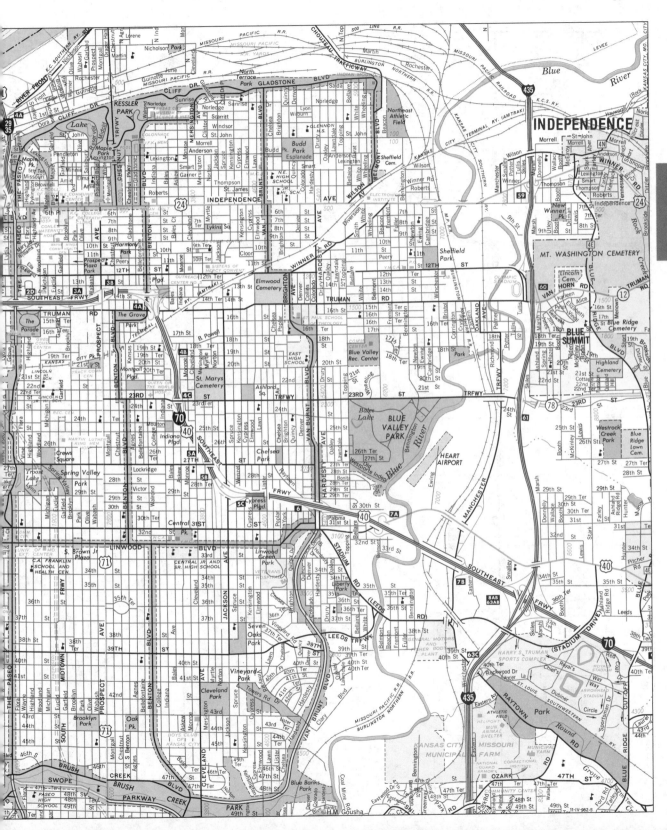

CENTRAL KANSAS CITY

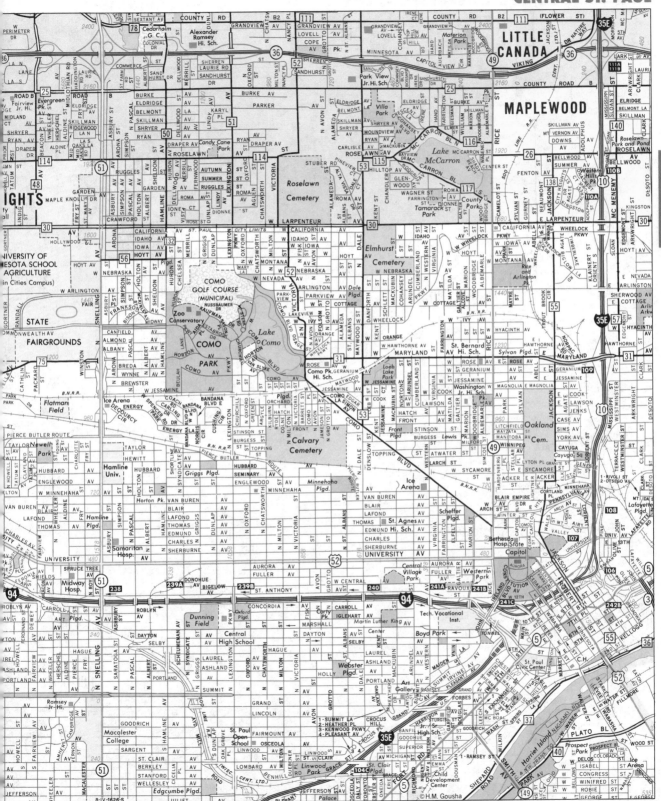

© H.M. Gousha

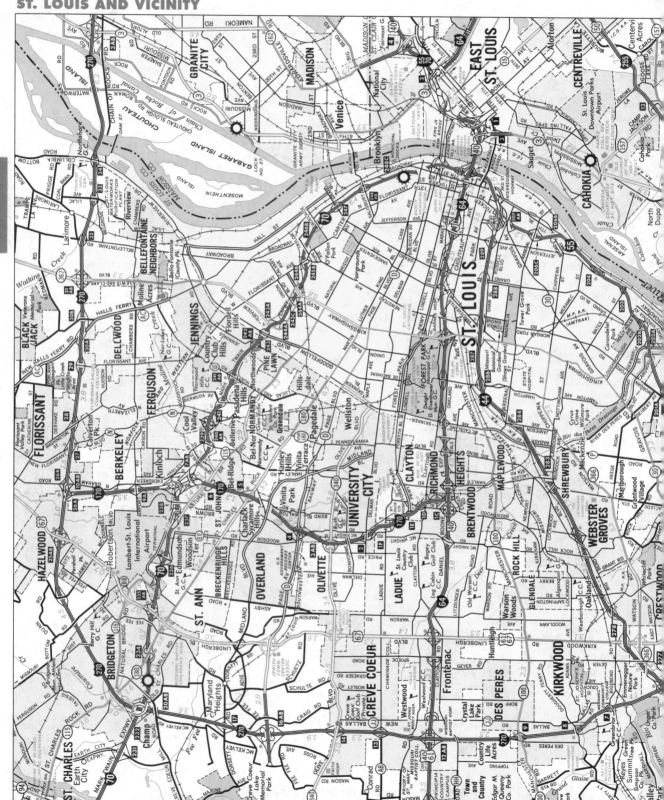

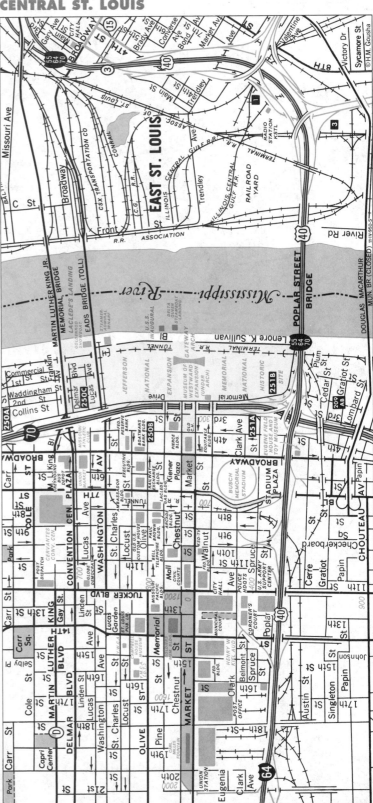

WEST SOUTH CENTRAL

Arkansas - Louisiana - Oklahoma - Texas

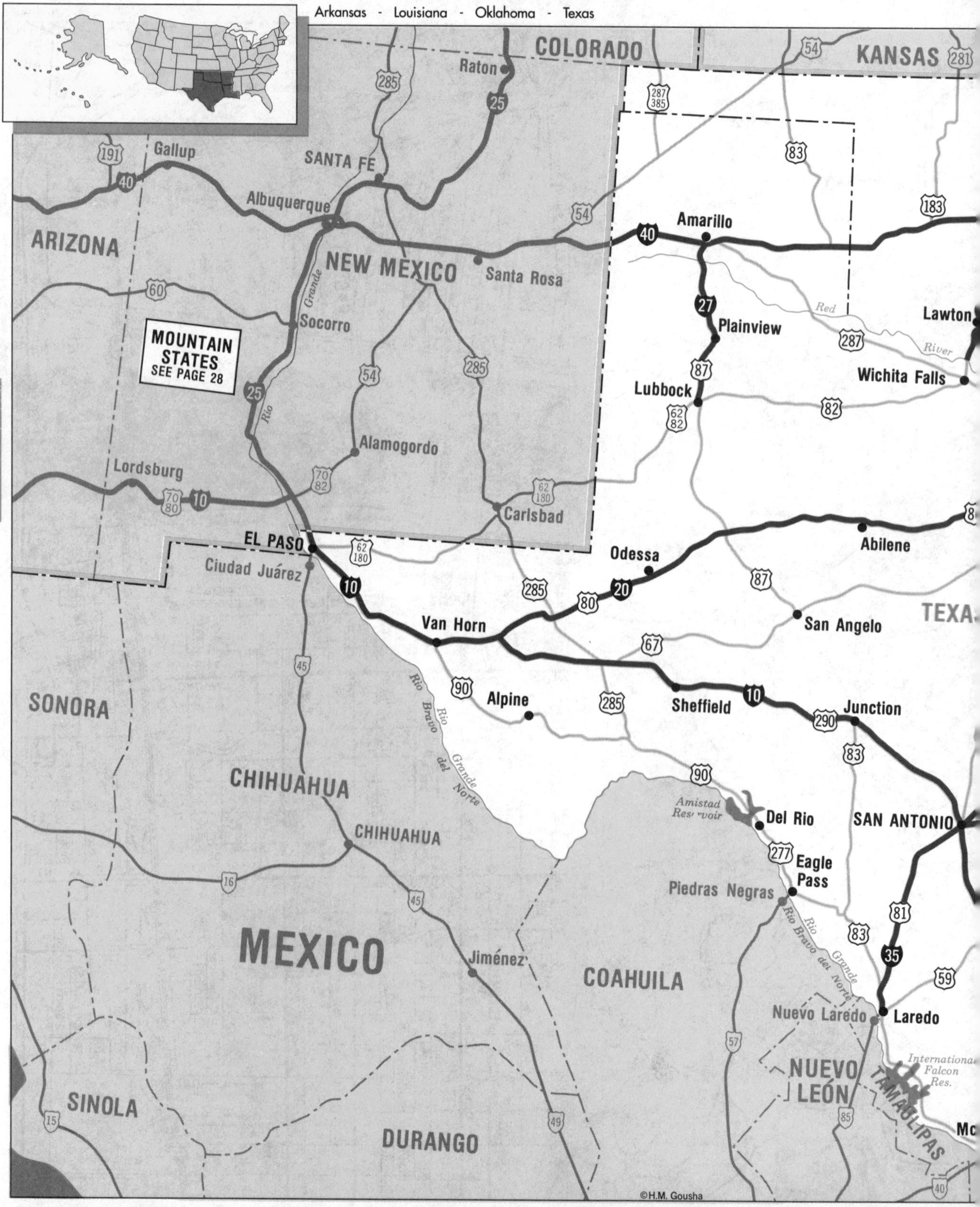

COLORADO

KANSAS

Raton

SANTA FE

Gallup

Albuquerque

ARIZONA

NEW MEXICO

Santa Rosa

Amarillo

Lawton

Plainview

MOUNTAIN
STATES
SEE PAGE 28

Socorro

Lubbock

Wichita Falls

Alamogordo

Lordsburg

Carlsbad

EL PASO

Odessa

Abilene

Ciudad Juárez

TEXAS

Van Horn

San Angelo

SONORA

Alpine

Sheffield

Junction

CHIHUAHUA

Amistad
Reservoir

Del Rio

SAN ANTONIO

CHIHUAHUA

Eagle
Pass

Piedras Negras

MEXICO

Jiménez

COAHUILA

Nuevo Laredo

Laredo

International
Falcon
Res.

SINOLA

NUEVO
LEÓN

DURANGO

TAMAULIPAS

©H.M. Gousha

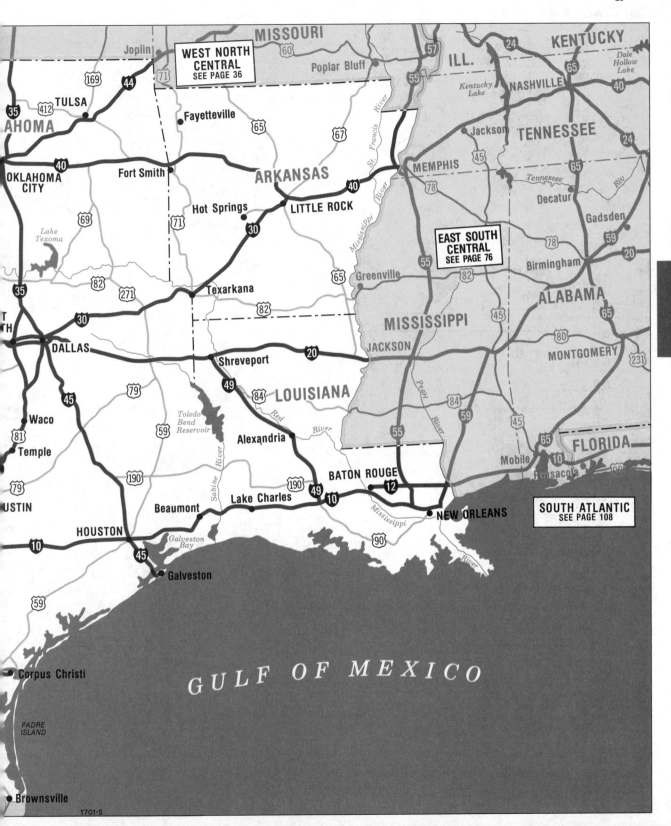

MISSOURI

WEST NORTH
CENTRAL
SEE PAGE 36

Joplin
Poplar Bluff

KENTUCKY

ILL.

Dale
Hollow
Lake

NASHVILLE

Kentucky
Lake

Fayetteville

TULSA

AHOMA

TENNESSEE

Jackson

ARKANSAS

MEMPHIS

Decatur

Gadsden

OKLAHOMA
CITY

Fort Smith

LITTLE ROCK

Hot Springs

St. Francis River

Mississippi River

EAST SOUTH
CENTRAL
SEE PAGE 76

Tennessee Riv.

Birmingham

Lake
Texoma

Greenville

ALABAMA

Texarkana

MISSISSIPPI

DALLAS

Jackson

Shreveport

MONTGOMERY

LOUISIANA

Toledo
Bend
Reservoir

Red River

Waco

Alexandria

FLORIDA

Temple

Pearl River

Mobile

Pensacola

Baton Rouge

Lake Charles

Sabine River

Beaumont

NEW ORLEANS

SOUTH ATLANTIC
SEE PAGE 108

HOUSTON

Galveston
Bay

Mississippi River

Galveston

USTIN

Corpus Christi

GULF OF MEXICO

PADRE
ISLAND

Brownsville

1701-S

© H.M. Gousha

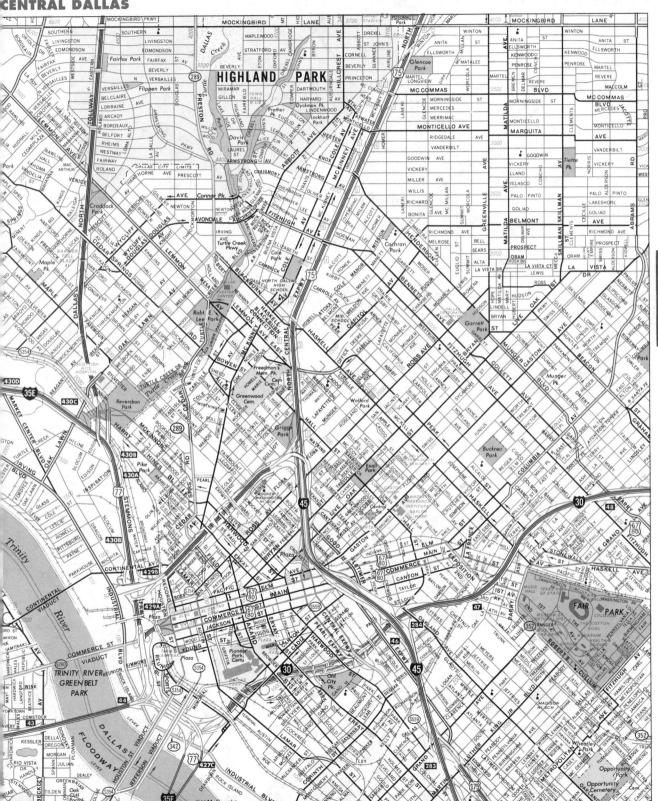

© H.M. Gousha

6-SF-1054-S

DALLAS- FORT WORTH AND VICINITY

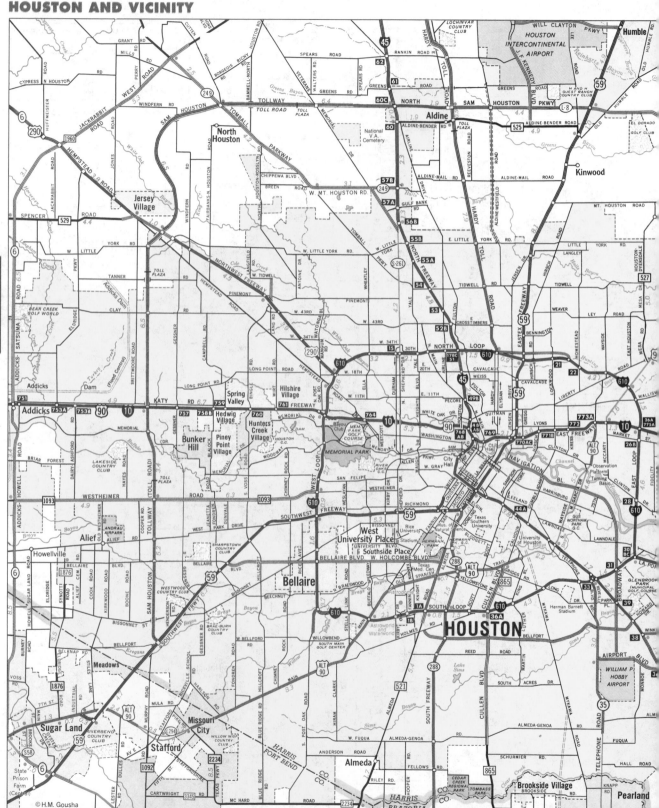

©H.M. Gousha

CENTRAL HOUSTON

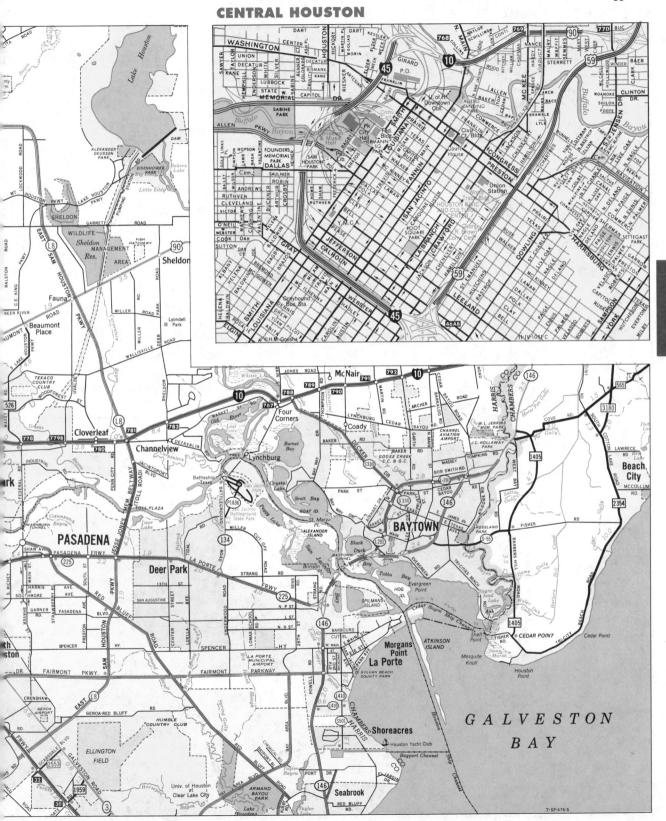

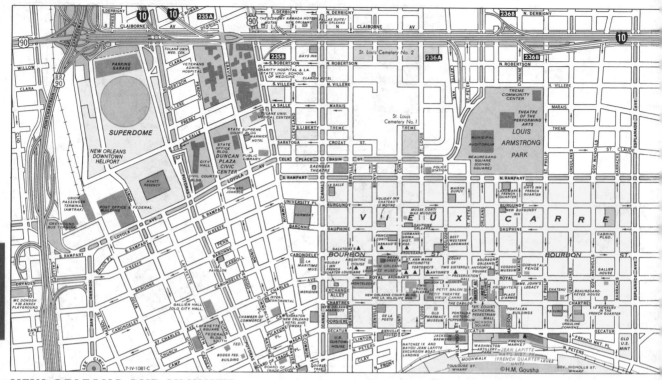

NEW ORLEANS AND VICINITY

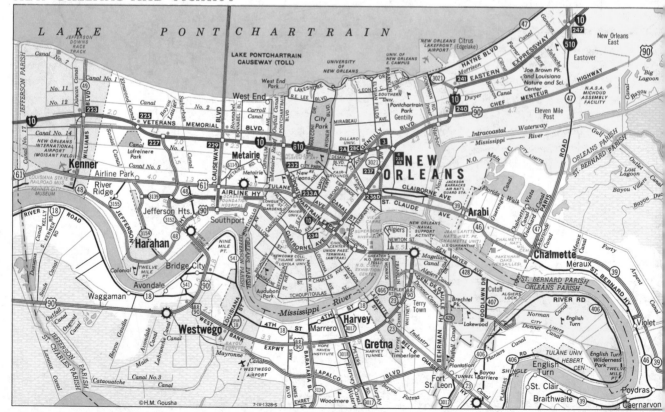

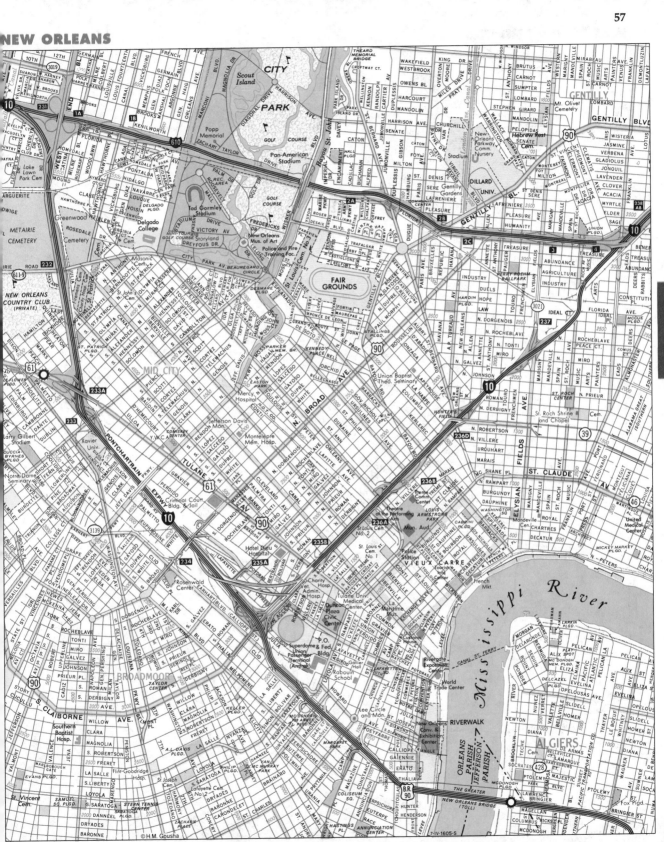

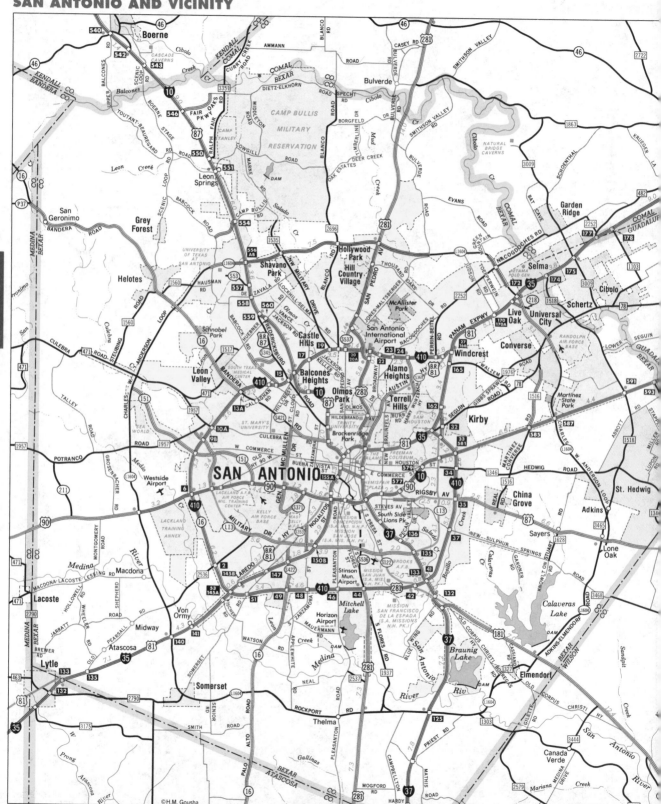

©H.M. Gousha

5-SF-1520-S

CENTRAL SAN ANTONIO

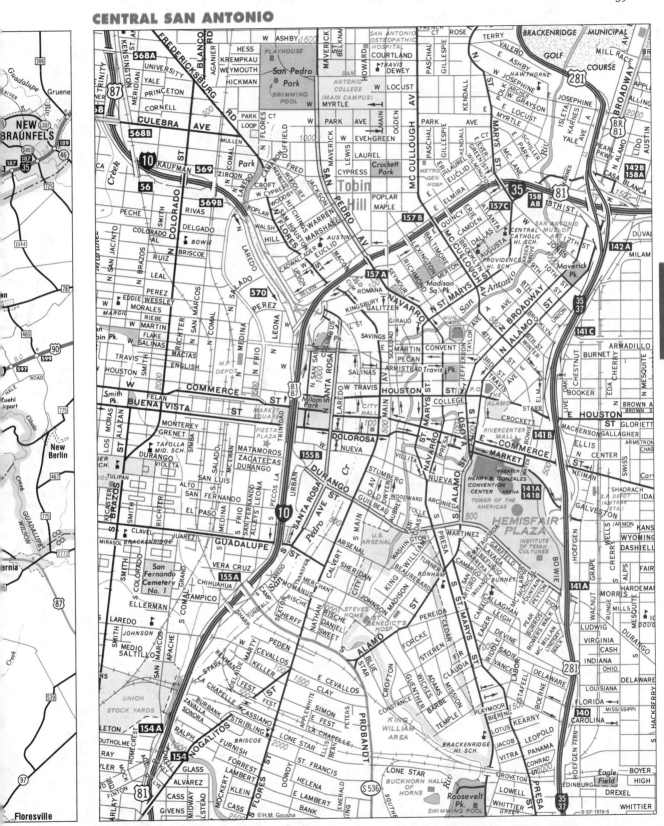

©H.M. Gousha

5-SF-1519-S

QUÉBEC

North Bay

Temiscamingue

Lac

Sudbury

TORONTO

Lake Ontario

Erie

Georgian Bay

Lake Huron

DETROIT

94

69

75

96

LANSING

MICHIGAN

96

31

Sault Ste. Marie

75

31

Lake Michigan

2

MILWAUKEE

CANADA

ONTARIO

Superior

Lake

Green Bay

43

41

41

94

43

Marquette

MICHIGAN

41

94

Thunder Bay

41

29

Green Bay

Lake Nipigon

Wausau

WISCONSIN

90
94

MADISON

Pigeon River

Northern Light Lake

61

2

29

94

River

Mississippi

90

River

Rainy Lake

International Falls

53

Duluth

St. Croix River

ST. PAUL

MINNEAPOLIS

Waterloo

MINN.

2

61

35

35

11

17

11

11

17

12

17

17

69

11

61

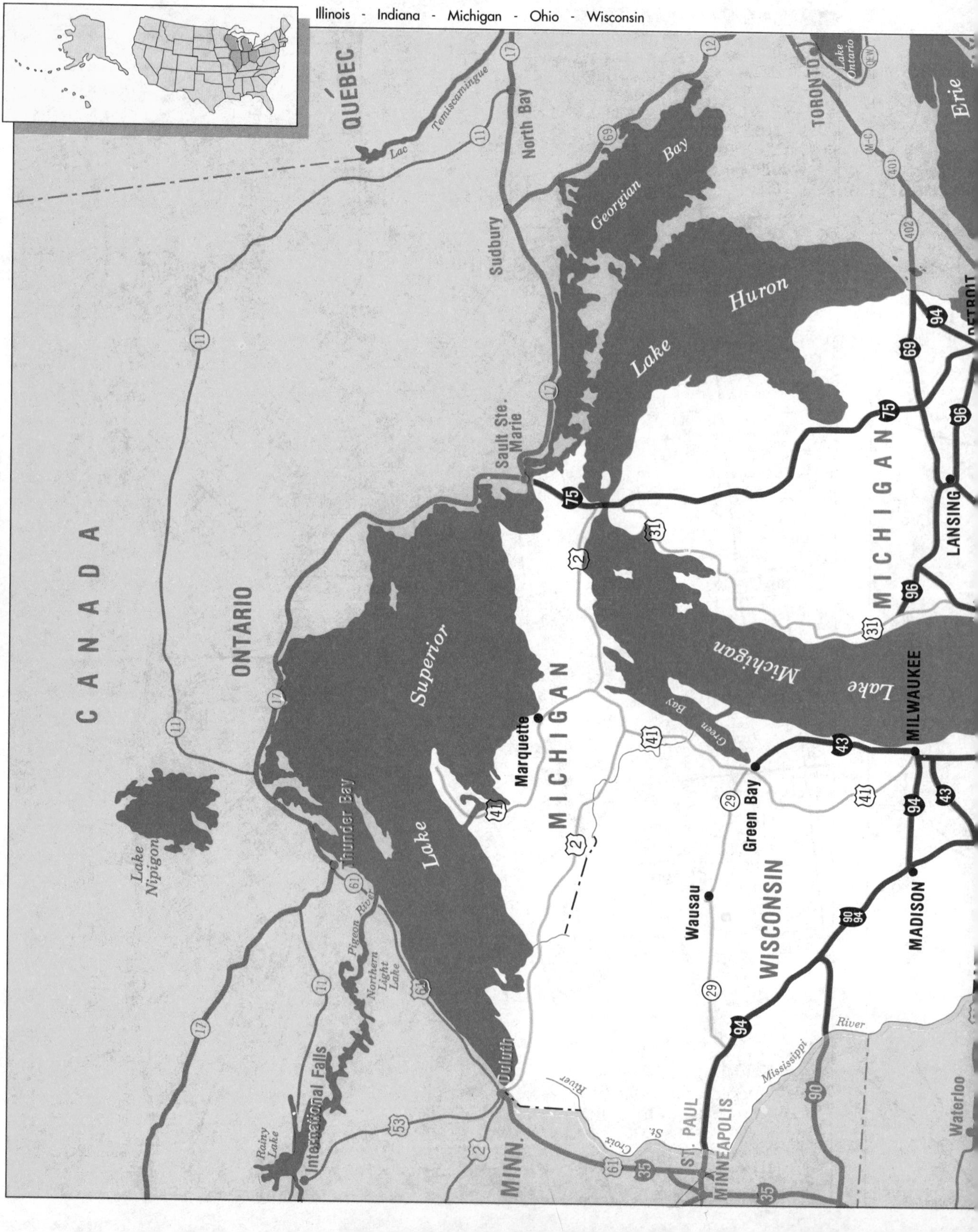

61

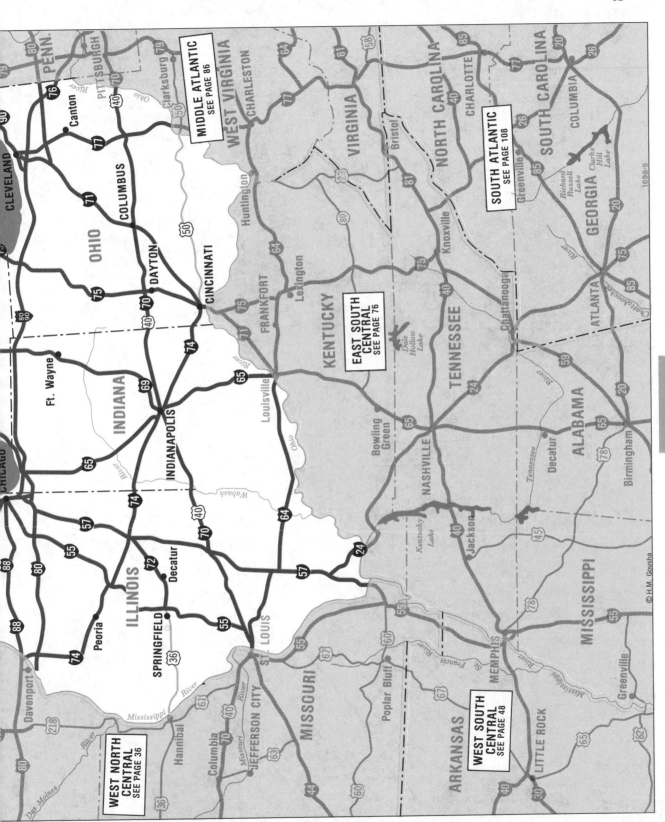

MIDDLE ATLANTIC
SEE PAGE 86

SOUTH ATLANTIC
SEE PAGE 108

EAST SOUTH
CENTRAL
SEE PAGE 76

WEST SOUTH
CENTRAL
SEE PAGE 48

WEST NORTH
CENTRAL
SEE PAGE 36

© H.M. Gousha

©H.M. Gousha

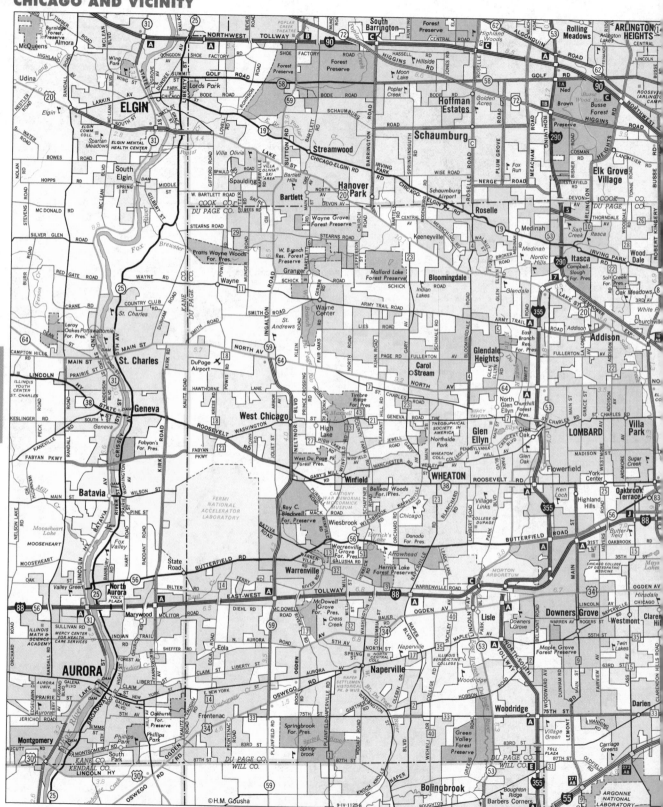

©H.M. Gousha

9-IV-1125-6

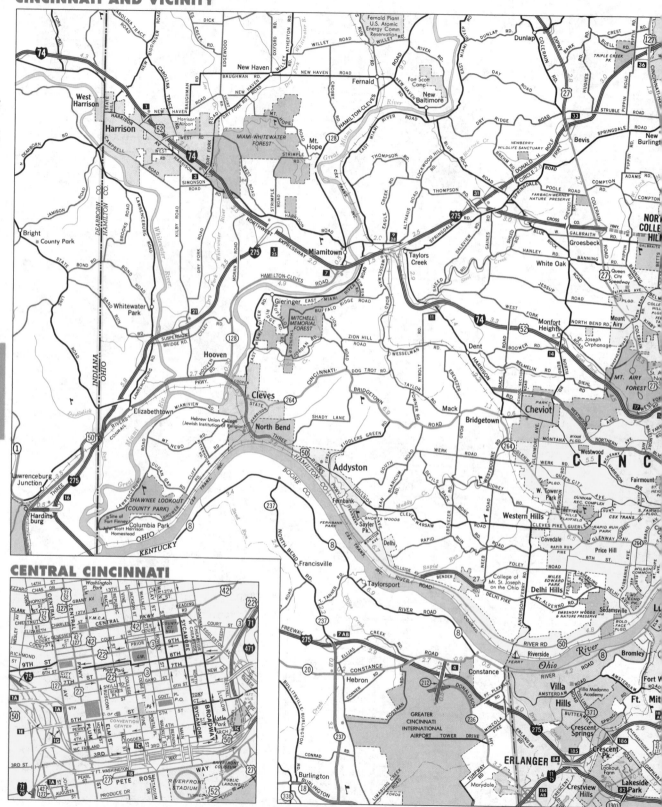

CENTRAL CINCINNATI

©H.M. Gousha
IV-1-781-S

CENTRAL CLEVELAND

CLEVELAND AND VICINITY

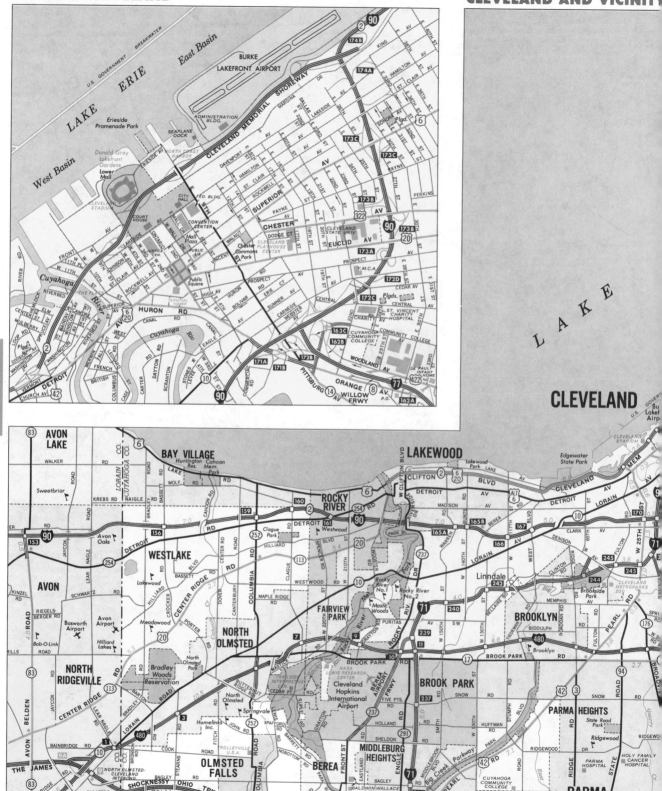

CLEVELAND

©H.M. Gousha

TAYLOR-MAY RD

©H.M. Gousha

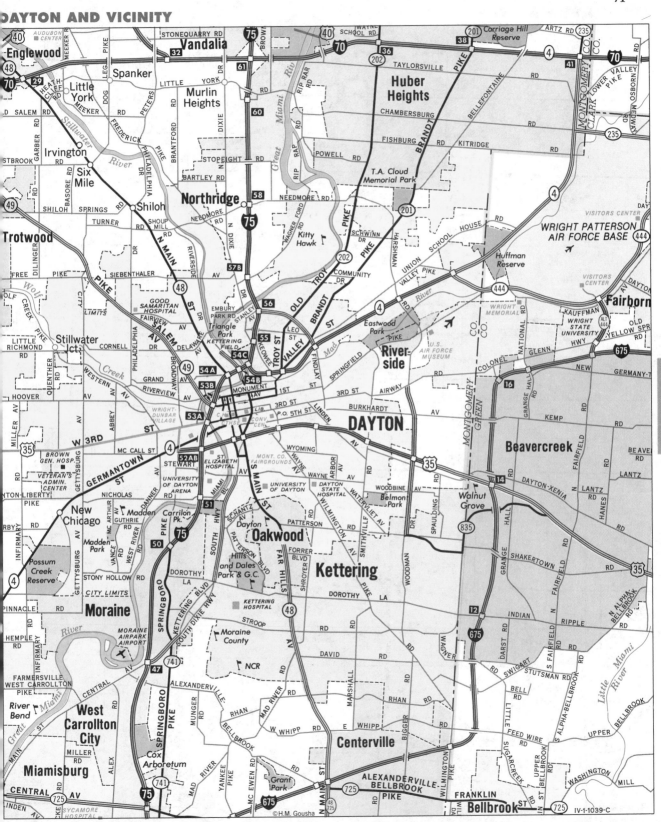

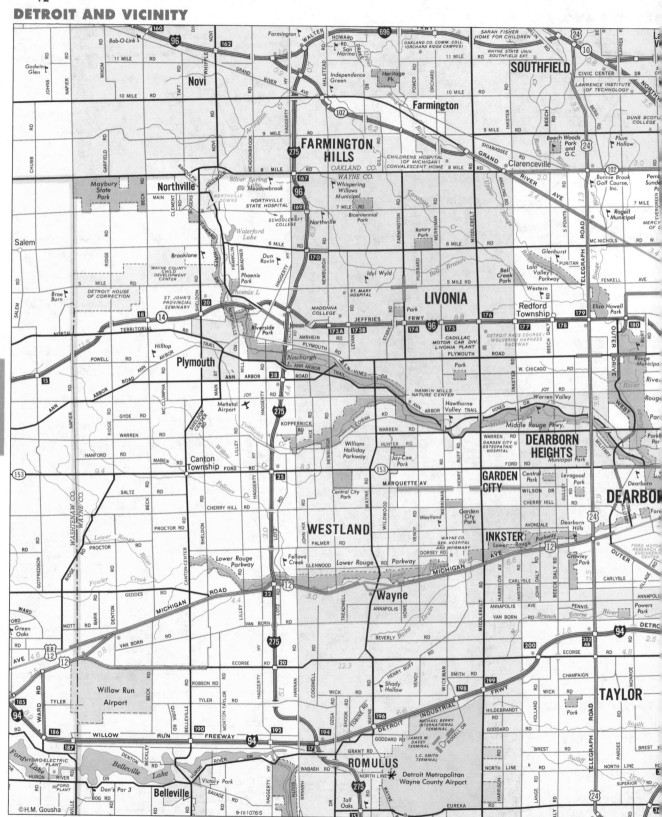

©H.M. Gousha

9-IV.1076-5

BOSTON HARBOR HOTEL℠
AT ROWES WHARF

Detroit Airport— 275 N.
to 696 East. Go 10-12
Miles to Woodward Ave
(M1). Woodward N into
Birmingham.

Follow downtown signs —
Left on 3rd Sign.

Townsend Hotel
100 Townsend St.
Birmingham, MI

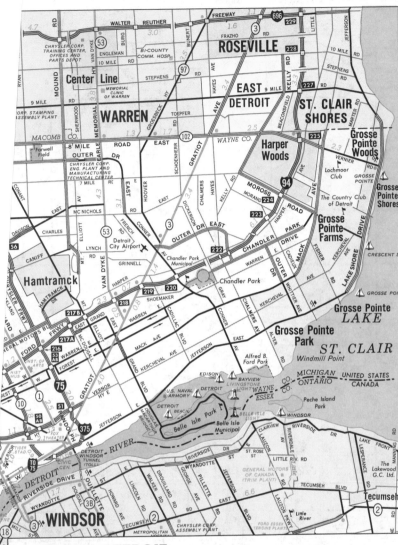

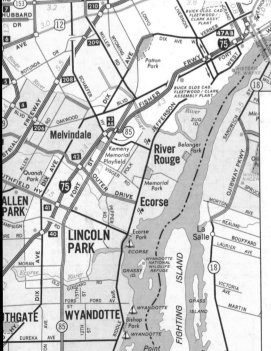

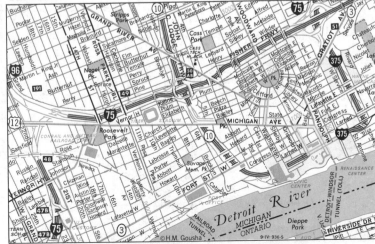

CENTRAL DETROIT

73

CENTRAL MILWAUKEE

LAKE

MICHIGAN

Milwaukee Bay

JONES ISLAND

WEST MILWAUKEE

N HARBOR DR.

University of Wisconsin - Milwaukee

Washington Park

Jackson Park

Forest Home Cemetery

Mitchell Park

Menomonee River

Kinnickinnic River

©H.M. Gousha

7-SF-952-S

EAST SOUTH CENTRAL

Alabama - Kentucky - Mississippi - Tennessee

MIDDLE ATLANTIC
SEE PAGE 86

EAST NORTH CENTRAL
SEE PAGE 60

WEST NORTH CENTRAL
SEE PAGE 36

WEST SOUTH CENTRAL
SEE PAGE 48

WEST VIRGINIA

VIRGINIA

NORTH CAROLINA

OHIO

KENTUCKY

TENNESSEE

INDIANA

ILLINOIS

MICHIGAN

MISSOURI

Lake Erie

Lake Michigan

CLEVELAND

COLUMBUS

DAYTON

CINCINNATI

Huntington

CHARLESTON

Bristol

Lexington

FRANKFORT

Louisville

Bowling Green

NASHVILLE

Knoxville

Chattanooga

Paducah

Jackson

MEMPHIS

ST. LOUIS

SPRINGFIELD

Decatur

Peoria

Hannibal

Poplar Bluff

Ft. Wayne

INDIANAPOLIS

CHICAGO

Davenport
Quad Cities

Iowa City

Dale Hollow Lake

Kentucky Lake

Ohio River

Tennessee River

Mississippi River

Missouri River

Wabash River

Francis River

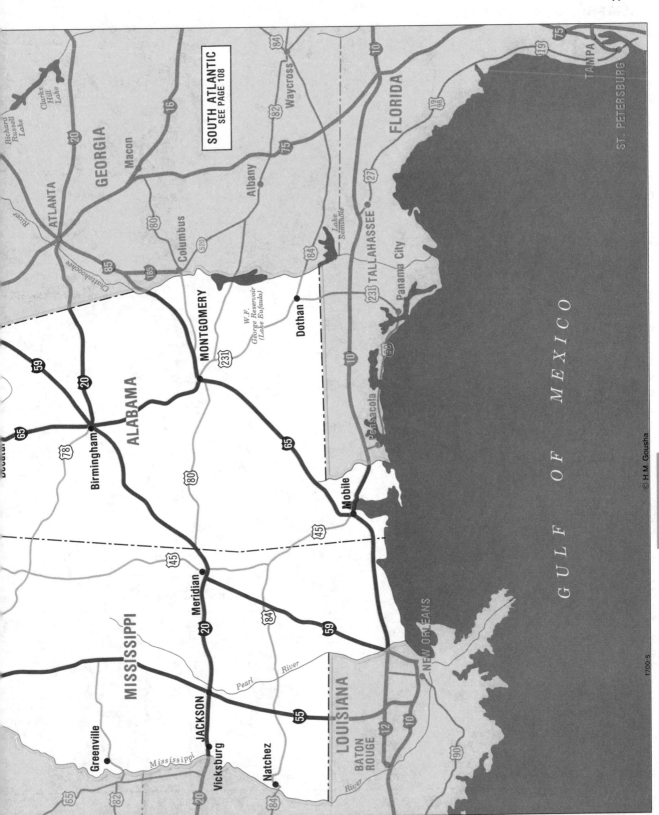

SOUTH ATLANTIC
SEE PAGE 108

GEORGIA

Richard Russell Lake
Clarks Hill Lake

ATLANTA
Chattahoochee River
Macon
16
20
80
Columbus
520
Albany
Waycross
84
82
75
185
85

FLORIDA
Lake Seminole
TALLAHASSEE
Panama City
27
231
98
99
10
75
19
TAMPA
ST. PETERSBURG

ALABAMA
MONTGOMERY
231
W.F. George Reservoir (Lake Eufaula)
Dothan
59
20
65
78
Birmingham
80
65
Mobile
45
Pensacola
10
98

GULF OF MEXICO

MISSISSIPPI
45
20
Meridian
84
59
JACKSON
Greenville
Vicksburg
Natchez
Mississippi River
Pearl River
55

LOUISIANA
BATON ROUGE
NEW ORLEANS
12
10
90

65
82
20
84

© H.M. Gousha

1700-S

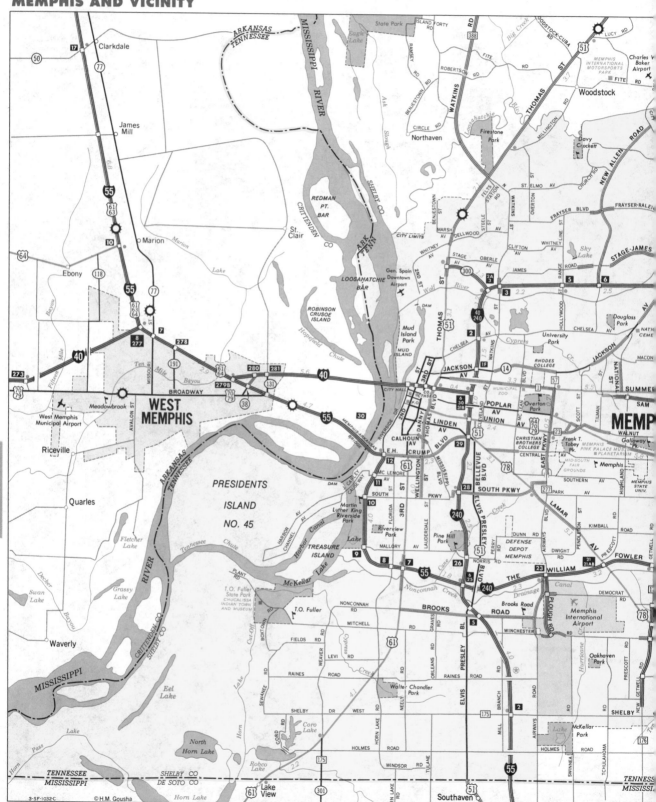

CENTRAL MEMPHIS

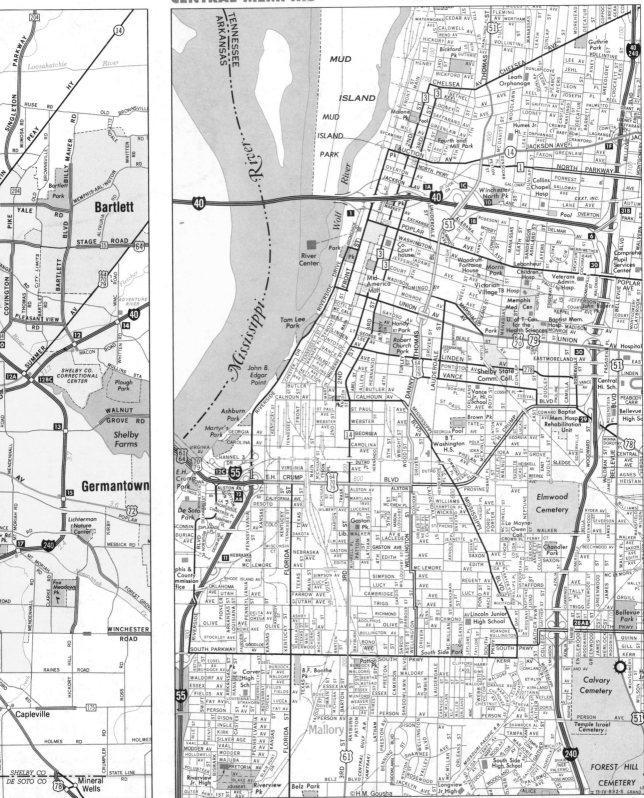

NEW ENGLAND

Connecticut - Maine - Massachusetts - New Hampshire - Rhode Island - Vermont

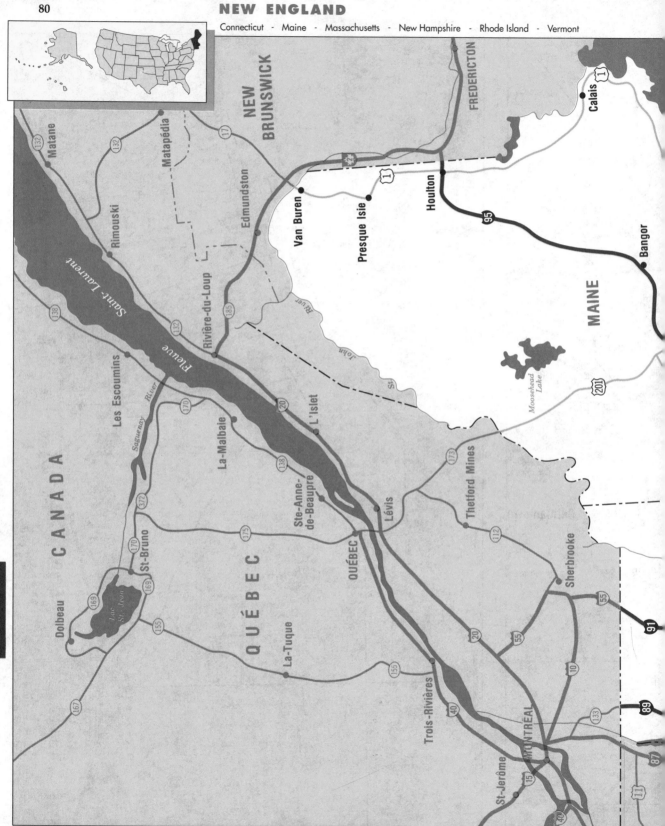

ATLANTIC OCEAN

Lake Placid

73

Lake Champlain

MONTPELIER

VERMONT

7

Rutland

93

91

5

87

Schenectady

90

ALBANY

87

7

Pittsfield

River

Connecticut

MASSACHUSETTS

89

9

2

5

Springfield

84

HARTFORD

7

15

CONNECTICUT

84

95

495

Bridgeport

New Haven

New London

6

395

95

95

Lake Winnipesaukee

NEW HAMPSHIRE

16

CONCORD

4

Manchester

93

BOSTON

495

90

95

3

Provincetown

6

New Bedford

PROVIDENCE

RHODE ISLAND

195

195

38

Newport

1

95

495

PORTLAND

Portsmouth

2

MIDDLE ATLANTIC SEE PAGE 86

1695-S

© H.M. Gousha

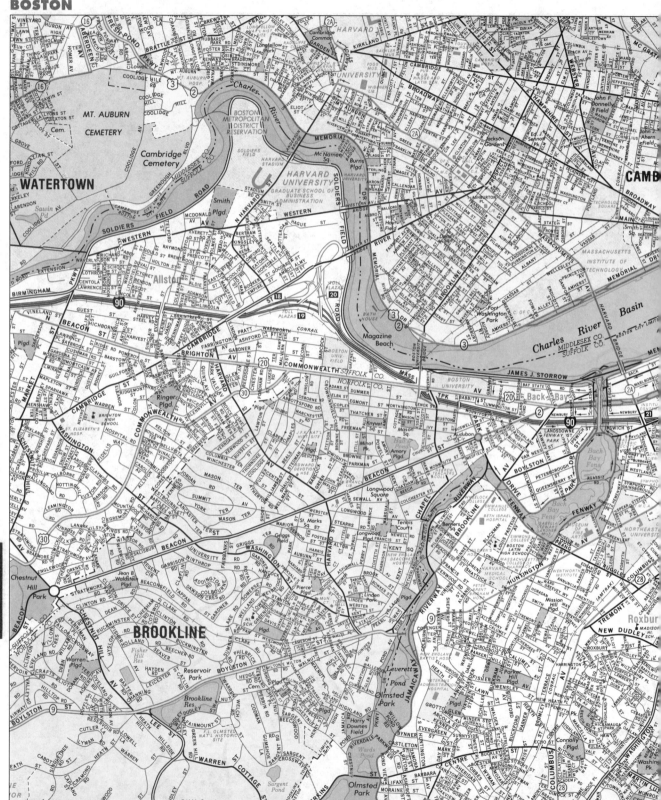

7-SF-1582-S   ©H.M. Gousha

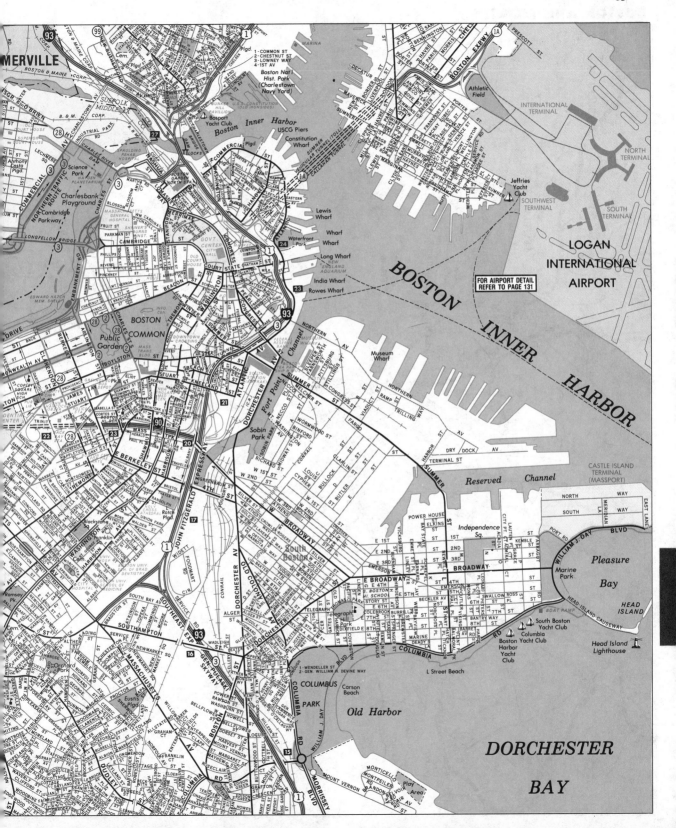

©H.M.Gousha

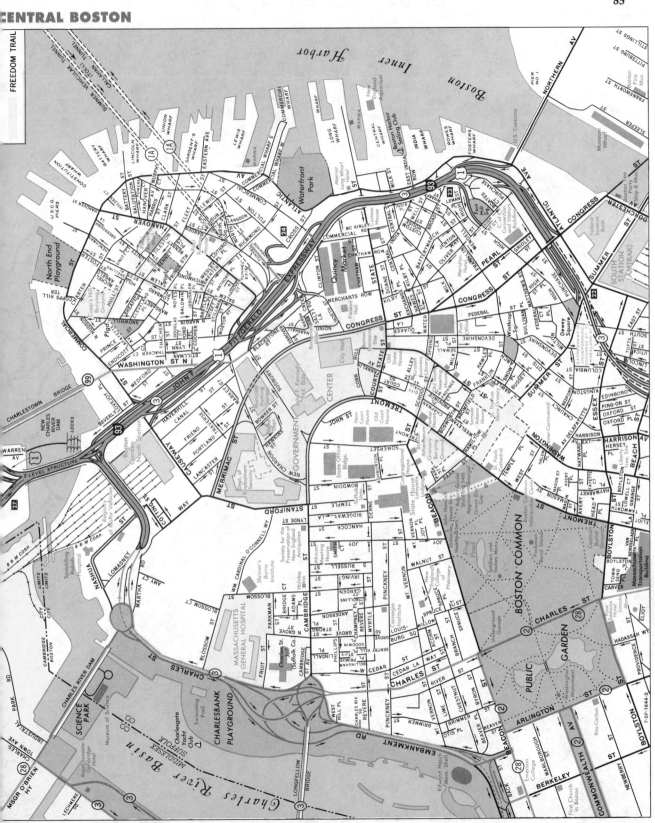

NEW ENGLAND
SEE PAGE 80

EAST NORTH
CENTRAL
SEE PAGE 60

QUÉBEC

CANADA

ONTARIO

OTTAWA

MONTPELIER

N.H.

VT.

MASS.

CONN.

R.I.

NEW YORK

N.J.

MD.

PENNSYLVANIA

OHIO

MICH.

Montréal

Ottawa

Toronto

North Bay

Sault Ste. Marie

Schenectady

Albany

Hartford

Concord

NEW YORK

Newark

Trenton

PHILADELPHIA

Atlantic City

Wilmington

Hagerstown

Allentown

Scranton

Binghamton

Utica

Watertown

Syracuse

Rochester

Buffalo

Niagara Falls

HARRISBURG

Altoona

PITTSBURGH

Erie

CLEVLELAND

Akron

Canton

Detroit

Port Huron

Lansing

Toledo

COLUMBUS

Dayton

Lake Ontario

Lake Erie

Lake Huron

Georgian Bay

Long Island Sound

Hudson River

Delaware River

Rivière des Outaouais

Ohio River

Conn. River

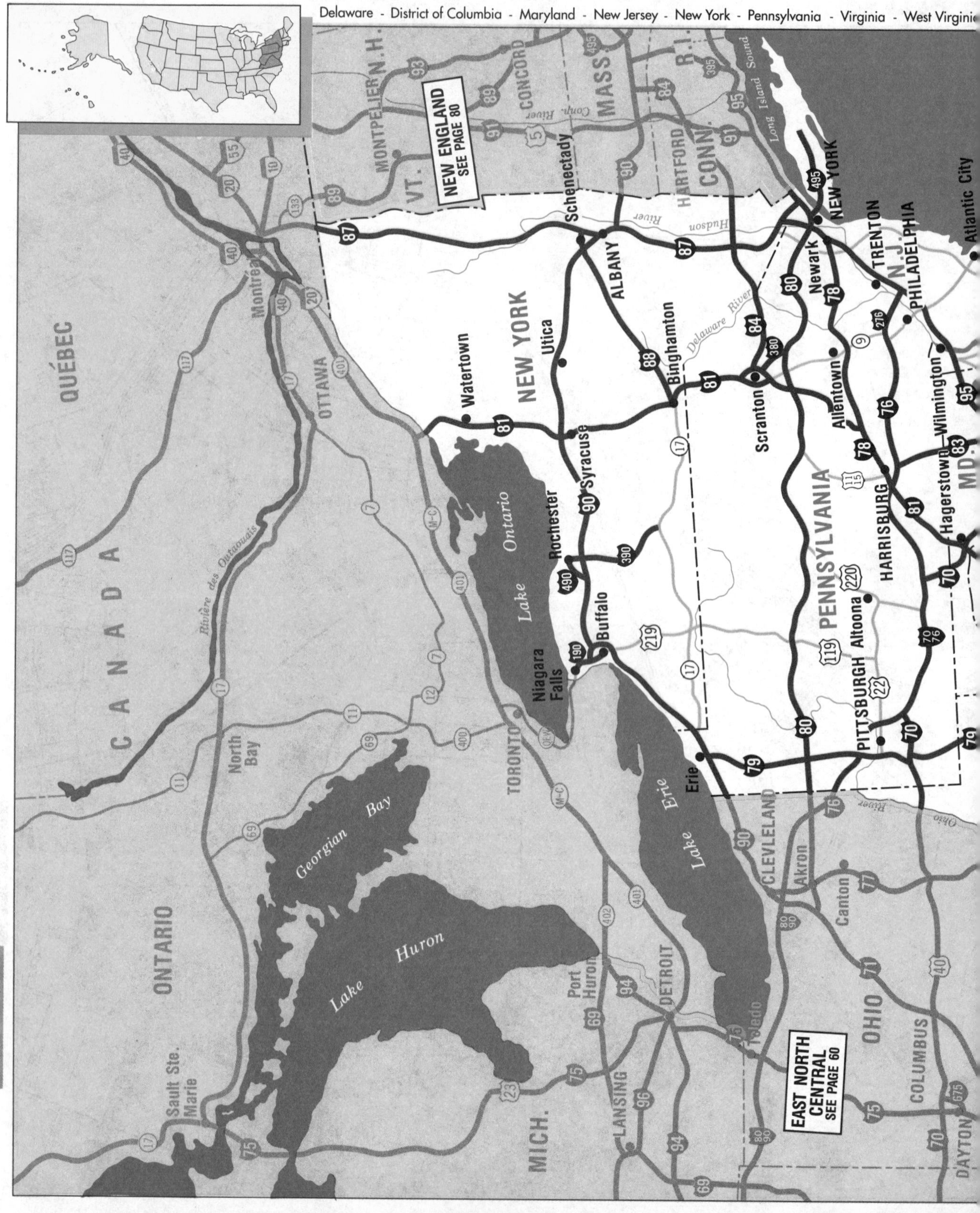

ATLANTIC OCEAN

DEL.

Chesapeake Bay

WASHINGTON D.C.

NORFOLK
Portsmouth
Newport News

Albemarle Sound
Pamlico Sound
Onslow Bay
Wilmington

Charlottesville

VIRGINIA
RICHMOND
Lynchburg
Roanoke

66
29
64
60
95
13
85
58
58
360
29
58

RALEIGH
Durham
NORTH CAROLINA
Greensboro
Winston-Salem
CHARLOTTE

117
40
117
15
40
95
40
85
64
85
77

WEST VIRGINIA
CHARLESTON
Huntington

81
64
77
64

KENTUCKY
FRANKFORT

64
71

EAST SOUTH CENTRAL
SEE PAGE 76

TENN.
Knoxville

40
75
75
81

SOUTH CAROLINA
COLUMBIA
Lake Marion
Santee River
Charleston
Savannah River
Savannah

20
95
26
26
26
117
101
16

SOUTH ATLANTIC
SEE PAGE 108

GEORGIA
ATLANTA
Macon
Columbus
Albany
Waycross

85
20
85
16
80
570
82
75
84
82

FLA.

95
82
84
10

1696-S
© H.M. Gousha

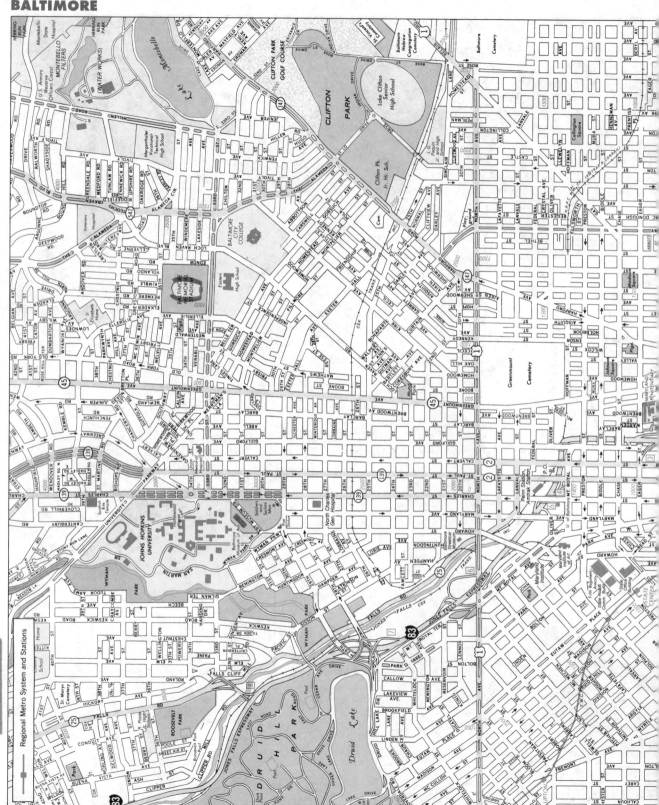

Regional Metro System and Stations

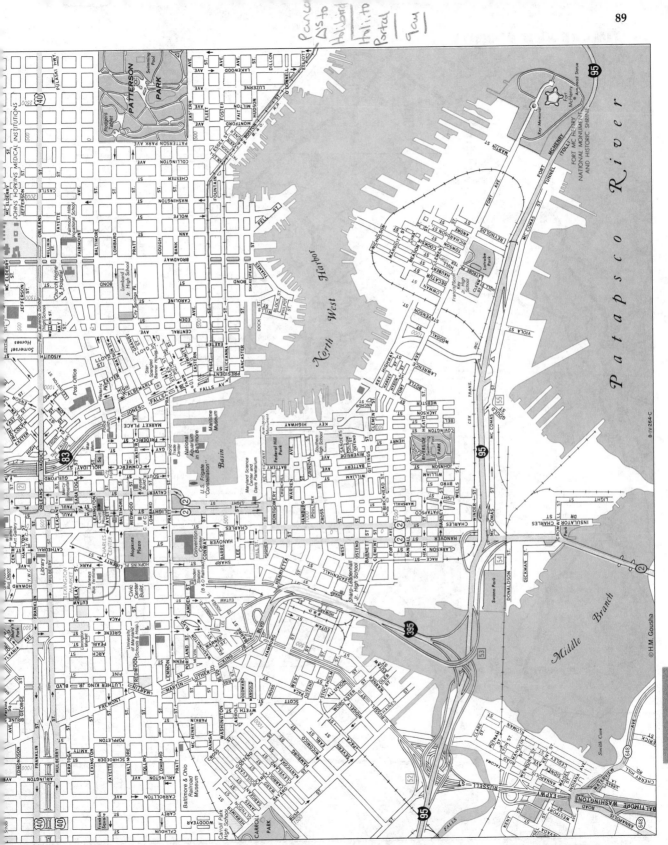

BALTIMORE AND VICINITY

CENTRAL BALTIMORE

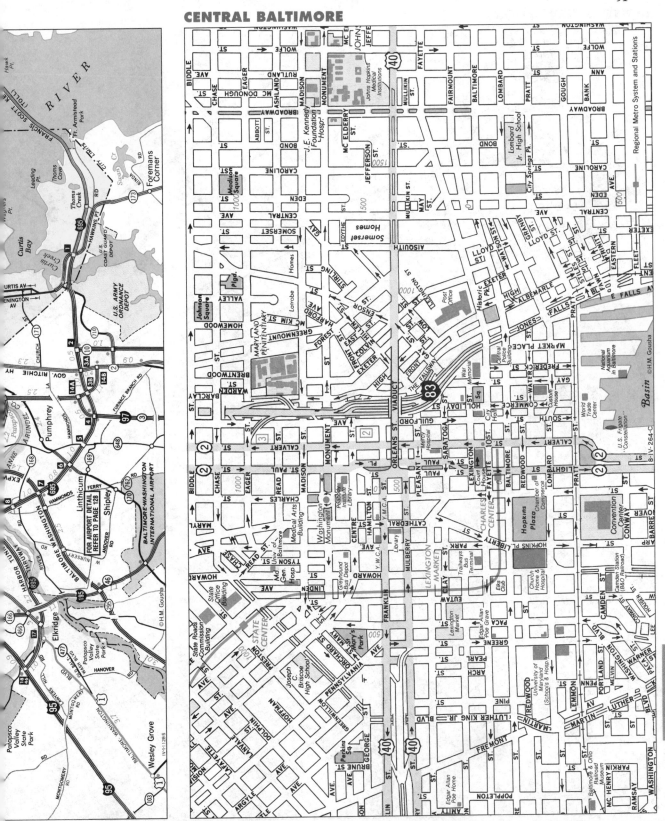

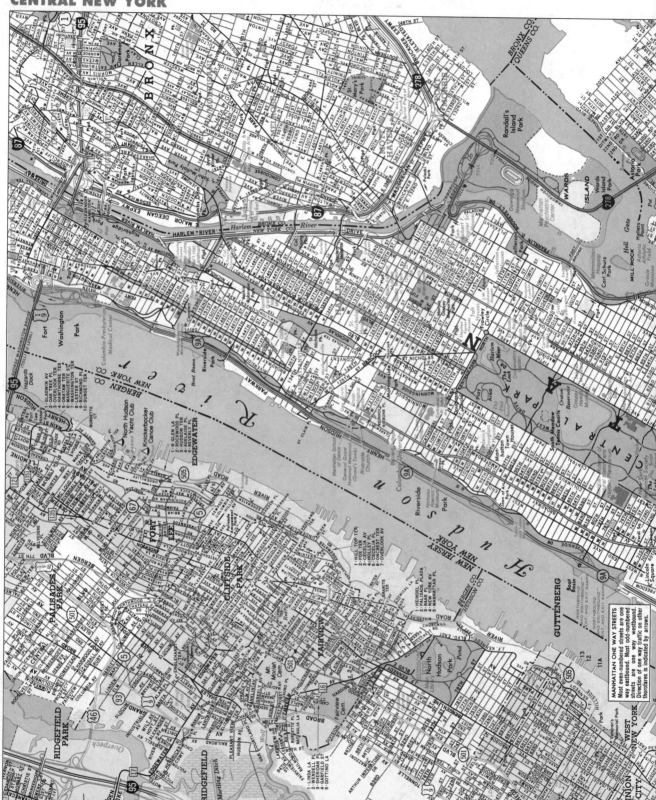

©H.M.Goushá

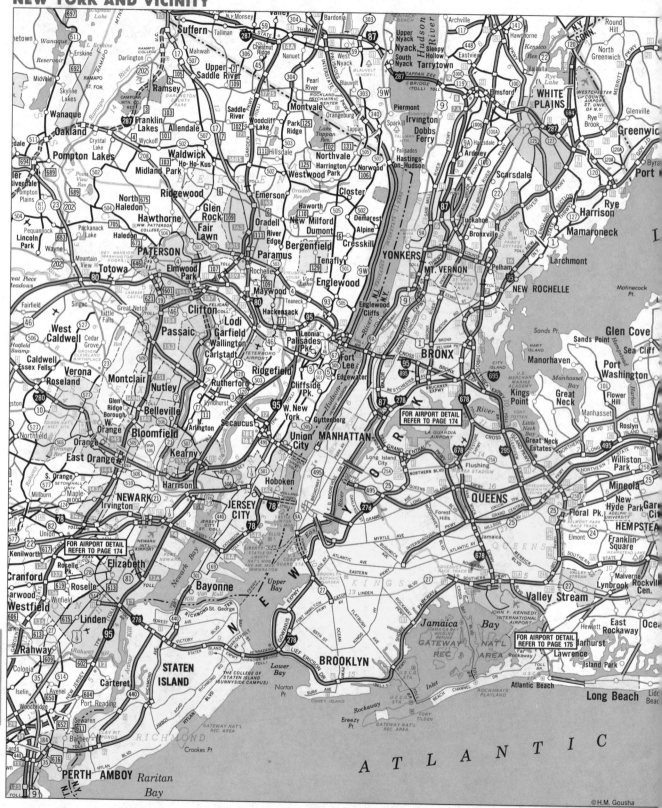

© H.M. Gousha

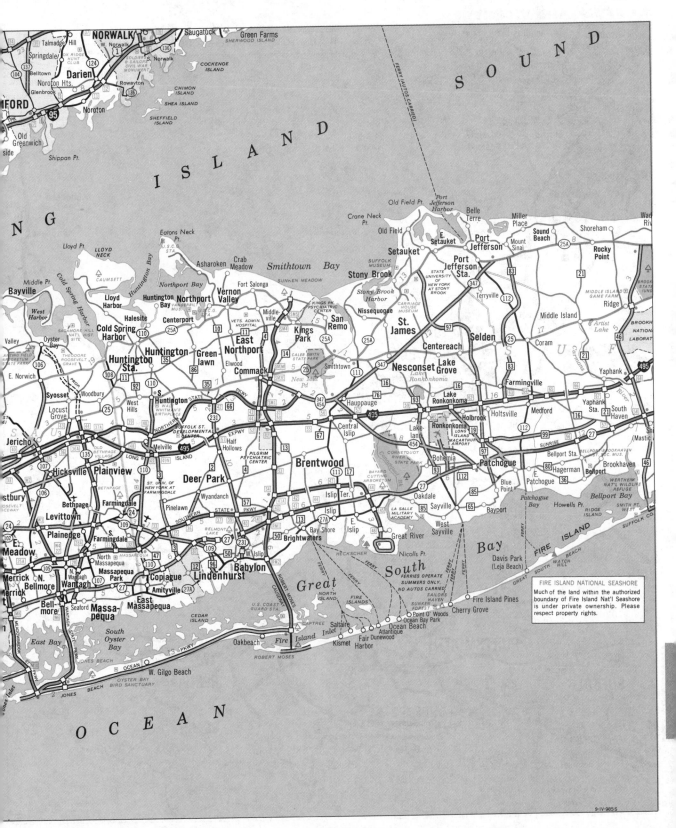

FIRE ISLAND NATIONAL SEASHORE

Much of the land within the authorized
boundary of Fire Island Nat'l Seashore
is under private ownership. Please
respect property rights.

9-IV-985-5

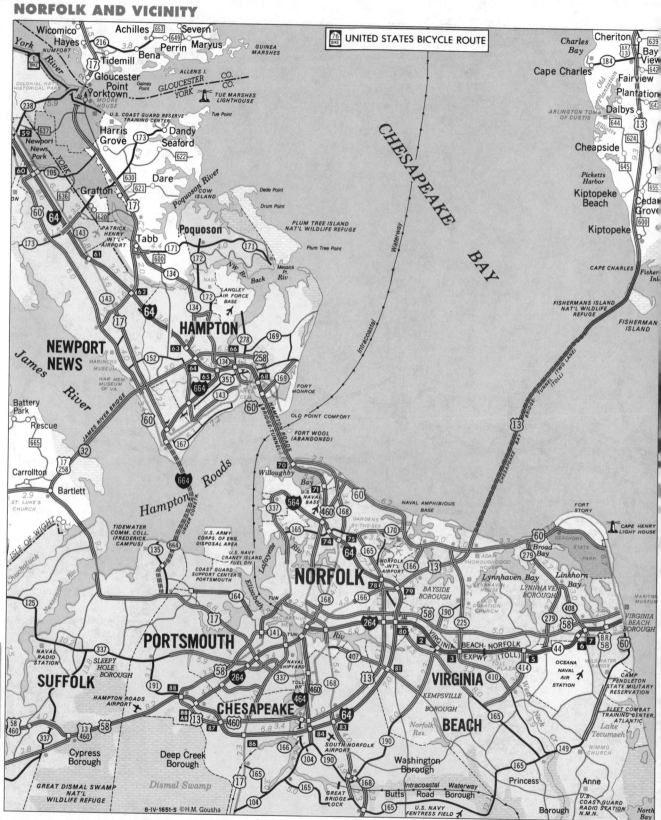

76 BIKE UNITED STATES BICYCLE ROUTE

8-IV-1651-S ©H.M. Gousha

CENTRAL NORFOLK

U.S. NAVY

Elizabeth River

Edgewater

Norfolk Yacht and Country Club (Private)

Faye Point

Tanner Point

Lafayette River Branch Clinic U.S. Navy

Lafayette River

Edgewater Park Haven

Larchmont

Larchmont Rec. Cen.

Old Dominion University

Lamberts Point

Powhatan Athletic Field

Lamberts Point

Ghent Point

Colonial Place

Tidewater Boat Club BOAT RAMP

NORFOLK

Park Place

Lafayette Park

Virginia Zoological Park

Talbot Park

North Branch

Wayne Creek

NORVIEW AV

Lakewood Park Athletic Field

Lakewood

Fairmount Park

Lafayette

LAFAYETTE BLVD

Ballentine Place

Norfolk and Western Ry. Station

Jeff Robertson Pk

St. Marys Cemetery

Barraud Park Athletic Cen.

Ghent

Norfolk Little Theater

Eastern Virginia Med. School Pub. Health Dept.

Norfolk Gen. Hosp.

Botetourt Gardens

Elmwood Cemetery

Calvary Cemetery

Huntersville

VIRGINIA BEACH

Brambleton

FORT NORFOLK (U.S. Army Eng. Dist. Hdqtrs.)

MIDTOWN TUNNEL

Pinners Point

Intracoastal Waterway

NORFOLK CITY LIMITS PORTSMOUTH CITY LIMITS

Norfolk Boat Club

City Hall Av

Town Point Park

WATERSIDE DR

U.S. NAVAL REGIONAL MEDICAL CENTER

Hospital Point

Holcomb

Scotts Creek

Oak Grove Cemetery

Parkview

London

Norfolk

CITY HALL AV

PARK AV

NORFOLK STATE UNIVERSITY

Presidential Pkwy

Chesterfield Heights

Eastern Branch Elizabeth River

Riverside Memorial Cemetery

Berkley

Berkley Neighborhood Rec. Cen.

Campostella

Indian River Road

DOWNTOWN TUNNEL

© H.M. Gousha

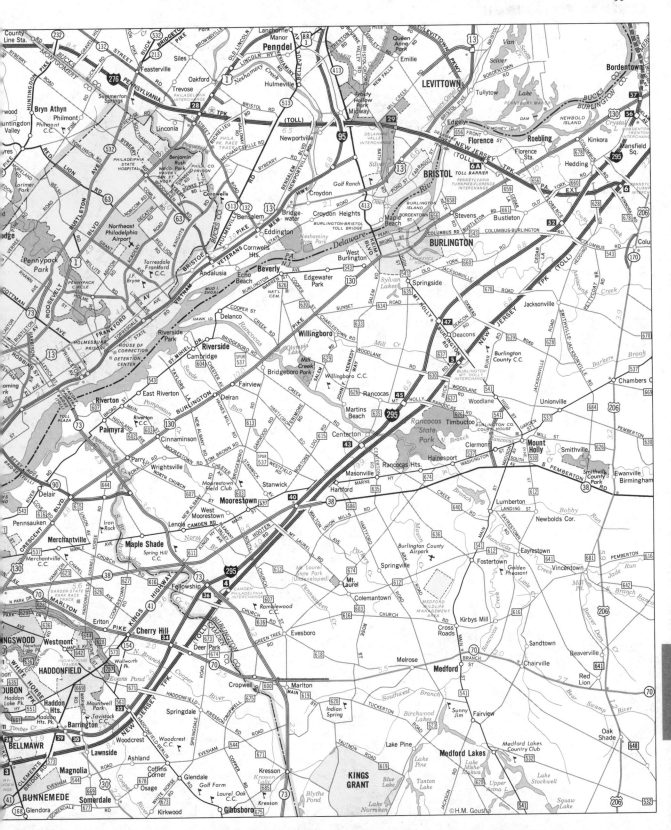

©H.M. Gousha

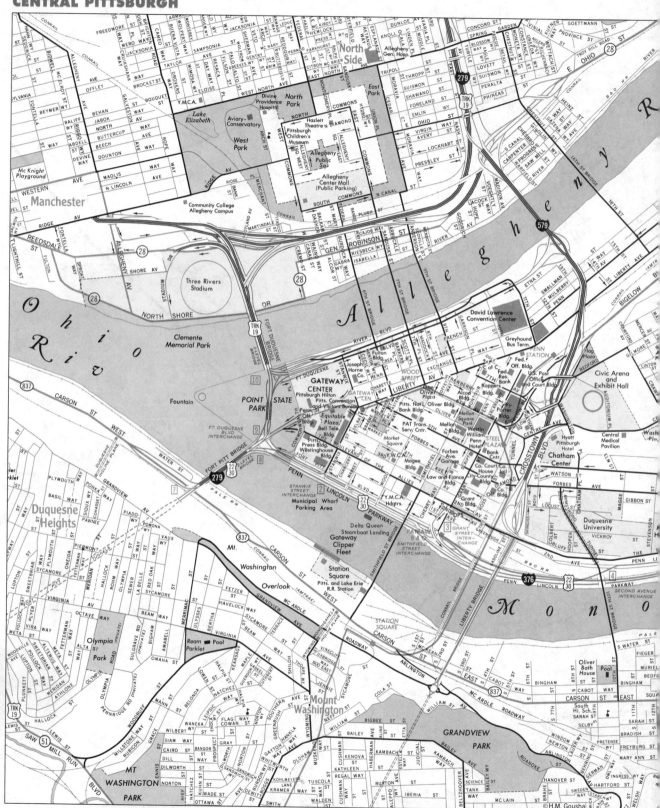

PAT System and Stations

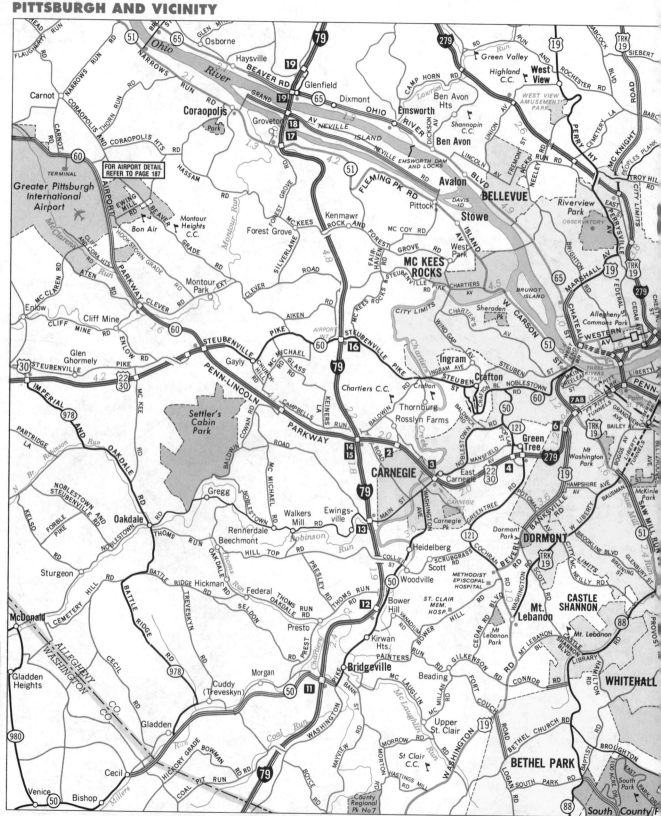

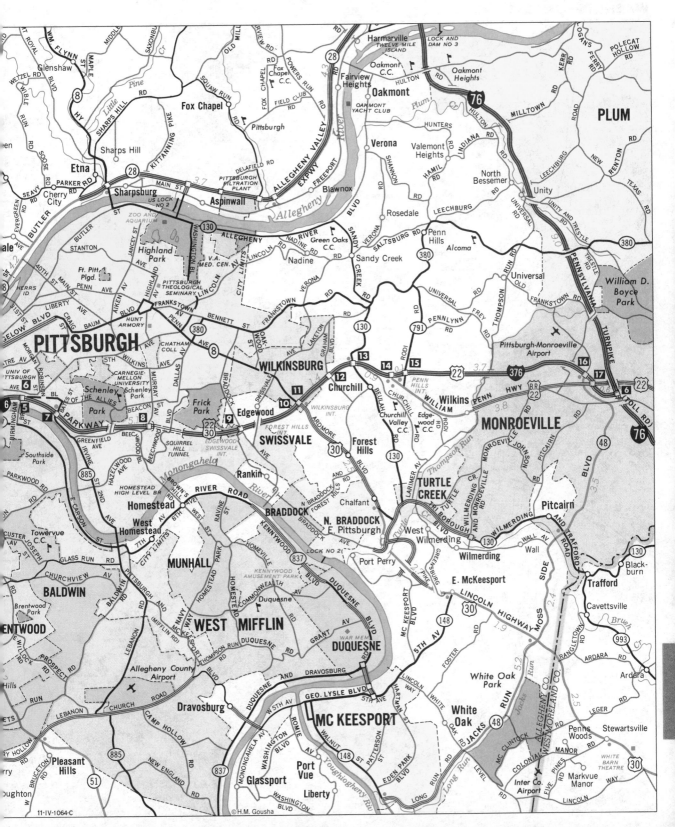

11-IV-1064-C   ©H.M. Gousha

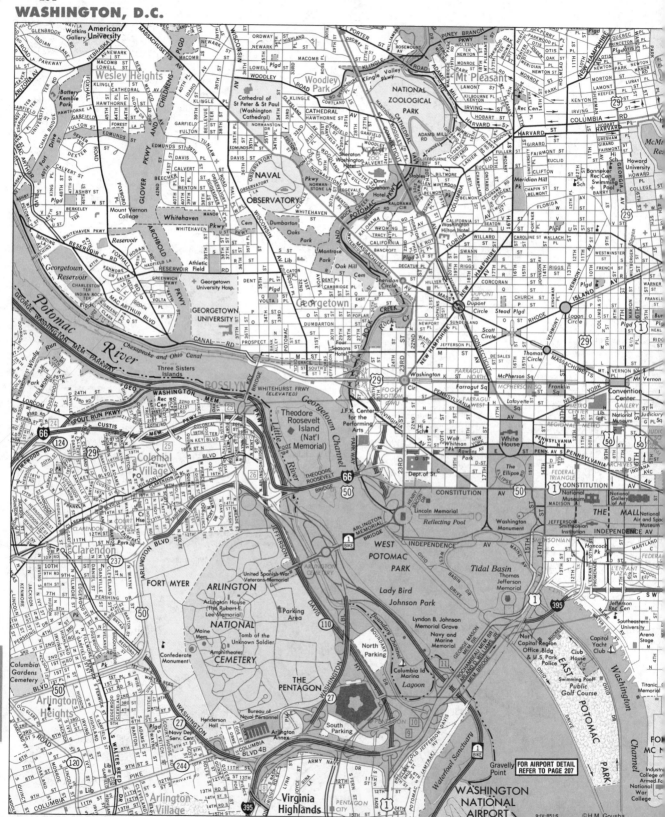

FOR AIRPORT DETAIL REFER TO PAGE 207

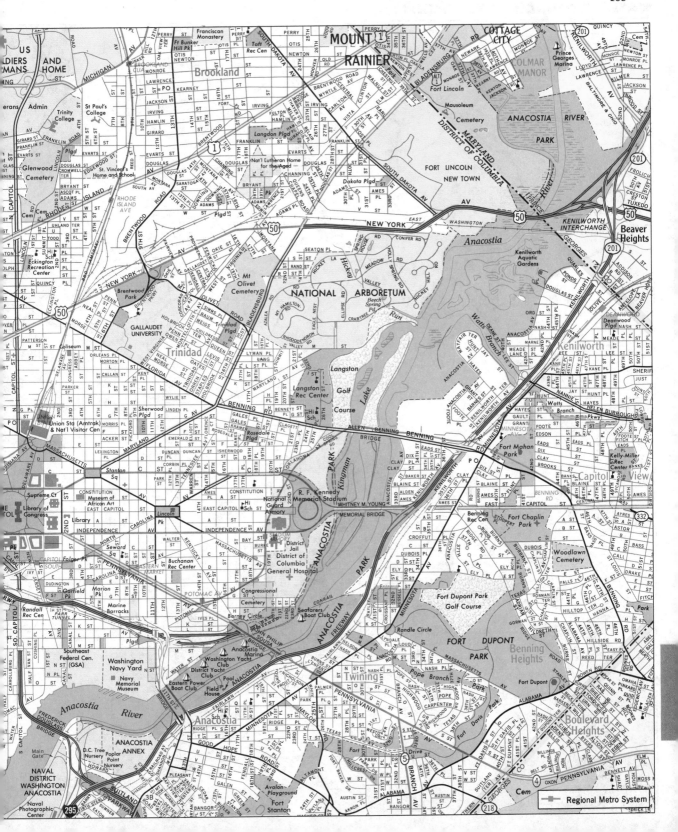

Regional Metro System

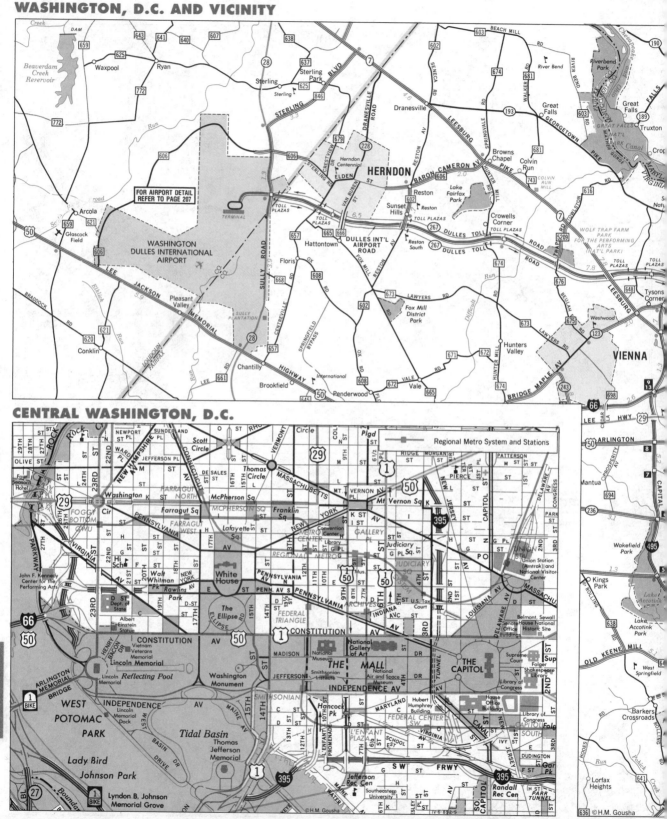

CENTRAL WASHINGTON, D.C.

SOUTH ATLANTIC

Florida - Georgia - North Carolina - South Carolina

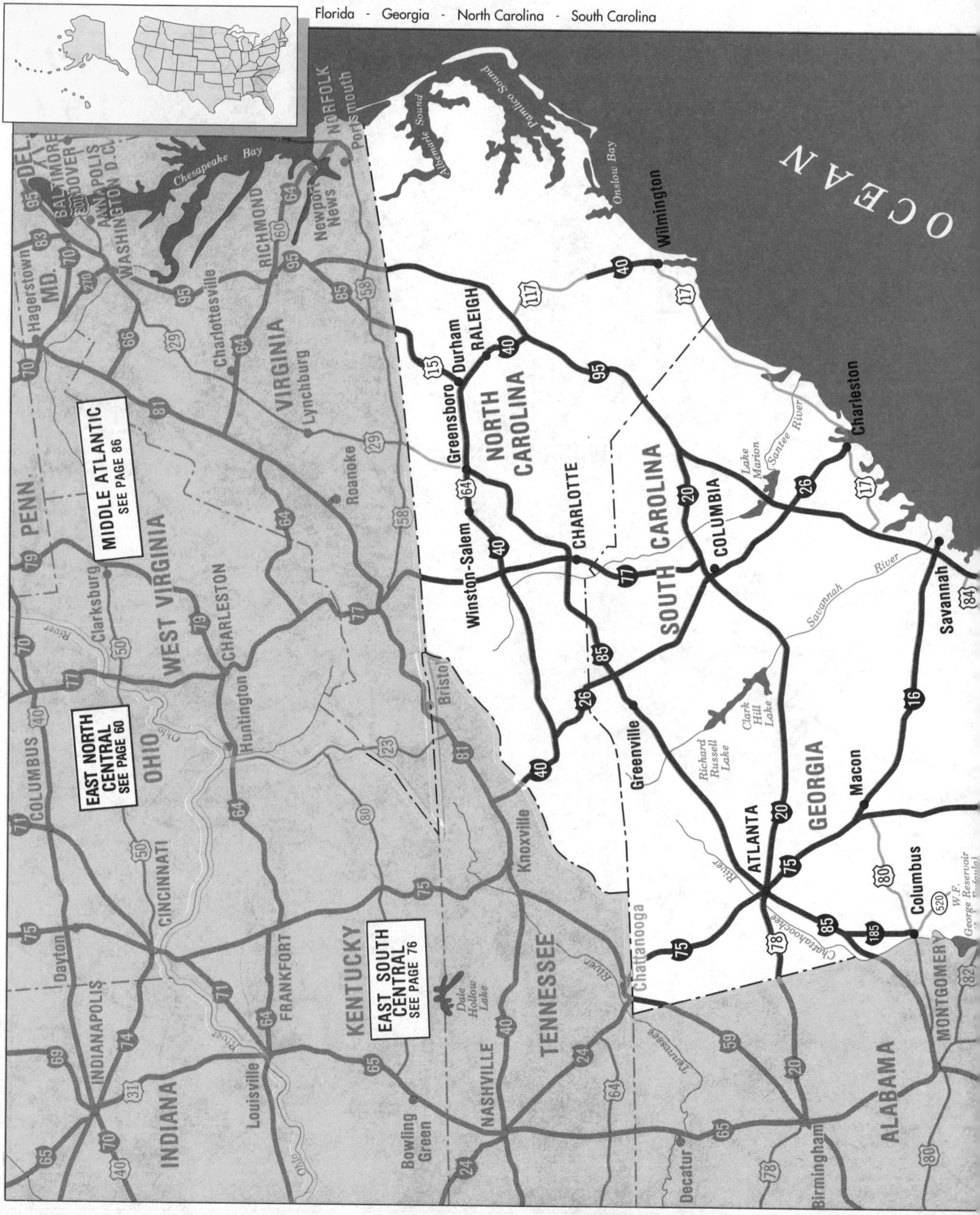

OCEAN

NORFOLK
Portsmouth
Newport News
Wilmington
Charleston
Savannah

Chesapeake Bay
Albemarle Sound
Pamlico Sound
Onslow Bay

DEL.
Baltimore
ANNAPOLIS
DOVER
WASHINGTON D.C.
MD.
Hagerstown
Richmond
Charlottesville
VIRGINIA
Lynchburg
Roanoke

95
83
70
210
66
29
64
85
58
60
95
117
40
40
95
17
15
Durham
RALEIGH
Greensboro
NORTH CAROLINA
64
Winston-Salem
40
CHARLOTTE
77
85
26
40
Greenville
77
Bristol
81

17
26
17
Charleston
Lake Marion
Santee River
SOUTH CAROLINA
20
COLUMBIA
Savannah River
River
Savannah
84
16

PENN.
70
81
79
WEST VIRGINIA
Clarksburg
CHARLESTON
79
77
Huntington
50
70
71
23
81

OHIO
COLUMBUS
40
50
Cincinnati
71
74
Dayton
69
31
INDIANA
Indianapolis
65
70
40

FRANKFORT
KENTUCKY
64
Louisville
65
Bowling Green
24
Nashville
TENNESSEE
40
64
24
Knoxville
75
Dale Hollow Lake
59
20
Chattanooga
75
78
85
ALABAMA
Birmingham
78
80
Decatur
65
MONTGOMERY
82

GEORGIA
Clark Hill Lake
Richard Russell Lake
Macon
ATLANTA
75
20
85
185
Columbus
80
520
W.F. George Reservoir
Chattahoochee River

MIDDLE ATLANTIC
SEE PAGE 86

EAST NORTH CENTRAL
SEE PAGE 60

EAST SOUTH CENTRAL
SEE PAGE 76

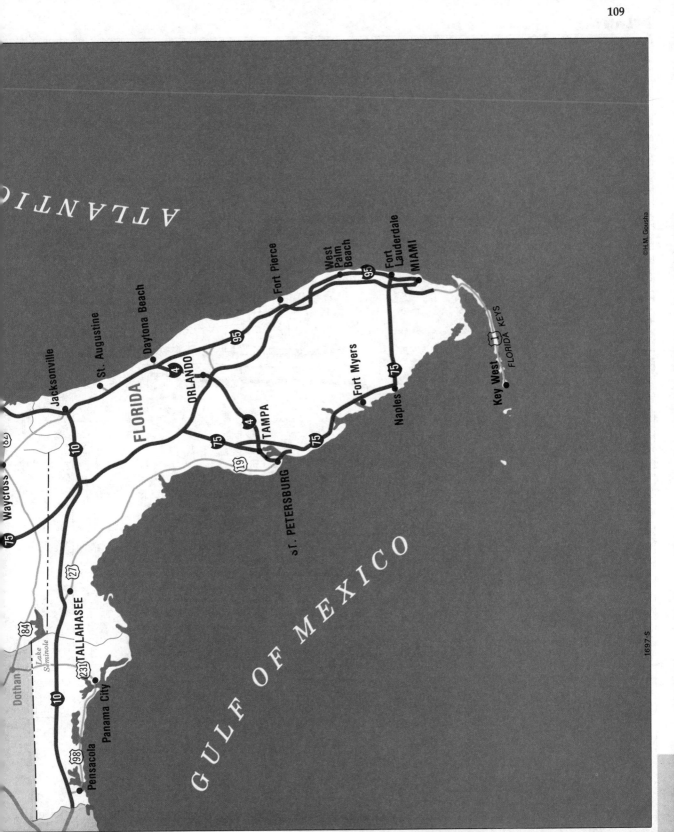

©H.M. Gousha

1697-S

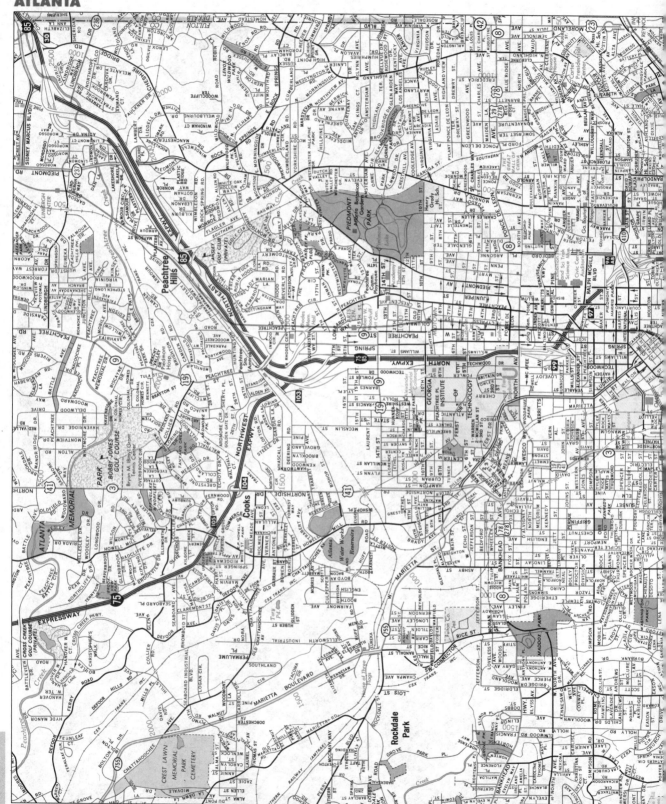

ATLANTA AND VICINITY

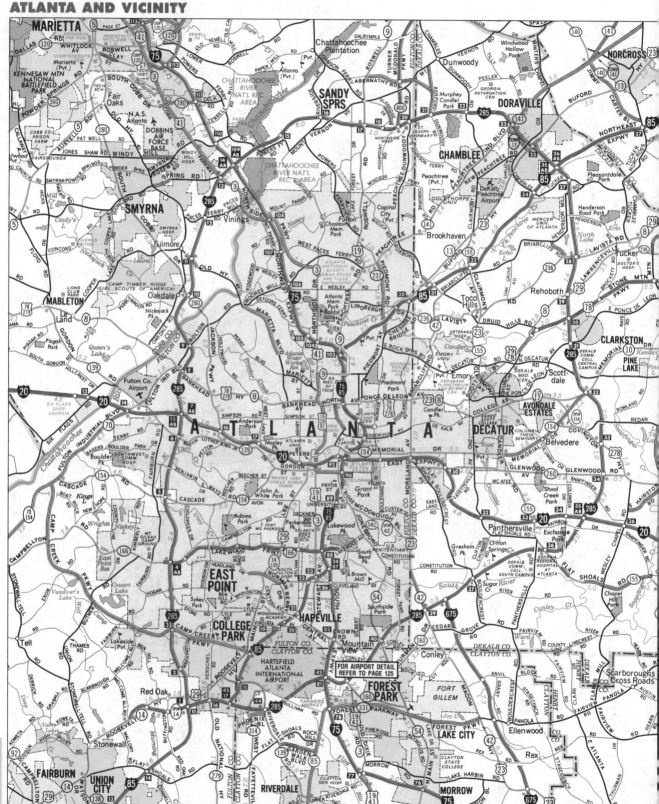

CENTRAL ATLANTA

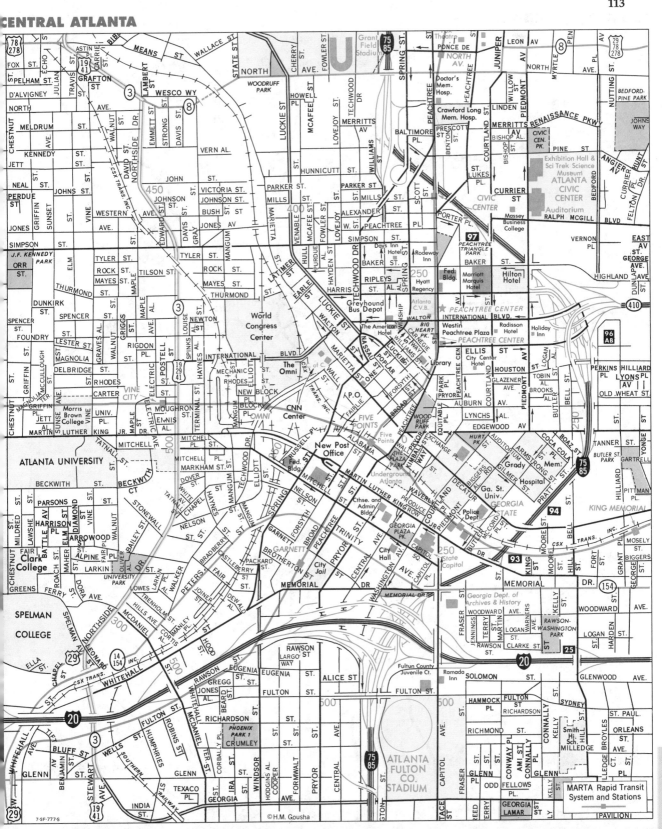

© H.M. Gousha

7-SF-777-S

MARTA Rapid Transit
System and Stations

© H.M. Gousha

11-IV -1600-S

CENTRAL CHARLOTTE

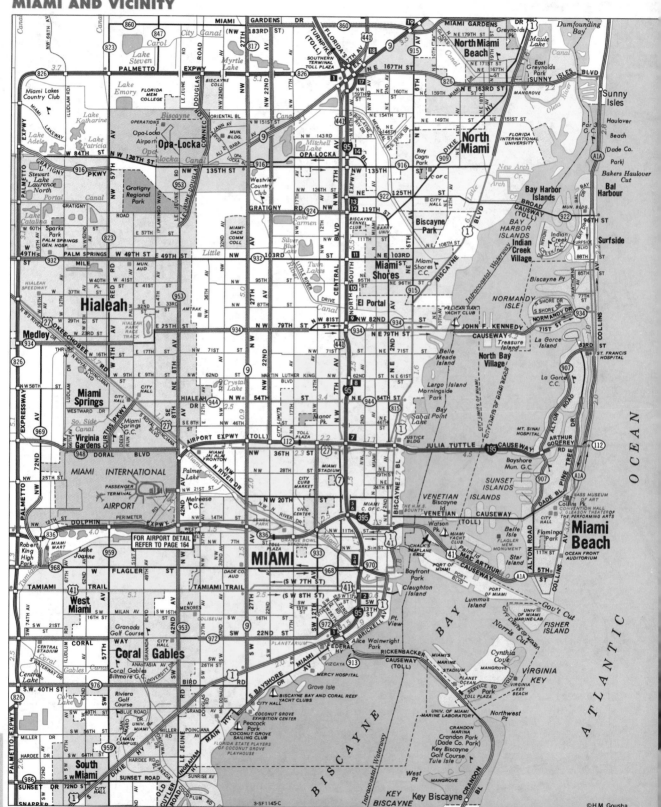

3-SF1145-C

©H.M.Gousha

Metro Rail System and Stations

©H.M. Gousha

12.IV-856-S

ORLANDO AND VICINITY

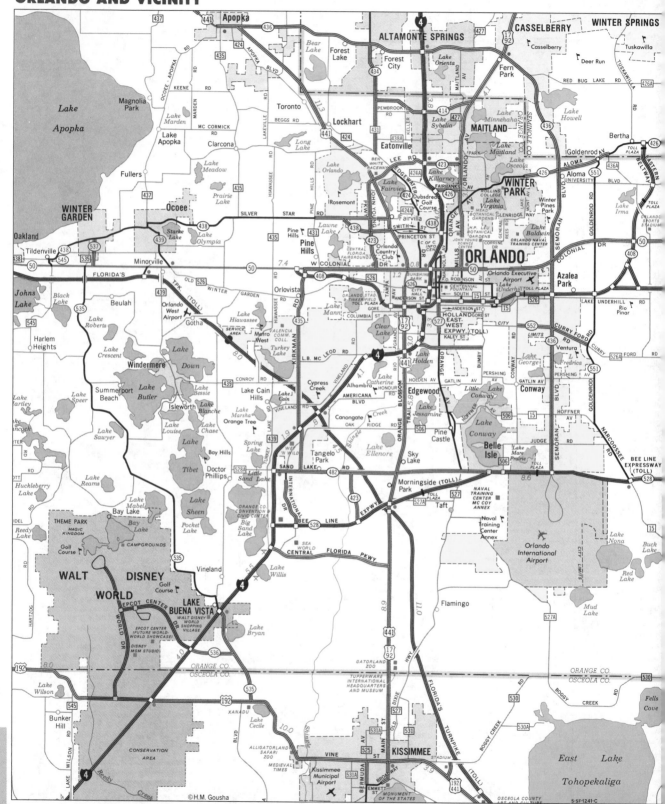

©H.M. Gousha

5-SF-1241-C

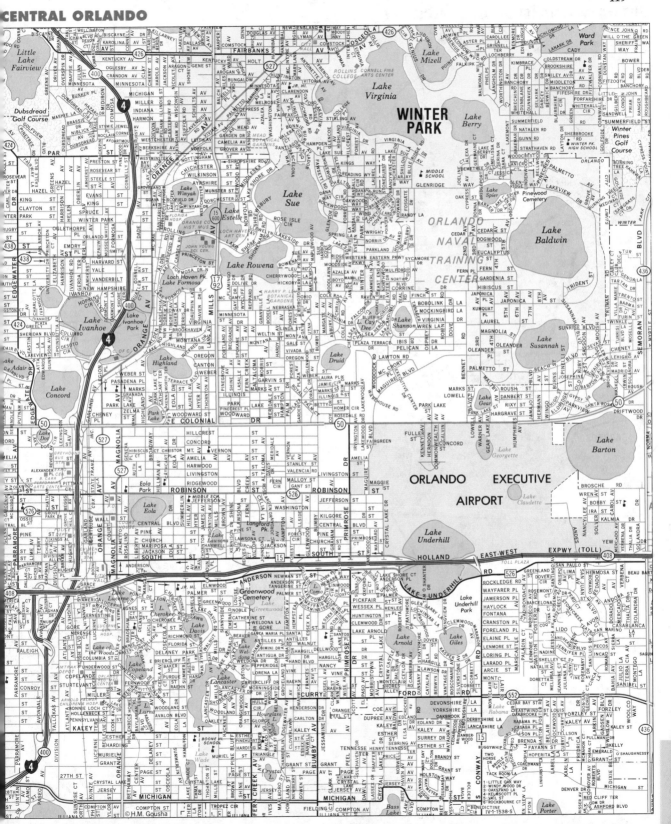

© H.M. Gousha

©H.M. Gousha

CENTRAL RALEIGH

ST. PETERSBURG-TAMPA AND VICINITY

CENTRAL TAMPA

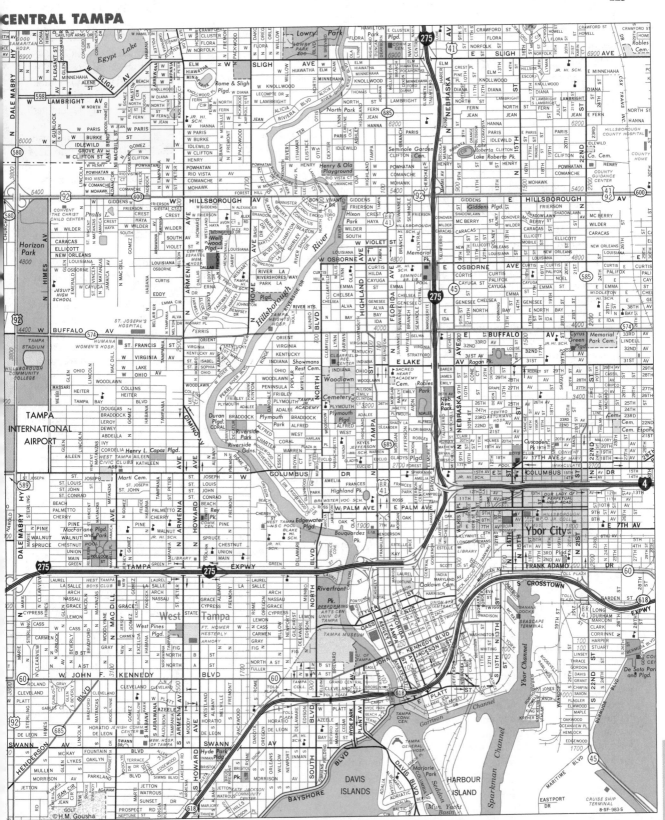

ATLANTA

Area Code: 404
Time Zone: Eastern
Weather: 976-1221
Police: 658-6666
Emergency: 911

Atlanta is both the Old South and the New South. Historically, this city prospered as the crossroads for 4 railroads, and today nobly bears the title of hometown to Dr. Martin Luther King, Jr. Outside Atlanta are graceful pre-Civil War homes that General Sherman spared from his traveling bonfire. Friendly and courteous customs still abide in Atlanta. Yet, Atlanta's Hartsfield International is one of the world's busiest airports. Peachtree Center, which has a network of glass skyways connecting its skyscrapers epitomizes Atlanta's new business image. A young workforce finds Atlanta so attractive that their numbers alone designate the city as a growth region. And top executives polled about the best cities in the U.S. for business elected Atlanta as the number one city. Ted Turner knew a good thing when he established Cable News Network (CNN) here. And Coca-Cola began the real thing in Atlanta decades ago. Not bad for a city that arose from ashes in 1866.

Business Profile
Population: 2,804,000
Population Growth (1980-1989): 31.1%
Unemployment Rate: 5.7%
Fortune 500 Corporate Headquarters: 20

General Information Sources
Atlanta Convention and Visitors Bureau: 521-6600
The Atlanta Chamber of Commerce: 880-9000

Getting There
By Air: Hartsfield Atlanta International
Airport general information: 530-6600
Once you've landed: Atlanta International Airport has domestic flights arriving at 2 terminals, North and South. Each terminal contains 4 concourses, A through D. International flights are handled at the North Terminal which has a special international concourse. International travelers have a long hike from their concourse to Customs. Luckily, signs are clearly posted and baggage carts are free. Transportation between concourses is available on the transportation mall, a computer-operated train which provides quick and free rides to and from domestic gates and baggage claims.
Atlanta Airport Shuttle, 524-3400 provides a 30- to 40-minute ride to downtown hotels at a cost of $7. It leaves from the North Terminal ground transportation area every 20 minutes.

FLYING TIMES
(in hours)
FROM
Atlanta
TO
Chicago: **2**
Los Angeles: **5**
New York: **3**
Miami: **1¾**

Metropolitan Atlanta Rapid Transit Authority (MARTA), 848-4711, provides a direct train ride from the airport to Five Points, the center of downtown Atlanta. The train is located in the South Terminal near the baggage claim and Delta Airlines. It operates 5am-1:30am daily, leaving every 12 minutes. The cost is 85 cents.
A taxi ride to downtown takes 20 to 30 minutes and costs $13.50. Taxis are: Checker Cab Co., 351-1111; Yellow Cab, 521-0200; Rapid Taxi, 691-6666.
Limousines (private): Service is available with 24-hour reservations. A-1 Limousine Services, 299-2388; Carey Limousine of Atlanta, 681-3366; Sun Belt Limousine, 524-3400.
Directions Downtown: Take I-85 north when leaving the airport. Atlanta is 9 miles north of the airport. Take the International Boulevard exit for points downtown.
Overland Adventures: *Route Map:* I-85 is Atlanta's girdle, encircling the city and offering rapid superhighway driving around the center of the city. Three interstate highways also converge in Atlanta, merging with its in-town freeways and beltways: I-75 runs northwest to Tennessee and southeast to Florida; I-85 travels northeast to North Carolina and southwest to Alabama; I-20 is Atlanta's east and west bisector, stretching east to South Carolina and west to Alabama.
Driving Regulations: Right turn on red is permitted unless otherwise stated. Seatbelts are required.
Bottleneck Busters: Atlanta has notorious rush-hour traffic from 7:30am-9:00am and between 4:30pm-6pm. However, during regular hours, the efficient highway system enables rapid traveling. Watch for some tie-ups due to construction of buildings in the downtown area.
Trains: Amtrak Atlanta/Brookwood Station, 1688 Peachtree St. N.W., 881-3060. Traveling north to Washington, D.C. and south to New Orleans, Amtrak makes a daily stop in Atlanta.
Bus Service: Greyhound/Trailways Lines Bus Terminal, 81 International Blvd., 522-6300
Public Transportation: Metropolitan Atlanta Rapid Transit System (MARTA), 848-4711. A combination bus and rapid rail network, MARTA operates a north-south rail line and an east-west rail line centrally joined at Five Points. Its 145 bus routes hook up with 29 rapid rail stations. MARTA operates from 5:30am to 12:30am daily; the fare is 85 cents. Transfers are free but must be picked up at the time exact fare or tokens are deposited.
Road Service and Repairs: American Automobile Association, 875-7175; Metro Mobil Auto Repair, 244-9545; Robinson and Stephens, 624-1207
Parking Regulations: Street and garage parking are readily available.
Towed? Call Property Management Office, 658-6876

International Travelers
Georgia Council for International Visitors: 873-6170

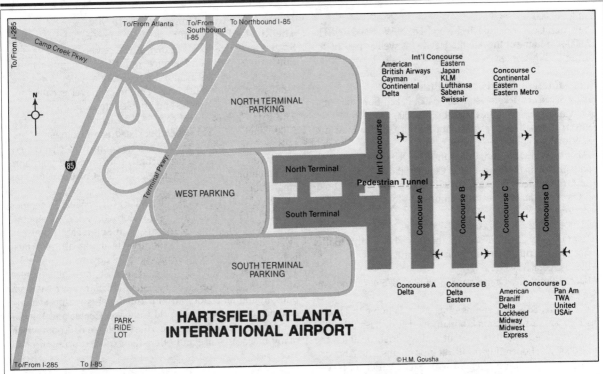

Int'l Concourse
American   Eastern
British Airways   Japan
Cayman   KLM
Continental   Lufthansa
Delta   Sabena
          Swissair

Concourse C
Continental
Eastern
Eastern Metro

NORTH TERMINAL PARKING

WEST PARKING

SOUTH TERMINAL PARKING

North Terminal

South Terminal

Pedestrian Tunnel

Concourse A   Concourse B   Concourse C   Concourse D

Int'l Concourse

PARK-RIDE LOT

HARTSFIELD ATLANTA INTERNATIONAL AIRPORT

Concourse A   Concourse B   Concourse D
Delta   Delta   American   Pan Am
               Eastern   Braniff   TWA
                              Delta   United
                              Lockheed   USAir
                              Midway
                              Midwest
                              Express

© H.M. Gousha

Foreign Currency Exchange: Hartsfield Atlanta Airport, North Terminal
Citizens and Southern National Bank, 35 Broad St. N.W., 581-2121
First Atlanta Bank, 2 Peachtree St., 332-6301
Translation Services: Hartsfield Atlanta International Airport, North Terminal
Berlitz Translation Services, 3400 Peachtree Rd. N.E., 261-5062
Inlingua Translation Service, 3384 Peachtree Rd., N.E., Suite 418, 266-2661
Consulates: Federal Republic of Germany: 659-4760
Japan: 892-2700
Mexico: 688-3258
Foreign Books and Periodicals: Oxford Books, 2345 Peachtree Rd. N.E., 262-3333

Business Visitor's Needs
Banking: Bank South, 55 Marietta St. N.W., 529-4111
Citizens & Southern Bank, 35 Broad St., 581-2009
Georgia Federal Bank, 20 Marietta St. N.W., 330-2400
Trust Company Bank, 25 Park Place N.E., 588-7711
Secretarial Services: Atlanta Freelance Secretarial Services: 880-9560
Executive Secretary: 955-0704
Secretaries Unlimited: 992-7309
Copying and Printing: Copy Center: 355-3355
Kinko's: 221-0000 (open 24 hours, M-F)
Kwik-Kopy: 875-6114

Messengers: Dependable Courier Service, Inc.: 763-1100
Georgia Messenger Service, Inc.: 681-3278
National Courier Systems: 873-6111
Telex Facilities: Telexcel: 988-0401
Medical Needs: Doctor referral: Medical Association of Atlanta: 881-1714
Dental referral: Georgia Dental Association: 458-6166
Pharmacy: Treasury Drugs: 876-0381
Hospitals: Georgia Baptist Medical Center: 653-4136
Crawford W. Long Memorial Hospital of Emory University: 686-4411
Piedmont Hospital: 350-2222

Convention Centers
Atlanta Civic Center, 395 Piedmont Ave. N.E., 523-6275. The Civic Center has seats for 4,600 people in the auditorium, many meeting rooms, and an 8-acre parking lot.
Atlanta Market Center, 240 Peachtree St. N.W., 220-3000 or 220-2216. The Market Center serves a dual function as the Atlanta Apparel Mart and the Atlanta Merchandise Mart, with 186,000 sq. feet available for exhibitions. In 1989 a showcase of communications and high-tech products called Inforum added another 100,000 sq. feet. Skywalks connect this facility to the Peachtree Center across the street.
Georgia World Congress Center, 285 International Blvd. N.W., 656-7676. The Center contains a 2,000-seat auditorium, a ballroom, 77 meeting rooms, and spectacular exhibition halls to-

taling 640,000 sq. feet.
The Omni Coliseum, 100 Techwood Dr. N.W., 681-2100. The 17,000-seat home of the Atlanta Hawks, as well as part of Ted Turner's CNN Center.

Entertainment, Sports, and Culture
Ticket Services: Ticketmaster: 249-6400. Peach Bowl Information (College Football Bowl Game): 586-8500
Sports: Baseball: Braves, Atlanta Fulton County Stadium, 577-9100
Basketball: Hawks, Omni Coliseum, 827-DUNK (827-3865)
Football: Falcons, Atlanta Fulton County Stadium, 261-5400
The Arts: Academy Theatre, 873-2518. The nation's second-oldest resident company features an original founder and a fine repertoire.
Alliance Theatre: 892-PLAY ((892-7529)
Atlanta Civic Center, 892-3303, houses The Atlanta Ballet whose season runs from November to April.
Atlanta Opera: 355-3311
Atlanta Symphony Orchestra: 876-HORN (876-4676); box office 892-2414
Fox Theatre, 881-2000, among other roles, is home to Theatre of the Stars, a production company which utilizes this 1929 movie palace (with its Egyptian and Moorish designs, the world's largest operating theatrical pipe organs, and a historical registry status) as a splendid setting for a variety of plays.
The Robert W. Woodruff Arts Center, 892-3600, is home to the Alliance Theatre Company, Atlanta Symphony Orchestra, the Atlanta Opera, Studio Theatre, Richard H. Rich Auditorium, and Symphony Hall.

Dining: Four Stars and Our Stars
Four Stars: The Dining Room, Ritz-Carlton Hotel, 237-2700. An elegant dining experience, reservations are required and the menu is expensively continental, $32-$64. The setting surrounds diners in Waterford chandeliers, antiques, and original artwork.
Pano's and Paul's, 261-3662. Moderately expensive continental menu, $12.50-$25.50. Specialties include crème brulée, own baking, and desserts. Chef-owned; Victorian decor. Reservations required.
Nikolai's Roof, 659-3282. On the 30th floor, wrapped in elegance and bathed in background music, diners can enjoy the expensive Russian and French menu which includes faisant à la Normandy and canard au muscadet. Reservations.
Our Stars: La Grotta, 231-1368. The Northern Italian menu is moderately priced. Outdoor dining, background music, and specialties like vitello tonnato are notables at La Grotta. Reservations are required.
Trotter's, 237-5988. With a 1920s club ambiance, this continental menu featuring seafood and veal is moderately priced. Reservations and valet parking.

Home Away from Home: Where to Stay
The Ritz-Carlton Atlanta, 181 Peachtree St. N.E., 659-0400. Singles are $155-$175. Located in the center of Atlanta, this hotel offers very good service and attracts many business travelers. Amenities include transportation, valet, concierge, tennis, golf, and health club. The luxury level is called the Ritz-Carlton Club, singles and doubles are $195.
The Ritz-Carlton Buckhead, 3434 Peachtree Rd. N.E., 237-2700. Singles are $135-$199. Buckhead is a fashionable location and this hotel is properly decked out with chandeliers and marble pillars. Pianist, jacuzzi, pool, and exercise room are amenities. The luxury level, the Ritz-Carlton Club, has singles for $199.
Stouffer Waverly, 2450 Galleria Parkway, 953-4500. Singles are $125-$130. Tennis, golf, health club, concierge, transportation, and shopping arcade are available. This hotel has sweeping views of Georgia countryside and an atrium which is 14 stories tall. About 12 miles north of downtown.
Westin Peachtree Plaza, 210 Peachtree St., 659-1400. Singles are $125-$160. A spectacular 73-story circular tower has been built around an 8-story atrium. This hotel is within walking distance of the Georgia World Congress Center and the Atlanta Market Center. It contains the Peachtree Ballroom which many businesses use and offers the expected array of hotel amenities.

Keeping Your Tone Away from Home
Joggers: For jogging information, contact the Atlanta Track Club, 231-9066. Biking and hiking are available at Piedmont Park, 872-1507.
Health Clubs: Atlanta Health and Racquet Club: 952-3200
Peachtree Center Athletic Club: 523-3833
Sportslife: 262-2120
Public Golf Courses: Bobby Jones Golf Course: 355-1009
North Fulton (in Chastain Park): 255-0723
Stone Mountain Golf Course: 498-5717

Shopping
Fashionable Buckhead is home to Lenox Square which has the best shopping in Atlanta. You will find Neiman Marcus, Macy's, and Rich's department store, Brooks Brothers, and specialty shops. Phipps Plaza has Lord and Taylor, Saks Fifth Avenue, and boutiques. For the tourist in all of us, don't miss the spectacular Underground Atlanta. The Underground was just completed in 1989—it is a huge underground/above ground shopping and entertainment marketplace. Other suburban malls are Perimeter Center, Southlake, Shannon, Towne Center, and Gwinnett Place. The sales tax for Georgia is 6%.
Florists: Bussey Florist: 378-6264
Dan Martin Flowers Inc.: 261-1161
Flowers Unlimited: 457-3757 and 800-548-9694 (corporate clients only)

BALTIMORE

Area Code: 301
Time Zone: Eastern
Weather: 936-1212
Police: 396-2525
Emergency: 911

Baltimore has blossomed as a middle child between New York and Washington, D.C. Easily overlooked in the past, this major port city has a revitalized Inner Harbor, a renovated Charles Street Center, some gentrified urban dwellers, and a reasonable cost of living compared to its sister cities like Philadelphia. Located here are such companies as General Motors, Procter and Gamble, and McCormick, king of the spice industry. Johns Hopkins Medical Center is a leader in biotechnology. City services are in order; the crime rate is on the way down. And you won't want to miss the National Aquarium (567-3810) with its tropical rain forest and outstanding marine life.

Business Profile
Population: 2,358,000
Population Growth (1980-1989): 7.2%
Unemployment Rate: 4.8%
Fortune 500 Corporate Headquarters: 6

General Information Sources
Baltimore Convention and Visitors Association: 659-7300
Visitor's Information Center (Inner Harbor, Summer): 837-INFO (837-4636)
Baltimore Economic Development Corporation: 837-9305
Office of the Mayor: 396-3100

Getting There
By Air: Baltimore-Washington International Airport (BWI) general information, 859-7111; ground transportation desk, 859-7545
Once you've landed: BWI's central terminal has 5 Piers (A through E) from which domestic and foreign flights are handled. Because of its close proximity to Baltimore and Washington, D.C., BWI serves both cities.
A taxi ride to downtown Baltimore will cost about $13 and take about 20 minutes. However, a taxi ride to Washington, D.C. will cost about $37, take 45 minutes and require an agreed-upon price prior to departure. Some taxi services are: G.T.P. Inc. (BWI), 859-1103; Owings Mills Taxicab, 486-4000; Sun Cab, 235-0300; Yellow Cab, 685-1212.
Airport Connections Limousine and Van Service, 859-7545, travels to many downtown hotels. Located at BWI's Ground

Transportation, vans run from 5:30am until 11pm M-F, and hourly on the weekends. The cost is $5.75 one way and $10 round trip. For door-to-door service, call 441-2345.
Airport Connections also accommodates the needs of those traveling to Washington, D.C. Leaving hourly, open daily, at a cost of $12, vans travel to the Washington Hilton, Capital Hilton, and Greenbelt Terminal, which is the company's transfer station. Travelers can make connections with buses going to the city at Greenbelt Terminal, right outside the Capitol, and on the Washington-Baltimore Parkway.
The Mass Transit Administration (MTA), 539-5000, has bus service to and from BWI and downtown Baltimore. The No. 16 Howard and Druid Hill bus departs at the MTA sign on the lower level of the central terminal. The bus debarks at Charles and Lombard Sts., and the ride takes about 55 minutes; fare, $1.15. Four buses run in the morning and 4 in the afternoon, M-F. One morning and 1 afternoon bus are available on Sat.; no buses run on Sun. MTA also provides bus connections between BWI and National Airport (in Washington) every hour, Sun.-F. The cost is $12 and the ride takes about 80 minutes.
Free shuttle service is provided between the airport and the rail terminal Amtrak's BWI Station, 674-1167. Ask at Ground Transportation about the shuttle's frequency.
Limousines (private): Service can be reserved with 24-hour notice: Carey National Limousine, 837-1234; International Limousine, 636-4700.
Directions to Downtown Baltimore: Follow the airport signs and bear right when the road splits. Follow the signs for Baltimore and the Baltimore Washington Parkway (I-295). Baltimore is 10 miles north of BWI, and both I-295 and eventually I-95 travel through the center of Baltimore.
Directions to Downtown Washington, D.C: Once on the Baltimore Washington Parkway (I-295 S), Washington is 25 miles or about half an hour south of BWI. The New York exit is handy for a direct downtown route.
Overland Adventures: *Route Map:* Baltimore has a network of interstates and tunnels that enable a driver either to enter the city or bypass the downtown area. Encircling the city is the Baltimore Beltway I-695 which interchanges with all major approach routes. Traveling north and south through Baltimore is I-95. A fast way to circumvent downtown Baltimore when traveling I-95 is to take the Harbor Tunnel Thruway (I-895) which goes around the city and under the harbor. This route feeds back into I-95 north and south of the city. Finally, Baltimore's direct connection with neighboring Washington, D.C. is its Baltimore Washington Parkway, I-295, which runs north and south between the cities.
Driving Regulations: Right turns on red lights are permitted unless otherwise indicated. Seat belts are mandatory; beltless drivers may be fined $25.

FLYING TIMES
(in hours)
FROM
Baltimore
TO
Chicago: 2¼
Los Angeles: 5
New York: 1
Atlanta: 1½

Bottleneck Busters: Rush hour traffic between the hours of 7:30am-9:30am and 4:30pm-6:30pm slows the pace in and around Baltimore. Try listening to WBAL-AM 1090 news talk radio for traffic and road updates.

Trains: Amtrak, Penn Station, 1500 N. Charles St., 291-4260, and BWI Station, Anne Arundel County, 674-1167. BWI Station handles local commuter service between Baltimore and Washington and regular passenger service. For further information call 800-USA-RAIL (800-872-7245). Amtrak also provides inner city rail service, commuter service, and regular passenger service: the MARC provides local commuter service along the Baltimore/Washington corridor. The coach fare is $10. The service begins at Penn Station, stops at BWI Station and travels on to Union Station in Washington, D.C.. Amtrak also has connections to major northeast corridor cities.

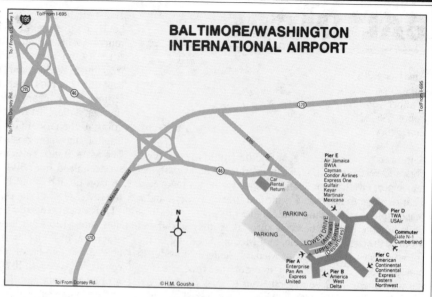

BALTIMORE/WASHINGTON INTERNATIONAL AIRPORT

Bus Service: Greyhound/Trailways Lines, 210 W. Fayette St. and 5625 O'Donnell St., 744-9311

Public Transportation: Mass Transit Administration (MTA), 539-5000. MTA has both bus and Metrorail (subway) service and operates 70 bus routes and 14 miles of rail. Most bus routes operate 24 hours daily; the base fare is $1. Metrorail's main station is called Charles Center Station and is located on the corner of Charles and Baltimore Sts. A 28-minute ride for $1.50 will go as far northwest as Owings Mills with many stops along the way. The service operates M-Sat., but not on Sun.

Trolleys are a convenient way to get around the center of Baltimore. The Charles St. route runs north and south from the Mount Vernon district to the Inner Harbor. The Inner Harbor trolley runs east and west to Fells Point. Operating about every 15 minutes and costing 25 cents, trolley rides are available daily from 11am to 7pm. For further information call Baltimore Trolley Works, 396-4393.

Glass-encased skywalks link the Inner Harbor to downtown hotels and stretch from Hopkins Plaza to Harborplace so that pedestrians can walk 14 blocks without having to cross any streets.

Water Taxis are a fun way to explore the harbor, 547-0090.

Road Service and Repairs: AAA Road Service, 462-1600; Brooklyn Servicenter, 355-8330; Eastern Exxon Servicenter, 633-5900

Parking Regulations: Street parking is difficult during business hours, but there are many parking garages especially east of the harbor. The cost is between $6 and $7 per day.

Towed? Call 396-9958

International Travelers

Foreign Currency Exchange: Ace Currency Exchange, 230 Park Ave., 752-7451

Maryland National Bank, Baltimore and Light Sts., 244-5000

Tele-Trip, BWI Pier C, Mutual of Omaha Service Center, 859-5997

Translation Services: Berlitz Translation Service, 2 N. Charles, 752-0767

Translingua Inc., 1320 Lafayette Ave., 744-7582

Foreign Books and Periodicals: News Center, Harborplace, 301 S. Light St., 685-1804

Business Visitor's Needs

Banking: The Bank of Baltimore, Baltimore and Charles Sts., 244-3360

Citibank, 6 St. Paul Center, 800-431-1350

First National Bank of Maryland, City Hall Plaza, Holiday and Fayette Sts., 625-9737

Provident Bank of Maryland, 114 E. Lexington St., 576-2872

Secretarial Services: Able Temporaries: 685-8189

ExecuType Business Centers: 542-2755

Kelly Services: 298-4490

Copying and Printing: Copy Cat Printing: 889-4800

ExecuType Business Centers: 542-2755

Kinko's: 625-5862 (open 24 hours)

Messengers: Dial Courier Network, Inc.: 269-5347

Maryland Messenger Service, Inc.: 837-5550

Telex Facilities: Western Union: 800-779-1111

Medical Needs: Doctor referral: Greater Baltimore Medical

Center: 828-4262
Dental referral: Dental Society: 752-3318
Pharmacies: Revco Drug Stores: 744-1422
Rite Aid Discount Pharmacies: 574-8750
Hospitals: Harbor Hospital Center: 347-3200
Johns Hopkins Hospital: 955-5000
St. Agnes Hospital: 368-6000
Maryland General Hospital: 225-8000

Convention Centers

Convention Center/Festival Hall, 1 W. Pratt St., 659-7000. Located in the scenic Inner Harbor area, this facility has 165,000 sq. feet of exhibit space and 45,000 sq. feet of meeting room space. The Convention Center and downtown hotels are connected to the Inner Harbor via a skywalk system.
Baltimore Arena, 201 W. Baltimore St., 347-2010. The arena is host to many forms of entertainment; it has 14,000 seats. Complete with built-in stage, the modern facilities and sound system make this an exhibitor's dream.

Entertainment, Sports, and Culture

Ticket Services: Ticketcenter: 481-6000
Sports: Baseball: Baltimore Orioles, Memorial Stadium, 338-1300
Box Lacrosse: Baltimore Thunder, Baltimore Arena, 347-2000
Hockey: Baltimore Skipjacks, Baltimore Arena, 727-0703
Indoor Soccer: Baltimore Blast, Baltimore Arena, 528-0100
The Arts: Call 837-INFO (837-4636) for current Arts information.
Center Stage, 332-0033, houses theatrical productions. Center Stage's resident troupe performs classical and contemporary plays.
Lyric Opera House, 832-1200, ext. 2137 or 685-5086, has great acoustics, important for the Baltimore Opera and other musical productions.
Morris A. Mechanic Theatre, 625-1400, hosts Broadway numbers and stage productions.
The Joseph Meyerhoff Symphony Hall, 783-8000, is the Baltimore Symphony Orchestra's home.
Peabody Conservatory of Music, 659-8100, is America's oldest music school. The Conservatory hosts musical programs.

Dining: Four Stars and Our Stars

Brass Elephant, 547-8480. With a choice of 5 dining areas, the Brass Elephant serves an Italian menu, has reasonable prices and the stained glass windows and marble fireplaces are impressive.
Haussner's, 327-8365. European ambiance with the added flair of original artwork. Haussner's German/American menu is reasonably priced and offers such choices as seafood and sour beef.
Pimlico (Pikesville), 486-6776. Pimlico's offers a varied menu; the grilled swordfish and Imperial crab are specialties. Quite reasonable, the background music, entertainment, and free valet parking are nice perks.

Tio Pepe, 539-4675. Tio Pepe is chef-owned and the menu offers such wonders as whole suckling pig and roast baby pheasant with grape sauce. Spanish menu and Spanish decor.

Home Away from Home: Where to Stay

Hyatt Regency Baltimore, 300 Light St., 528-1234. Single rooms cost $119-$145; Luxury Level singles cost $160-$175. On the harbor, the Hyatt offers concierge, valet parking, health club facilities, tennis, and airport transportation.
Radisson Plaza Lord Baltimore, Baltimore and Hanover Sts., 539-8400. Single rooms $80-$160; Luxury Level singles $90-$135. This classic hotel was built in 1928 and has been restored so that such touches as murals, carved moldings, and pillars abound. Such amenities as valet parking and health club facilities are provided.
Omni International, 101 Fayette St., 752-1100. Single rooms are $74-$104. Amenities include pool with poolside service, airport transportation, exercise room, and a business center.
Society Hill, 58 W. Biddle St., 837-3630. For a cozy almost inn-like experience, this 4-story hotel has a winding staircase, antique decor, and a Victorian building. Singles $65-$75.

Keeping Your Tone Away from Home

Joggers, Hikers, and Bikers: Baltimore has many parks, and most of them have trails for walking and jogging. For further information call the Department of Recreation and Parks, 396-7901. Short hikes through nature trails can be found at Druid Hill Park, 396-6106, which is home to the Baltimore Zoo. Also the Cylburn Arboretum, 396-0180, has fine nature trails. For information about bicycling trails, contact the Bicycling Hotline, 333-1663.
Health Clubs: Baltimore Racquet and Fitness Club: 625-6400
Downtown Athletic Club: 547-6984
Public Golf Courses: Carroll Park Golf Course: 685-8344
Clifton Park Golf Course: 243-3500
Forest Park Golf Course: 448-4653

Shopping

The place to shop in Baltimore is Harborplace's 2 pavilions on Pratt and Light Sts. Over 100 shops offer fine clothing selections and handmade gifts from around the world. Antique Row has blocks of antique buys. Try the Lexington market complex for a taste of what shopping was like 200 years ago—135 merchants display food and wares. Or, for mall shoppers who are also seeking department stores, try the Convention Center Mall. Don't forget Charles St. which offers boutiques and clothiers.
Florists: Federal Hill Florist: 837-4380
Michael Anthony Florist of Baltimore: 576-7600
Roland Park Florist: 435-2100

BOSTON

Area Code: 617
Time Zone: Eastern
Weather: 936-1234
Police: Metro: 523-1212; State: 566-4500
Emergency: 911

The economy of Boston is heavily diversified, with a base of finance and insurance, retail trade and industry, business and medical services, higher education, and tourism. Investment in construction of commercial structures, medical, educational and cultural facilities, and housing in the city has been increasing in the last few years.

Boston's harbor, which covers over 30,000 acres, is one of the world's largest and busiest, with millions of tons of cargo handled each year. It is a major economic asset to the city. More than 5,000 manufacturing firms make Boston a major industrial center as well. It is a favorite of conventioneers and business travelers because it has so much to offer with its historical heritage, sightseeing opportunities, and cultural and entertainment choices.

Business Profile
Population: 2,861,000
Population Growth (1980-1989): 2%
Unemployment Rate: 3.4%
Fortune 500 Corporate Headquarters: 12

General Information Sources
24-hour Service and Information (Mayor Raymond Flynn's office): 725-4500
Greater Boston Convention & Visitors Bureau Inc.: 536-4100
Greater Boston Chamber of Commerce: 227-4500
National Park Visitors Center: 242-5642

Getting There
By Air: Logan Airport Public Information Office: 561-1800
Logan Airport Ground Transportation Hotline: 800-235-6426
Pan Am, 800-221-1111, and Trump Airlines, 800-247-8786, run hourly air shuttles to New York City, Trump on the hour and Pan Am on the half-hour.

Once you've landed: Free shuttle buses connect all airline terminals with the MBTA Blue Line, the fastest way to downtown. Three buses circulate regularly and come every 8-12 minutes. Call the Logan Airport Hotline (above) or the MBTA at 800-392-6100.

Buses and van limousines leave from most of the major downtown hotels and are available at the terminals. Fees range from $3.25 to $6.50. Among them, American International Rent-a-

Car, 569-3550; and City Transportation, 236-1888.

Limousines (private): Reservations 24 hours in advance are recommended. Standard Limousine, 569-3880; Takumi Limo Service, 738-6244 (drivers speak Japanese).

Taxis can be hired both at the hotels and at the airport. Fares should range around $10 to a downtown hotel. (Property that is lost or missing after a taxi ride should be reported to the Boston police department's Hackney Carriage Unit, 536-8294.)

Airport Water Shuttle: 800-235-6426. Leaves every 15 minutes M-F (except major holidays) from 6am to 8pm from Rowes Wharf (High St. and Atlantic Ave.). Free shuttle bus operates from airport ferry dock to all terminals. On weekends, it runs every half-hour from 12pm to 7:30pm (Pick-up from the airport dock is on the quarter hour, 12:15pm to 8:15pm.)

Helicopter Service: Individual arrangements through Hub Express, 800-962-4744

Directions Downtown: Follow signs for exiting the airport complex, and look for signs leading to Boston/Central Artery. You'll be on I-93. It will take you inside a tunnel (stay in right lane). Take first right when you get outside tunnel—almost a U-turn (DON'T go back onto I-93 north). You'll be in downtown Boston on Northern St.

Overland Adventures: *Route Map:* I-95 runs north-south along the eastern coast and circles west around downtown Boston. I-93 (Central Artery) runs north-south through the heart of Boston. I-90 (Massachusetts Turnpike) runs east-west into downtown Boston.

Driving Regulations: No seat belt law. Right turn allowed on red except where indicated.

Bottleneck Busters: Boston is a city under constant reconstruction and redevelopment. Projects currently affect traffic in Cultural District, Boston Historic Waterfront, and Back Bay.

Trains: Amtrak trains run downtown into South Station, Summer St. and Atlantic Ave., 482-3660 or 800-872-7245

Bus Service: Greyhound/Trailways Lines Terminal, 10 St. James Ave., 423-5810. Continental Trailways Terminal, 55 Atlantic Ave., 426-7838. Both companies operate state, interstate, and Canadian travel.

Public Transportation: Massachusetts Bay Transportation Authority (MBTA), 722-3200, operates all the subways, trolleys, city buses, and commuter trains (which run 5am to 12:30am).

Road Service and Repairs: If you break down on the Massachusetts Turnpike, stay with your car. A police cruiser should pass by any given stretch of road within 10 minutes, and they will contact repair or towing operators for you. Other services (like AAA) are not allowed on the turnpike, so don't bother with a call. Tow trucks are stationed every 20 miles. The Turnpike Authority's number is 973-7300.

Parking Regulations: Most downtown hotels have their own

FLYING TIMES (in hours)	
FROM Boston	
TO	
Chicago:	3½
Los Angeles:	5½
New York:	1
Miami:	3¼

parking garages or arrangements with off-street lots. Street parking with 1-hour meters is the norm, but beware: cars in Boston are heavily ticketed and regularly towed after 60 minutes, so note down the time when you park. Check for signs indicating no parking between 6:30pm and 6:30am., or between 4pm and 6pm. The tow trucks are out immediately. *Towed?* Call the Department of Public Utilities, 727-3559

International Travelers

Foreign Currency Exchange: BayBank, Terminal C at Logan Airport, 569-1172; Terminal E, 567-2313

Deak International, 160 Franklin St., 426-0016

Translation Services: Berlitz Translation Services, 437 Boylston St., 266-6858

Europacific Translations, 872 Massachusetts Ave., 354-6110

Consulates and International Organizations: As one of the major political and financial cities in the U.S., Boston has many foreign consulates and representatives, many of them clustered along Boylston St.; they are listed in the phone book's blue pages.

Foreign Books and Periodicals: Asian Books, 12 Arrow St., 354-0005

Harvard Coop, 1400 Massachusetts Ave., 492-1000

Schoenhof's Foreign Books, 76-A Mt. Auburn St., 547-8855

Business Visitor's Needs

Banking: Bank of New England, 28 State St., 742-4000

Shawmut Bank, 100 Federal St., 292-2000 (call for other locations)

Full Service Assistance: Boston Mimeo and Stenographic Service: 482-4696

Office Plus: 367-8335

The Skill Bureau: 423-2986 or 661-6699

Secretarial Service: Accountemps: 951-4000

Kelly Services: 890-7778

Copying and Printing: Copy Cop: 267-9267 (call for other locations)

Sir Speedy Instant Printing: 267-9711 (call for other locations)

Fax and Telex Facilities: Boston Telex: 576-5788

Kinko's: 491-2859 (Also provides word processor time rental and other services.)

Messengers: Choice Courier: 787-2020

Marathon Messenger: 266-8990

Medical Needs: Doctor referral: Massachusetts Medical Society: 893-4610

Dental referral: Massachusetts Dental Society: 508-651-7511

Pharmacy: Phillips Drug: 523-4372 (open 24 hours)

Hospitals: Massachusetts General: 726-2000 (no credit cards)

Brigham and Women's Hospital: 732-5636

Mt. Auburn: 492-3500

Convention Centers

The phone numbers given for each facility should be able to

tell you if special transportation arrangements have been made to the major hotels.

Bayside Exposition Center, 200 Mount Vernon St., 825-5151. 200,000 sq. feet of exhibition space.

John B. Hynes Convention Center, 900 Boylston St., 954-2000. 190,000 sq. feet of exhibition space, a 4,000-seat auditorium with full stage facilities, 25 permanent meeting rooms (one even holds up to 800), and several smaller rooms seating from 25-350.

World Trade Center, Commonwealth Pier, 439-5000. Huge 875,000-sq.-foot exhibition, conference, and meeting complex.

Entertainment, Sports, and Culture

Ticket Services: Tickets for most events and games can be charged with a phone call to the box offices or to Teletron, 720-3434 or 800-382-8080.

Sports: Baseball: Red Sox, Fenway Park, 267-8661

Basketball: Celtics, Boston Garden, 227-3200 or 227-3206

Football: New England Patriots, Sullivan Stadium (Foxboro), 509-543-1776

Hockey: Bruins, Boston Garden, 227-3200 or 227-3206

The Arts: Bostix provides half-price tickets on same-day performances, Faneuil Hall Marketplace, 723-5181.

Boston Ballet Company: 964-4070

Charles Playhouse: 426-6912

Colonial Theatre: 426-9366

Loeb Drama Center: 547-8300

Metropolitan Center: 542-3600

Opera Company of Boston: 426-5301

Shubert Theatre: 426-4520

Wilbur Theatre: 423-4008

Concert Halls: Berklee Performance Center: 266-7455
Boston Center for the Arts: 426-7700
Symphony Hall: 266-1492
Wang Center for the Performing Arts: 482-7393
Museums: Boston Center for the Arts: 426-5000
Hichborn Museum: 523-1676
Museum of Fine Arts: 267-9300

Dining: Four Stars and Our Stars

Le Marquis de Lafayette, 451-2600. Elegantly appointed room with Waterford chandeliers. French menu. Very expensive. Closed Sundays.
Jasper's, 523-1126. On the waterfront. Contemporary New England menu with deco decor. Intimate dining. Dinner to $45.
Cafe Budapest, 266-1979. Hungarian menu, old-world elegance. Dinner from $21.
Maison Robert, 227-3370. French menu, specializing in fish, white veal, lamb. Two dining areas, Bonhomme Richard the more elegant. Dinner to $40.
Julien, 451-1900. Nouvelle; the specialty is breast of duck. Renaissance garden decor. Dinner to $60.
Biba, 426-7878. Eclectic, moderately-priced menu. Right on the Public Garden—great view.
No Name, 338-7539. Specializes in fresh fish, seafood only. View of ocean and fishing boats.
Felicia's, 523-9885. Italian menu and furnishings, fresh pasta of course. Dinners to $15.
Grill 23, 542-2255. American, meaty. Oriental rugs and antique furnishings. Moderate.
Tatsukichi, 720-2468. Sushi and sashimi are the specialties here, and the Foreign Affairs Lounge active for cocktails.

Home Away from Home: Where to Stay

Bostonian, Faneuil Hall Marketplace, 523-3600 or 800-343-0922. Every convenience. Singles start at $175.
Four Seasons, 200 Boylston St., 338-4400. Classic elegance, overlooks public gardens, gift shop. Singles start at $185.
Marriott-Copley Place, 110 Huntington Ave., 236-5800 or 800-228-9290. Singles and doubles start at $185, Luxury Level singles $195 and up (private lounge, continental breakfast, concierge service, etc.).
Hotel Meridien, 250 Franklin St., 451-1900 or 800-543-4300. In the financial district. Has everything including shopping arcade. Singles start at $195.
Ritz-Carlton, 15 Arlington at Newbury St., 536-5700 or 800-241-3333. Grooming shops, shopping arcade, everything else. Singles start at $195. Ritz-Carlton Club level includes afternoon tea, breakfast, evening cocktails, the works. Singles start at $325.
Copley Square, 47 Huntington Ave., 536-9000 or 800-225-7062. Worn, but some charm left. Houses Cafe Budapest. No room service, but free coffee in rooms, and fitness arrange-

ments made for you if you wish. Singles start at $86.
Boston Park Plaza Hotel and Towers, 50 Park Plaza at Arlington St., 426-2000 or 800-225-2008. Grooming shops, garage parking. Singles start at $110.
Beacon Street Guest House, 1047 Beacon St., 232-0292. 14-room inn with some shared baths, rooms $30-69. Continental breakfast included.

Keeping Your Tone Away from Home

Joggers and Bikers: Casual joggers and bikers head for the Esplanade's paths along the Charles River. For bike rental try Community Bike, 542-8623. Almost all the major hotels have fitness clubs and many have pools. The desk may be able to make reservations for court sports and tell you where to pick up a game of basketball.
Health Clubs: Boston Athletic Club: 269-4300
Boston Racquet Club: 482-8881
YMCA: 536-7800
YWCA: 536-7940
Public Golf Courses: Fresh Pond Golf Club: 354-9130
Martin Golf Course: 894-4903
Ponkapoag Golf Course: 828-0645

Shopping

Go to Copley Place for Neiman Marcus and designers like Ralph Lauren, Gucci, Yves St. Laurent, and Tiffany's. Nearby is Downtown Crossing, older but with more department stores. One of them, Filene's, is known for terrific bargains on expensive clothing. For pricey antique shops, art galleries, and boutiques, Newbury St. in the Back Bay area offers the best selection and the most stylish window shopping.
Faneuil Hall is filled with bars, shops, and restaurants, but may have more of a touristy gift selection. And for that lover of books and records, nothing beats Harvard Square in Cambridge, with its Garage and Galleria (malls of small shops) and the Harvard Coop.
Florists: Greenhouse: 437-1050
Victorian Bouquet: 367-6648
Winston Flowers: 536-6861

CHARLOTTE

Area Code: 704
Time Zone: Eastern
Weather: 359-8466
Police: 336-2351
Emergency: 911

Charlotte is proud of a history that stretches from its Revolutionary War heritage to a modern-day reputation that has brought powerhouses like Fieldcrest/Cannon Mills, Duke Power, and Nucor to its doorstep. It also hosts the World Seniors Golf Tournament, Jazz Charlotte, and the World 600 races. The city's restored Fourth Ward is a symbol of a venerable and distinguished city. Charlotte has so much going for it, it's no wonder that its residents are some of the most friendly and self-assured city dwellers around!

Business Profile
Population: 389,650
Population Growth (1980-1989): 16%
Unemployment Rate: 3.2%
Fortune 500 Corporate Headquarters: 1

General Information Sources
Charlotte Convention and Visitors' Bureau: 334-2282
Charlotte Chamber of Commerce: 377-6911
Visitor Information Center: 377-INFO (377-4636)

Getting There
By Air: Charlotte/Douglass International Airport general information: 359-4013
Once you've landed: The airport sports a new International Complex offering 21 commuter gates and 4 international gates. Yellow Cab Limousine provides rides from the airport to downtown hotels. The cost is $4, the ride is 20 to 25 minutes. Service runs from 7:00am to 11pm daily. Call about weekend service, 332-6161.
A taxi cab takes about 15 minutes and costs about $11; additional passengers ride for $2 extra and additional bags are 50 cents. A Circle Cab Co., 375-1010; Charlotte Checker, 333-1111; Yellow Cab, 332-6161.
Limousines (private): Service available with 24-hour reservations: Executive Transportation, 347-0211
Directions Downtown: When leaving the airport take the Airport Freeway. Turn left at the first stoplight. This road will dead end so turn right onto Wilkinson Blvd. Charlotte is 8 miles east of the airport. Eventually, Wilkinson Blvd. becomes the John Belt Parkway. A central downtown exit would be College St.

FLYING TIMES
(in hours)
FROM
Charlotte
TO
Chicago: 2
Dallas: 2½
New York: 1½
Miami: 2

Overland Adventures: *Route Map:* Charlotte's routes are conveniently near, but do not intersect the city's business area. I-277 is the beltway running north and south around downtown. I-77 travels north as far as Cleveland, OH and south to Columbia, SC. I-85 travels west to Atlanta, GA and east to Petersburg, VA. U.S. 74 is an east to west route connecting Charlotte to the coast at Wilmington, NC
Driving Regulations: Right turn on red is permitted unless otherwise indicated. Seat belts are mandatory, a $25 fine will be issued to passengers who fail to wear seatbelts.
Bottleneck Busters: Since Charlotte's major interstates don't go through the city, and beltway I-277 travels around the downtown area, traffic problems are few.
Trains: Amtrak, 1914 N. Tryon St., 376-4416
Bus Service: Greyhound/Trailways Lines, 601 W. Trade St., 527-9393
Public Transportation: Charlotte Transit System, 336-3366, provides local bus service for 70 cents one way and express service for a $1 one way. No-fare zones are possible in uptown Charlotte on Tryon and Trade Sts. between the hours of 9am and 3pm.
Road Service and Repairs: For service call: AAA Carolina Motor Club, 377-3600; AAA Wrecker Service, 398-2222
Parking Regulations: Both street parking and lot parking are abundant.
Towed? Call Beaty's, 338-9360; Hunter's, 375-9357; S and R, 333-4555

International Travelers
International Organizations: International House, 322 Hawthorne Lane, 333-8099
Foreign Currency Exchange: First Citizens Bank, Charlotte/Douglass International Airport (across from concourse C), 335-4340
First Union National Bank, 301 S. Tryon St., 374-6025
Translation Services: Berlitz Translation Services, 6512 Six Forks Rd., Raleigh, 919-870-9521
Carolina Translation Service, 1431 Sterling Rd., 375-5267
International House, 322 Hawthorne Lane, 333-8099
Foreign Books and Periodicals: Newsstands International, Providence Square Shopping Center, 365-0910

Business Visitor's Needs
Banking: BB&T, 200 S. Tryon St., 342-7000
North Carolina National Bank, 101 S. Tryon St., 374-5000
United Carolina Bank, 212 S. Tryon St., 377-6506
Secretarial Services: Executive Support: 342-3205
Kelly Services: 372-3440
Copying and Printing: Kinko's: 358-8008
Kopy Korner Printing: 554-7060
Kwik-Kopy Printing: 332-6521
Messengers: Transit Express Co.: 338-9000

Tryke Express: 333-4800 or 333-1604
Telex Facilities: Pack It Services: 588-7447
Western Union: 800-325-6000
Medical Needs: Doctor referral: Presbyterian Hospital Free
Physician Referral: 371-4111
Dental referral: Charlotte Dental Society: 358-8303
Pharmacies: Eckerd Drugs: 375-5556
Revco Drugs: 375-4930
Hospitals: Carolinas Medical Center: 355-2000
Presbyterian Hospital: 371-4000
University Memorial Hospital: 547-9200

Convention Centers

Charlotte Convention Center, 101 S. College St., 332-5051. The Charlotte Convention Center exhibit space totals 134,000 sq. feet. In addition, this facility boasts 2 auditoriums, 2 banquet areas and many meeting rooms.
The Merchandise Mart, 2500 E. Independence Blvd., 333-7709, is also available for exhibits and shows.

Entertainment, Sports, and Culture

Ticket Services: Teletron, 800-543-3041; Ticketron (walk-in) at Camelot Music Stores
Sports: Baseball: Charlotte Knights, Knights Castle, 332-3746 or 803-548-8051
Basketball: Charlotte Hornets, Charlotte Coliseum, 376-6430
Racetrack: Charlotte Motor Speedway, NASCAR and SCCA racing, 455-2121
The Arts: Ovens Auditorium, 372-3600, is home to Charlotte Symphony Orchestra (which also features a summer Pops in the Park series), Opera Carolina, and the Oratorio Singers of Charlotte. Charlotte City Ballet and the Charlotte Choral Society also perform here.
Spirit Square Center for the Arts, 376-8883, is a multi-purpose center which among other functions is home to Charlotte City Ballet Company, Charlotte Choral Society, and Charlotte Repertory Theatre.

Dining: Four Stars and Our Stars

Lamp Lighter, 372-5343. This French-American restaurant is housed in a 1910 Spanish revival home. Specialties include beef Wellington and raspberry cognac. Dinners are moderately priced.
Reflections, 377-0400. Elegant dining and reservations required. Features a continental menu, pianist, and free parking. Moderately priced.
Morrocrofts, 364-8220. An English club motif, regional cuisine, and background music make this restaurant decorative yet comfortable. Moderately priced.

Home Away from Home: Where to Stay

Park, 2200 Rexford Rd., 364-8220. Single rooms are $99-$109. Amenities include a pool with poolside service, health club,

golf privileges, concierge, and transportation. The Park is quite a beautifully decorated spot.
Guest Quarters, 6300 Morrison Blvd., 364-2400. Single rooms cost $110-$160. Private patios and balconies make this hotel special. Amenities include pool with poolside service, tennis and golf privileges, health club, and free airport transportation.

Keeping Your Tone Away from Home

Joggers: Keeping joggers and walkers in mind, Charlotte developed a series of linearly connected parks which skirt local creeks and make for scenic walking or jogging routes. Call Charlotte City Parks and Recreation Department, 336-2464, for further information.
Health Clubs: YMCA: 333-7771
YWCA: 525-5770
Public Golf Courses: Pawtuckett Golf Club: 394-5909
Renaissance Park Golf Course: 357-3375

Shopping

Charlotte has a variety of shopping experiences. Have fun at centrally located City Fair with its marketplace atmosphere and multi-level shopping. Eastland Mall offers 123 shops and several major department stores. Specialty clothing shops featuring brand names are the focal point of Midtown Square, an enclosed shopping plaza. Probably the most extensive and expensive shopping can be found at Southpark Mall and the adjacent Specialty Shops on the Park: the mall has 115 specialty shops and department stores; The Specialty Shops on the Park are 20 exclusive shops linked to a plaza of prestigious hotels. And for antique hunters, try Waxhaw Antique Village south of Charlotte in Waxhaw. You'll enjoy the turn-of-the-century village tableau, too.
Florists: Charlotte Flower Shop: 334-8860
Elizabeth House of Flowers: 342-3919

CHICAGO

Area Code: 312; 708 for suburbs
(Telephone numbers in this section are within the 312 calling area unless noted otherwise.)
Time Zone: Central
Weather: 976-1212
Police: Metro: 744-4000
Emergency: 911

Back in 1916 Carl Sandburg called Chicago the "city of the big shoulders." The description still holds true today. He also called it "hog butcher for the world, tool maker, stacker of wheat, player with railroads and the nation's freight handler." Today he would have to add something about the city's predominate stake in the world's financial futures trading and merchandising industries, as well as the real estate fortunes that have been built from Chicago. The city is home to the world's tallest skyscraper (the Sears Tower, 1454 ft.), and the world's largest commercial building (The Merchandise Mart). But Chicago isn't all bulk and swagger; its cultural facilities offer as urbane and sophisticated an experience as any world-class city. And the large immigrant population adds spice and diversity to Chicago's neighborhoods.

Business Profile
Population: 6.2 million
Population Growth (1980-89): 3%
Unemployment Rate: 5.4%
Fortune 500 Corporate Headquarters: 42

General Information Sources
Chicago Chamber of Commerce: 580-6900
Chicago Convention and Tourism Bureau: 567-8500
International Visitors Center: 645-1836
The Mayor's Office of Inquiry and Information: 744-4000

Getting There
By Air: O'Hare International, 686-2200; multilingual service, 686-2304 (the world's busiest airport).
Midway Airport, 5700 S. Cicero Ave., 767-0500. Served by 6 commercial airlines; also used by corporate and private aircraft.
Meigs Field, 15th St. at Lakefront, 744-4787. Primarily used by private and corporate aircraft; served by one commercial carrier.
Once you've landed: Landing at O'Hare: A taxi ride downtown takes about 50 minutes and costs between $18 and $22. Taxis are located on the lower level of each domestic terminal. There is also a Super Saver Shared Ride program which allows 3 O'Hare passengers to share a ride downtown or to the

Near North Side. Passengers are charged a flat rate of $12 each. Shared rides leave from the lower front of Terminal 3.
Regular bus service is run by Continental Air Transport, 454-7799 or 454-7800. Buses connect O'Hare with downtown Chicago (serving nearly all Chicago hotels), the Near North Side and the Northwest suburbs. Buses leave for downtown every half-hour from 6am to 10pm; during peak hours they leave every 15 minutes. One way ticket from O'Hare to Loop, Gold Coast, or North Loop locations $9, round trip $16.
Free Courtesy buses are provided by about 30 hotels in the O'Hare area.
Chicago Transit Authority provides train service, 836-7000; this service operates in the median strip of the Kennedy Expressway and takes riders from the airport to downtown. Riders enter the Loop through the Dearborn subway station. The trip takes about 35 minutes.
Limousines (private): Agencies suggest customers make reservations 2 to 3 days in advance. The fare downtown runs between $45 and $60, plus 15% tip. The price to other locations is $32 an hour (plus tip); there is a 2-hour minimum. There are limousine booths on the lower level of both domestic terminals; these are for customers with reservations. Chauffeurs meet passengers in the baggage claim areas. Limousine services: American Limousine, 708-920-8888; Chicago Limousine Service, 726-1035; Delaware Cars & Limousines, 337-2800; La Salle Livery Limited, 238-8888.
Directions Downtown: From O'Hare, take I-190 to I-90/Kennedy Expressway. O'Hare is 18 miles west of downtown.
Overland Adventures: *Route Map:* I-80, one of the country's main east-west routes, connects with I-55 to the west and I-94 from the east to provide access to Chicago. The city has several major highways that lead into the city center: I-90/I-94 (called Kennedy Expressway north of I-290 and the Dan Ryan Expressway south of I-290); I-290 (Eisenhower Expressway); I-55 (Stevenson Expressway); and the Indiana Toll Road (I-80/90). In Chicago's Loop, the intersection of State St., and Madison St. is the beginning point for city addresses; State divides the east and west addresses, and Madison the north and south. The city is organized in a grid system.
Bottleneck Busters: Rush hour is a headache. It is in full swing by 6:30am, and all expressways entering the city are usually clogged. When it's not winter, with the requisite snow and ice that make driving dangerous and slow, roads are constantly under construction. Try to avoid the Loop highways during rush hour. I-94/Dan Ryan Expressway is expected to be undergoing construction work for the next few years. Most radio stations have constant traffic updates, including WBEZ-FM 91.5, the NPR station, and WGN-AM 720.
Taxis: It is fairly easy to hail a cab on the street in the downtown business area. Major cab companies include: Checker

FLYING TIMES
(in hours)
FROM
Chicago
TO
Los Angeles: 4
New York: 2
Miami: 3

Taxi, 829-4222; Flash Cab, 561-1444; Yellow Cab, 829-4222.

Trains: Amtrak, Union Station, 210 S. Canal St., 558-1075. Illinois Central, 111 E. Wacker Dr., 819-7500

Bus Service: Greyhound/Trailways Lines Bus Station, 74 W. Randolph St., 781-2900

Public Transportation: Chicago Transit Authority (CTA), 836-7000, runs the city's extensive subway and bus system.

Road Service and Repairs: AAA Emergency 24-hour service, 372-1818 or 800-262-6327

Towed? Call Police Department Auto pound and tow records, 744-5513

International Travelers

Foreign Currency Exchange: Foreign Currency Exchange, O'Hare Airport, Terminal 4 (8am-8pm daily)

Deak International, 111 W. Washington, 236-0042; and 500 W. Madison, 993-7545

International Visitor's Center, 520 N. Michigan Ave., 645-1836

World's Money Exchange, 6 E. Randolph, Suite 204, 641-2151

Translation Services: AATIL, Inc., 79 W. Monroe St., Suite 1310, 236-3366

Berlitz Translation Services, 2 N. La Salle, 372-6055; Water Tower Place, 845 N. Michigan Ave., 943-4262

Inlingua Translation Service, 20 N. Michigan Ave., Suite 560, 641-0488

Japan Communications, 676 St. Clair, Suite 1900, 549-5569

Consulates: There are more than 50 countries represented by a consulate in Chicago. Some of the major ones are listed below. Check the Yellow Pages for more.

Canada: 427-1031	Israel: 565-3300
France: 787-5359	Japan: 280-0400
Germany: 263-0850	People's Republic of China: 346-0287
Ireland: 337-1868	Poland: 642-4102

Foreign Books and Periodicals: Kroch & Brentano Bookstore, 29 S. Wabash St., 332-7500.

Six Corners Newsstand, 4002 N. Milwaukee, 685-4955 (open 24 hours)

Other Services: Chicago Multilingua Graphics, 1014 Davis St., Evanston, 708-864-3230 (foreign language typesetting)

Business Visitor's Needs

Banking: American National Bank & Trust of Chicago, 33 N. LaSalle, 661-5000

Exchange National Bank, 120 S. LaSalle, 781-8000

First National Bank of Chicago, 1 First National Plaza, 732-4000

Harris Trust & Savings Bank, 111 W. Monroe St., 461-2121

Full Service Assistance: AAA Office Services: 751-1234

HQ-Headquarters Companies: 372-2525 (call for other locations)

The Professional Suite: 641-2341

Secretarial Services: Executive Support Systems: 929-0266

LaSalle Secretarial Service: 346-4255

Copying and Printing: Minuteman Press: 368-0577

Pip Printing: 236-9033 (fax service; call for other locations)

CHICAGO O'HARE INTERNATIONAL AIRPORT

© H.M. Gousha

Sir Speedy: 419-0014; fax 419-0016 (call for other locations)

Fax and Telex Facilities: Many of the businesses listed in "Copying and Printing," above, have fax facilities, as well as: Express Telex: 372-0359

Instant Printing Corp.: 726-6275; fax 726-6279 (call for other locations)

Messengers: American Courier Services: 625-3600

Arrow Messenger Service: 489-6688; in the suburbs, 708-484-6688

Chicago Rush Delivery: 631-2060

Medical Needs: Doctor referral: Chicago Medical Society: 670-2550

Dental referral: Chicago Dental Society: 836-7300; emergency service, 726-4321

Pharmacy: Walgreen's: 664-8686 (open 24 hours; call for other locations)

Hospitals: Northwestern Memorial Hospital: 908-2000

Michael Reese Hospital: 791-2000

Rush Presbyterian St. Luke's: 942-5000

Convention Centers

McCormick Place-on-the-Lake., E. 23 St. and S. Lake Shore Dr., 791-7000. One of the world's largest convention centers. Exhibition space: 1.63 million sq. feet.

Apparel Center and ExpoCenter/Chicago, 350 N. Orleans St., 527-4141. Exhibition space: 140,000 sq. feet.

Rosemont O'Hare Exposition Center, 5555 N. River Rd., Rosemont, 708-692-2220. Exhibition space: 375,000 sq. feet.

Also, many hotels in Chicago have meeting facilities.

Entertainment, Sports, and Culture

Ticket Services: Ticketmaster: 559-1212

Sports: Baseball: Chicago Cubs, Wrigley Field, 878-CUBS (878-2827)

Chicago White Sox, Comiskey Park, 924-1000

Basketball: Chicago Bulls, Chicago Stadium, 943-5800

Football: Chicago Bears, Solider Field, 663-5408

Hockey: Chicago Black Hawks, Chicago Stadium, 733-5300

The Arts: Art Institute of Chicago: 443-3600

Ballet Chicago: 993-7575

Chicago Symphony Orchestra, Orchestra Hall: 435-6666

League of Chicago Theatres: Curtain Call 977-1755

Dining: Four Stars and Our Stars

Note: Reservations are essential for all of the following:

Ambria, 472-5959. Located in a 19th-century hotel/mansion, this restaurant offers nouvelle French cuisine. For a group of 4 or more, phone ahead to order the sampling menu, which will allow you to taste a bit of everything. Dinner only.

Cape Cod Room, 787-2200. This marvelous seafood restaurant is a Chicago institution.

Crickets, 280-2100. Located in the Tremont Hotel, this is often compared to New York's "21." A cadre of local business and social figures have made Crickets their home. French cuisine.

House of Hunan, 329-9494. Delicious Chinese food, elegant ambiance on Michigan's Magnificent Mile. The menu draws on dishes from all of China's culinary regions.

Le Perroquet, 944-7990. One of the city's best French restaurants. The private elevator that whisks you away to the dining room only adds to the aura of luxury. Lunch and dinner weekdays, dinner on Sat., closed Sun.

Pump Room, 266-0360. A local legend, the Pump Room serves continental and nouvelle cuisine. Scenes from Hitchcock's *North by Northwest* were shot here. Open daily.

Shaw's Crab House, 527-2722. Who would have thought that a first-class seafood place would be found a thousand miles from any ocean? Reservations suggested for lunch.

Spiaggia, 280-2750. Specializing in Northern Italian cuisine, this is the best Italian restaurant in Chicago. Imaginative menu, elegant surroundings. Located in One Magnificent Mile building, with a view of the lake.

Home Away from Home: Where to Stay

This is but a sampling of the city's many fine hotels.

Chicago Hilton & Towers, 720 S. Michigan Ave., 922-4400. An old-fashioned grand hotel. More than 1,600 rooms. Pool and full health facilities. Rooms $115-$200, suites from $200.

The Drake, 140 E. Walton Pl., 787-2200. Listed on the National Register of Historic Places, this is another grand old Chicago hotel. This renovated Italianate palace offers old-world charm accompanied by up-to-date facilities. The Vista Executive Club is the hotel's VIP floor. 600 rooms and suites. Rooms $155-$220, suites $300-$600, studio rooms $230-$300.

The Fairmont, 200 N. Columbus Dr., 565-8000. Luxurious and elegant, this hotel is a favorite with travelers. 700 rooms and suites, with a full service business center. Guests have privileges at a nearby health club. High tea is a popular event. Rooms $170-$235, suites $500-$650.

Hyatt Regency Chicago, 151 E. Wacker Dr., 565-1234. 2,000 rooms. Huge, elegant with every amenity. A favorite with conventions and meetings planners. The top 2 floors house the Regency Club, with deluxe rooms and services, including free breakfast and cocktails. Rooms $135-$185, suites $295-$1,750. Regency Club: rooms $184-$215, suites $1,100.

McCormick Center Hotel, 23rd St. at Lake Shore, 791-1900. A good choice if you're in town for a convention at McCormick Place. Three restaurants, health club with heated pool, sauna, and steam room. Rooms $99-$155, suites $270-$950.

Raphael, 200 E. Delaware Pl., 943-5000. 175 rooms and suites. Intimate, comfortable atmosphere. Health club privileges. Prices here are more moderate: rooms $95-$140, suites $120-$155.

Ritz Carlton, 160 E. Pearson St. in Water Tower Place, 266-1000. Contemporary, opulent, and sophisticated; at the top of Water Tower Place. 488 rooms and suites. Extensive health club facilities. Rooms $185-$240, suites $270-$2,000.

Swiss Grand Hotel, 323 E. Wacker Dr., 565-0565. A favorite with business executives, with its extensive fitness facilities (including a heated pool) and its full service business center. Rooms have 2-line telephones, large desks, other working essentials. Rooms $175-$450, suites $450-$2,500.

Keeping Your Tone Away from Home

Joggers and Bikers: The city's Parks Department maintains 20 miles of bicycling and jogging paths along Lake Michigan, and in Lincoln, Grant, Burnham, and Jackson Parks. Bike rentals available from Bicycles Chicago Rental (in Grant Park), 738-9754; Edgebrook Cycle & Sport, 792-1669; Village Cycle Center, 751-2488.

Shopping

Chicago's premier department store is Marshall Field & Co., whose flagship branch is at 111 North State Street.

The Magnificent Mile, located along North Michigan Ave. from the Chicago River to Oak St., is home to some of Chicago's glitziest stores, including Saks Fifth Avenue, Gucci, Tiffany's, Neiman Marcus, I. Magnin. Also along North Michigan is Water Tower Place, a 7-story vertical mall which houses shops like Lord & Taylor, Benetton, the Limited, and The Gap. Michigan Ave.'s other vertical mall is the Avenue Atrium, which is home to Bloomingdale's.

Oak St. has a strip of distinctive designer boutiques including Gianni Versace and Giorgio Armani. Lincoln Park, a fashionable neighborhood to the north of the Loop, also has several lovely specialty stores—Clark St. between Diversey and Armitage is a good starting place.

Local sales tax is 8%.

Florists: City Garden: 427-6600

Flowers by Clody: 327-1842

CINCINNATI

Area Code: 513
Time Zone: Eastern
Weather: 241-1010
Police: 765-1212
Fire/Life Squad: 241-2525
Emergency: Police, fire, ambulance: 911

Winston Churchill once described Cincinnati as America's most beautiful inland city. Now that's high praise. Located on the Ohio River, and built around several hills, Cincinnati is also widely known as an extremely livable city, with abundant cultural and recreational facilities. On rainy days, or on unbearably humid summer days (and Cincinnati has its share of both) Cincinnatians can use the city's Skywalk, an enclosed second story walkway, which connects the city's major department stores, the convention center, the downtown hotels, and more than 80 shops, banks, restaurants, and office buildings. Just across the Ohio River from Cincinnati are Covington and Newport, Kentucky, which are considered part of the metropolitan area.

The city has a diversified economy. Companies that call Cincinnati home include Procter and Gamble, Cincinnati Milacron, Kroger, US Shoe, American Financial, and Kenner Products.

Business Profile
Population: 1.5 million
Population Growth (1980-1989): 4.1%
Unemployment Rate: 5%
Fortune 500 Corporate Headquarters: 16

General Information Sources
Greater Cincinnati Convention and Visitors Bureau: 621-2142
Visitor Information Line: 421-INFO (421-4636)
Cincinnati Bell Yellow Pages: 333-4444. Stuck somewhere without a phone book? This is a talking yellow pages service.
City Hall: 352-3000
Chamber of Commerce: 579-3100

Getting There
By Air: Greater Cincinnati International Airport information: 606-283-3151. The airport is located across the river in northern Kentucky, about 13 miles southwest of the city.
Lunken Airport, 321-4132, is used for charter and private flights.
Charter airlines: Executive Jet Management, 871-2004; Sunbird Air Services, 322-2711
Once you've landed: A cab ride downtown takes about 30

minutes and costs about $22. The Jet Port Express, 606-283-3702, goes to several downtown hotels. It leaves every 30 minutes, from 6am-11pm; the trip costs $8 one way ($12 round trip) and takes about 30 minutes. Taxi services: Airport Taxi, 606-283-3260; Covington Yellow Cab, 606-431-6500.
Limousines (private): Cincinnati Limousine Service, 474-5870; Queen City Limousine, 851-4300. Reservations are essential.
Directions Downtown: Take Airport Rd. (KY 212) to I-275 to I-75 (and I-71) and then to downtown exits.
Overland Adventures: *Route Map:* I-275 circles the city, while Routes 71 and 75 are the main highways from central Ohio (71 leads to Columbus; 75 to Dayton and Detroit). The two merge in downtown Cincinnati, then split again south of the city. Route 74 is the largest highway from the west, and the main route to Indianapolis.
Driving Regulations: Right turn on red is legal in Cincinnati and Kentucky unless specifically prohibited by sign. Seat belts and child restraints mandatory.
Bottleneck Busters: Traffic is not a major problem in Cincinnati. There are occasional slowdowns on I-75/I-71, especially over the Brent Spence Bridge during the rush hour. Radio station WCKY-AM 1530 carries traffic reports.
Trains: Amtrak, 1901 River Rd., 800-872-7245
Bus Service: Greyhound/Trailways Lines Station, 1005 Gilbert Ave., 352-6000
Public Transportation: Queen City Metro bus service, 621-4455. Cheap and convenient.
Road Service and Repairs: AAA, 15 W. Central Pkwy., 762-3100; 24-hour Emergency Road Service, 762-3222
Parking Regulations: There is some metered parking downtown, but most drivers use the garages located under the large office buildings or private garages. There is a municipal garage at Fountain Square. Parking costs vary, but are in the $6-a-day range.
Towed? City of Cincinnati Auto Impoundment Unit, 352-6371

International Travelers
Foreign Currency Exchange: Central Trust Bank, 201 E. 5th St., 651-8057
Fifth Third Bank, 38 Fountain Sq. Plaza, main lobby on Skywalk level, 579-5300
Translation Services: Inlingua School of Languages, 602 Main St., Suite 400, 721-8782
Foreign Books and Periodicals: Cinti Fountain Square News, 426 Walnut St., 421-4049
Duttenhofer's, 214 W. McMillan, 381-0007

Business Visitor's Needs
Banking: Central Trust Bank, 201 E. 5th St., 651-8896

FLYING TIMES
(in hours)
FROM
Cincinnati
TO
Chicago: 1¼
Los Angeles: 4½
New York: 1½
Miami: 2¼

Fifth Third Bank, 38 Fountain Sq. Plaza, main lobby on Sky-walk level, 579-5300
Secretarial Services: Corporex Exec. Suites: 606-331-8840
Exec-Sec-Co.: 751-6943
Hyde Park Executive Services: 871-9399
Manpower Temp. Services: 621-0788
Copying and Printing: Pip Printing: 721-1611 (call for other locations)
Queensgate Express-Arnco Printing: 421-3445 (call for other locations)
Fax Facilities: Mail Boxes Etc. USA: 742-9490 (call for other locations)
Messengers: Cinti Express Delivery Service: 542-1900
Priority Dispatch: 421-3800
Medical Needs: Doctor referral: Academy of Medicine: 721-2345
Dental referral: Cincinnati Dental Society: 984-3443
Pharmacy: Walgreen's: 24-hour prescription service, 751-3444; store information, 751-1147
Hospitals: University of Cincinnati Hospital, 558-1000; physician referral, 558-7832
Christ Hospital: 369-2000
Good Samaritan Hospital: 872-1400
Jewish Hospital of Cincinnati: 569-2000

Convention Center
Dr. Albert B. Sabin Convention Center, 525 Elm St., 352-3750. 162,000-sq.-foot main floor, 41 meeting rooms, 30,000-sq.-foot ballroom.

Entertainment, Sports, and Culture
Sports: Baseball: Cincinnati Reds, Riverfront Stadium, 421-REDS (421-7337)
Football: Cincinnati Bengals, Riverfront Stadium, 621-3550
The Arts: Cincinnati Ballet: 621-5282
Cincinnati Opera: 241-2742
Cincinnati Symphony Orchestra: 381-3300
College Conservatory of Music: 556-4183

Dining: Four Stars and Our Stars
Maisonette, 721-2260. Cincinnati's finest French restaurant, and considered by some critics to be one of the best in the country. Reservations required. Lunch weekdays and dinner nightly except Sundays.
Pigall's French Restaurant, 721-1345. Classic French cuisine. Open for lunch and dinner daily except Sunday.
Lenhardt's, 281-3600. German-Hungarian menu features 11 varieties of schnitzel, chicken paprikash, sauerbraten-potato pancakes.
Skyline Chili, 241-2020. Move over, Texas, Cincinnati has its own specialty chili that comes with various toppings. Skyline has 50 branches throughout the area; listed is a downtown location.
Bacchus Restaurant, 421-8314. Continental and light nouvelle

cuisine, as well as regional American specialties.
Waterfront (Covington, KY), 606-581-1414. One of several riverboat dining establishments, Waterfront boasts gorgeous views of the downtown skyline. Grilled seafood, rotisserie selections.

Home Away from Home: Where to Stay
Cincinnatian Hotel, 601 Vine St., 381-3000. A smallish landmark hotel (147 rooms, some suites) which has been elegantly restored. Some rooms have balconies that overlook the 8-story atrium (and its marble staircase). Rates run from $165-$215 nightly.
Hyatt Regency Cincinnati, 151 W. 5th St., 579-1234. A large hotel (485 rooms, 22 stories) with complete health club and pool. VIP floor is available. Rooms $135-$160, studio rooms $125-$300, suites $225-$700.
Omni Netherland Plaza, 5th and Race Sts., 421-9100. Connected to the city's Skywalk; a beautifully restored old landmark. 621 rooms. Prices: $107-$170, suites from $175.
Westin, at Fountain Square, 621-7700. Modern, sophisticated glass high-rise with 460 rooms. Full fitness facilities, including pool and sauna. Connected to the Skywalk. Rooms $135-$188, suites $350-$1,500.

Keeping Your Tone Away from Home
Joggers and Bikers: Eden Park is popular with joggers. Also, the Convention and Visitors Bureau (621-2142) has information on jogging courses. Airport Playfield (Lunken Airport) has a bike trail; call 321-6500 to inquire about rental bikes.
Health Clubs: YMCA: 241-5348
Public Golf Courses: Avon Fields: 281-0322
California Golf Course: 231-4734
Reeves Golf Course: 321-2740

Shopping
Major downtown department stores include Gidding/Jenny for women and Saks Fifth Avenue. Sales tax in Cincinnati is 5 1/2 %.
Florists: The Dennis Buttelwerth Florist: 321-3611

CLEVELAND

Area Code: 216
Time Zone: Eastern
Weather: 931-1212
Police : 621-1234
Emergency: 911

Cleveland, known as the Great Lake City, extends 80 miles along Lake Erie. Located midway between New York and Chicago, Cleveland is connected to the Atlantic Ocean via the Saint Lawrence Seaway. It is the largest overseas cargo port on Lake Erie. Cleveland's location offers accessibility to outer markets, a low cost of living and a skilled labor force. Once labeled a smokestack city, Cleveland now sustains an emerging service sector, as witnessed by the development of such establishments as The Cleveland Clinic, renowned for its organ research, and Case Western Reserve University's polymer-chemistry department, known for its cooperative research with the plastics industry. Businesses like Ameritrust bank and Jones Day Reavis and Pogue law firm prosper alongside traditional industries like steel and oil. City officials note that information lags progress by six to nine months, so business people looking for easy information may find it a frustrating arena.

Business Profile
Population: 573,822
Population Growth (1980-1989): 0%
Unemployment Rate: 5%
Fortune 500 Corporate Headquarters: 17

General Information Sources
Mayor's Action Center: 664-2900
Greater Cleveland Growth Association: 621-3300
Convention and Visitors Bureau of Greater Cleveland: 621-4110
Fun Phone: 621-8860

Getting There
By Air: Cleveland Hopkins International Airport information and paging: 265-6030
Once you've landed: Rapid Transit Authority's (RTA) Windermere train leaves the airport station every 10 minutes during rush hours and every 20 minutes during normal hours. The Windermere runs from 4:30am to 12:20am; the cost to downtown Cleveland's Union Terminal at Public Square is $1. RTA 24-hour hotline, 621-9500.
Taxi cabs are located outside the luggage area. The ride from the airport to downtown Cleveland takes 20-35 minutes, a $16 ride. Americab, 881-1111; Yellow/Zone Cab, 623-1500.

FLYING TIMES
(in hours)
FROM
Cleveland
TO
Chicago: 1½
Los Angeles: 5
New York: 1½
Miami: 2¾

Hopkins Airport Limo can provide regular service to downtown as well as to other parts of Cleveland, 267-8282.
Limousines (private): Service requires 24-hour notice. Century Limousine, 234-4097.
Directions Downtown: From the airport take I-71 North 10 miles. Take the Ontario Street exit for downtown Cleveland.
Overland Adventures: *Route Map:* I-90 is the main east and west route. Continuing east, I-90 links Cleveland to Erie, Buffalo, and Toronto. Continuing west, I-90 links Cleveland to Toledo, Detroit, and Chicago. Heading south are Interstates 71 and 77. I-71 links Cleveland to Columbus and Cincinnati; I-77 links Cleveland to Charleston, WV. I-480 feeds into I-77, connecting Cleveland to Pittsburgh and Philadelphia. Lake Erie is north of Cleveland.
Driving Regulations: Turn right on red unless marked. Seatbelts are required.
Bottleneck Busters: During rush hour, avoid Chagrin Blvd., Chester Rd., 9th St. and Ontario St. Main Ave. bridge will be under construction soon.
Trains: Amtrak, 200 Cleveland Memorial Shoreway N.E., information and reservations, 696-5115 or 800-USA-RAIL (800-872-7245).
Bus Service: Greyhound/Trailways Lines, 1465 Chester Ave., fare and schedules, 781-1400.
Public Transportation: RTA Bus and Train Service covers the downtown area in 5 loops. Schedules and maps are located at many stops as well as at the information center at 2019 Ontario St., 621-9500. Downtown buses are 85 cents and express buses and trains are $1.
Road Service and Repairs: For 24-hour road service and towing call these AAA-approved services: Charlie's Towing, 234-5300 (near downtown); Rogers Towing, 235-1127 (near the airport). Auto Service Repair/Maintenance Information: dial 771-4070, then enter 1105. Travel Tips Information: dial 771-4070, then enter 1430.
Parking Regulations: Limited metered parking; parking lots and garages available.
Towed? Call 623-5064

International Travelers
Nationality Services Center of Cleveland, 1715 Euclid Ave., 781-4560. Translating and information available.
Foreign Currency Exchange: Huntington National Bank, 917 Euclid Ave., 344-0080
Society National Bank, 800 Superior Ave., 689-3000
Translation Services: Berlitz Translation Services, 815 Superior Ave. N.E., 861-0950
Consulates: The Canadian Consulate, 55 Public Square, 771-0150
Foreign Books and Periodicals: Grabowski Superette, 6405 Fleet Ave., 883-9549
Lansing Pharmacy, 3879 E. 71st St., 341-5090

Business Visitor's Needs

Banking: Large full service banks include National City, 1900 E. 9th St., 575-2000; and Ameritrust Company, 900 Euclid Ave., 737-5000.

Secretarial Services: Kelly Services: 243-8292
Olsten Services: 861-1900

Copying and Printing: Kinko's: 589-5679
Watt Printing: 696-5000

Messengers: Bonnie Speed Delivery: 696-6033
Executive Delivery Systems: 861-4560

Telex Facilities: Western Union: 800-325-6000

Medical Needs: Doctor referral: Mt. Sinai staff referral: 421-5555
Dental referral: National Dental Studios: 289-6900
Pharmacy: Revco Discount Drug Center: 621-6019 (call for other locations)
Hospitals: Mt. Sinai Medical Center: 421-4000
University Hospitals: 844-1000

Convention Centers

Cleveland Convention Center, 500 Lakeside Ave., 348-2200, has 375,000 sq. feet of exhibition space and a total of 13,605 seats. The convention center is within walking distance of downtown.

These hotels are also available with seating for 1,000 or more: Sheraton Cleveland City Center, 771-7600; and Stouffer's Inn on The Square, 696-5600.

Entertainment, Sports, and Culture

Ticket Services: For a complete run-down on available events call Ticketron: 524-0000

Sports: Baseball: Indians, Cleveland Stadium, 241-5555
Basketball: Cavaliers, Coliseum, 659-9107
Football: Browns, Cleveland Stadium, 696-5555
Soccer: The Crunch, Coliseum, 659-9107; box office 349-2090

The Arts: Cleveland Ballet, Cleveland Opera and Great Lakes Theater Festival: 241-6000 (summer only)
Cleveland Orchestra: 231-1111
Cleveland Playhouse: 795-7000. Theatrical productions, regular season.

Dining: Four Stars and Our Stars

There are no four-star restaurants in Cleveland, but try these three Cleveland sparklers:

French Connection, 696-5600. Elegant dining and fine French cuisine. Moderately expensive, reservations required. The restaurant is in Stouffer's Inn on The Square.

Sammy's, 523-5560, is chef-owned and its specialties include a raw bar, boule de neige, and fresh fish. In a restored 1850s warehouse.

Samurai Japanese Steak House (in Beachwood), 464-7575. Specialties include Teppanykai filet mignon and shrimp flambé. Moderately priced. Open daily; reservations required.

Home Away from Home: Where to Stay

Stouffer's Inn on The Square, 24 Public Square, 696-5600. Regular single rooms from $124; the Luxury level club floor has singles from $164. This is Cleveland's grandest hotel (it holds the only AAA 4-diamond rating in the city).

The Clinic Center, 2065 E. 96th St. at Carnegie Ave., 791-1900. Convention facilities; single rooms are $75 and up. Perks are high tea and lobby entertainment.

Sheraton Cleveland City Center, 777 St. Clair Ave., 771-7600. Offers a lake view and executive level rooms, singles $100, doubles $120. At the "concierge level" you get free coffee and *USA Today*.

Keeping Your Tone Away from Home

Joggers: Cleveland Metroparks has extensive trails for jogging and hiking: 351-6300

Health Clubs: YMCA: 344-0095
YWCA: 881-6878

Public Golf Clubs: Cleveland Metroparks has several locations: 351-6300

Public Beaches: Cleveland Lakefront State Parks: 881-8141

Shopping

Saks Fifth Avenue and fine men's clothing stores can be found in Beachwood Place mall, and La Place mall, both located on the East Side. May Co. and Higbee's on Public Square are traditional department stores. The Arcade and Tower City Center (in Terminal Tower) are historic landmarks housing specialty shops. For boutiquing go to Beachcliff Market Square on the West Side.

Florists: Alexander's Florist: 292-4500
Segelin's: 791-8900

Fruit Baskets: Feren's Gourmet Gifts: 431-8700

COLUMBUS

Area Code: 614
Time Zone: Eastern
Weather: 281-1111
Police: 645-4545
Emergency: 911

Columbus is Ohio's state capital with Dayton and Cincinnati as neighbors. Columbus prospers under its capital city responsibilities and is one of the best-run and most civic-minded cities in Ohio. Home to many of the nation's insurance companies and Ohio State University, Columbus has an educated work force and strongly supports the arts. This city has a mayor willing to fight the drug problem and a citizenry willing to work together to make Columbus a prosperous community.

Business Profile
Population: 1,662,000
Population Growth (1980-1989): 8.6%
Unemployment Rate: 5.0%
Fortune 500 Corporate Headquarters: 6

General Information Sources
Greater Columbus Convention and Visitors Bureau: 221-6623 or 800-234-COLS (800-234-2657)
The Columbus Area Chamber of Commerce: 221-1321
Recorded Information and Events: 221-CITY (221-2489)

Getting There
By Air: Port Columbus International Airport general information: 239-4004. Convention and Visitors Bureau information booth at the airport: 239-4343.
Once you've landed: A taxi ride from the airport to downtown Columbus takes about 20 minutes and costs about $11. German Village and Independent Taxi, 443-3663; Yellow Cab Co., 221-3800.
Airport Limousine service, 478-3000, leaves the airport every half-hour; the costs are $5.25 one way and $9.50 round trip. The van makes stops at major hotels and the bus station. Operates daily.
Limousines (private): Service is attainable with 24-hour reservations: American Limousine Service, 294-2623; Carey of Columbus Limousine Service, 228-5466.
Directions Downtown: Columbus is 7 miles west of the airport. Take International Gateway from the airport terminal. At the light, turn left onto Stelzer Rd. After 5 traffic lights, turn right onto Broad St. and follow it into downtown Columbus.

FLYING TIMES
(in hours)
FROM
Columbus
TO
Chicago: **1**
Los Angeles: **5**
New York: **1½**
Miami: **2½**

Overland Adventures: *Route Map:* Several interstates pass through Columbus. Its beltways are I-270 and I-670 which encircle the city. Traveling north and south is I-71, and traveling east and west is I-70. I-70 links Columbus with Dayton.
Driving Regulations: Right turn on red is permitted unless otherwise posted. Left turn on red is permitted when the turn is made from a one-way street onto another one-way street.
Bottleneck Busters: Watch out for road construction on the interstates. On I-70, I-71, and I-270, some exit and entrance ramps have been under construction and might be closed. In some places on the interstates, traffic narrows down to one lane. For up-to-date rush hour traffic reports, listen to radio station WFNY 94.7 FM; or try calling AAA traffic hotline, 431-STUK (431-7885).
Trains: Amtrak ticketing agent, 3000 E. Main St., 235-2371. (There is no Amtrak station in Columbus.)
Bus Service: Greyhound/Trailways Lines, 111 E. Town St., 800-528-0447
Public Transportation: Central Ohio Transit Authority (COTA), 228-1776. COTA has daily bus service along 96 routes. Local bus fare is 75 cents and express bus fare is $1. Catch a bus just about anytime on Broad St. or High St. Express bus terminals are on N. High St. and on 3rd St.
Road Service and Repairs: AAA Emergency Road Service, 431-3388; Noble's, 235-7377
Parking Regulations: In downtown Columbus, 2-hour metered street parking is possible, but most people use nearby parking garages where the fees are about $7 for the day.
Towed? Call Impounded Vehicles, 645-6400

International Travelers
International Services: International Visitors Council, Port Columbus International Airport, 231-9610
Foreign Currency Exchange: Ameritrust Co. NA, 33 N. 3rd St., 224-0670
BankOhio National Bank, 155 E. Broad St., 463-7100
Translation Services: Altco Translators, 1426 Ridgeview Rd., 486-2013
Asist Translation Service, 4663 Executive Dr., 451-6744
Foreign Books and Periodicals: National Newsstand and Books, 4005 E. Broad St., 433-0033
Newsstand, 3309 E. Broad St., 236-5632

Business Visitor's Needs
Banking: Bank One, Columbus, 100 E. Broad St., 248-5800
Huntington National Bank, 41 S. High St., 463-4902
Secretarial Services: Kelly Services: 221-6775
Olsten Temporary Services: 228-8114
Copying and Printing: The Ink Well: 221-1412
Kinko's: 294-7485 (open 24 hours)

Messengers: Lightning Delivery Service: 889-2915
Priority Dispatch, Inc.: 464-4545
Telex Facilities: Western Union: 221-0640
Medical Needs: Doctor referral: Ask-A-Nurse: 293-5678
Dental referral: Columbus Dental Society: 236-0972
Pharmacies: Rite Aid: 235-4101
Tweeters Drugs: 461-4404
Hospitals: Ohio State University Hospitals: 293-8000
Doctors Hospital: 297-4000
Grant Medical Center: 461-3232

Convention Centers
Ohio Center, 400 N. High St., 221-6700, has 90,000 sq. feet available in its exhibit hall, 2 ballrooms, and 31 meeting rooms. An expansion called Greater Columbus Convention Center, scheduled for completion in 1992, will be just north of the Ohio Center. 216,000 sq. feet of exhibit hall space, a ballroom, and 75 meeting rooms will make this a spacious convention facility.
Veterans Memorial, 300 W. Broad St., 221-4341, has 110,000 sq. feet of exhibit hall space, a large auditorium and 10 meeting rooms.

Entertainment, Sports, and Culture
Ticket Services: Ticketmaster: 221-1414
Regional Sports Update: Dial 899-8000, when asked, enter the 4 digit code 1310.
Sports: Baseball: Clippers (AAA farm team for the New York Yankees), Cooper Stadium, 462-5250
Golf: The Memorial Tournament at Muirfield: 889-6700. This PGA tournament is held in May, and the event is hosted by hometown golf course designer Jack Nicklaus.
Horse Racing: Beulah Park Jockey Club (Grove City): 871-9600
Scioto Downs: 491-2515
The Arts: Columbus Association for the Performing Arts (CAPA), 469-1045. CAPA is the owning organization for both the Ohio and Palace Theatres. These theaters are home to Columbus Symphony, BalletMet, and many other types of entertainment all of which thrive under the auspices of CAPA. Don't miss the Picnic with the Pops summer concert series featured by the Columbus Symphony.
Jazz Arts Group (JAG), 231-7836, performs at Battelle Auditorium and has internationally acclaimed artists.
Opera Columbus, 461-0022, is Columbus's grand opera company.
Players Theatre Columbus, Vern Riffe Center for Government and the Arts, 644-8425. This regional theater company has a mixed repertoire and presents programs in the facility's complex of 3 theaters.

Dining: Four Stars and Our Stars
Three Stars: Gourmet Market, 486-1114. The Gourmet Market is chef-owned, specializes in its own baking and fresh

seafood or veal, and the prices are moderately expensive. Reservations are required.
Peppercorn Duck Club, 463-1234. The continental menu features Long Island duckling and seafood. Moderate prices and nightly entertainment make this restaurant a good choice. Reservations are required.
Our Stars: Jotham's Riverside, 488-0605. This chef-owned restaurant features a French menu with such delights as caviar beluga malossoi and escalope de veau aux morilles. Prices are reasonable and reservations are required.

Home Away from Home: Where to Stay
Hyatt on Capitol Square, 75 E. State St., 228-1234. Single rooms cost $109-$135. Luxury level single rooms are $158. Amenities include concierge, airport transportation, and exercise facilities.
Hyatt Regency, 350 N. High St., 463-1234. Single rooms cost $99-$129. Luxury level single rooms are $149. Concierge and airport transportation are available. The Hyatt Regency has the Peppercorn Duck Club restaurant and nightly entertainment.
Stouffer Dublin, 600 Metro Place N., Dublin, 764-2200. Single rooms cost $104-$124. Although a bit out of the way from downtown Columbus, this hotel offers tennis and golf, health club, and an indoor pool.

Keeping Your Tone Away from Home
Joggers and Bikers: Antrium Park has both jogging and biking paths. For information contact City of Columbus Recreation and Parks, 645-7410. Sharon Woods (Westerville) and Blacklick Woods are 2 possibilities for joggers and bikers. For more information call Metropolitan Parks, 891-0700.
Health Clubs: Sawmill Athletic Club: 889-7698
YMCA: 224-1131
Public Golf Courses: Bridgeview Golf Club: 471-1565
Grove City Golf Club (Grove City): 875-2497

Shopping
Columbus City Center is a 3-level shopping center with many retail stores. Lane Avenue Shopping Center, north of Ohio State University, has over 100 stores. Short North Business Association has specialty shops and art galleries. The Continent/Home of the French Market features international shopping. And for antique lovers, try Ohio Antiques Center. Sales tax in Columbus is 5 3/4%.
Florists: Arlington Flowers and Gifts: 488-1843
DeSantis Florists: 451-4414

DALLAS – FT. WORTH

Area Code: Dallas, 214; Ft. Worth, 817
Time Zone: Central
Weather: 214-787-1111
Emergency: Dallas, 214-744-4444; Ft. Worth, 911

The Dallas-Ft. Worth area, or the Metroplex, as locals have dubbed the area that includes the 2 cities and their suburban neighbors, long ago moved beyond being just oil-driven. Today it is a major center for wholesale merchandise trade, particularly in the fashion industry, as well as a mecca for high-technology companies.

The 2 cities have a fierce rivalry. Dallas has traditionally been thought of as sophisticated and slick—as the cosmopolitan financial capital of Texas. Ft. Worth, with its stockyards and dependence on the agricultural industry, has been thought of as rough, rugged, and the embodiment of the West. But as the whole Dallas-Ft. Worth area grows (it has expanded an eye-popping 24% in the last 10 years), those distinctions are becoming murkier. And many businesses have a Metro number that can be dialed for free anywhere within the greater metropolitan area.

Corporations headquartered in the area include Tandy, American Airlines, Electronic Data Systems, and Texas Instruments. Note: Addresses in this section are in Dallas unless noted otherwise.

Business Profile
Population: 3.9 million
Population Growth (1980-1989): 24.2%
Unemployment Rate: 5.8%
Fortune 500 Corporate Headquarters: 34

General Information Sources
Dallas Convention & Visitors Bureau: 214-746-6677
Dallas Special Events Info-Line: 214-746-6679
Dallas Chamber of Commerce: 214-746-6600
Ft. Worth Chamber of Commerce: 214-336-2491
Ft. Worth Convention & Visitors Bureau: 214-336-8791

Getting There
By Air: Dallas-Ft. Worth Airport: 214-574-8888; multilingual airport info: 214-574-4420. The country's largest airport: the locals like to point out that it is bigger than all of Manhattan. D/FW is approximately 20 miles northwest of Dallas, and about 25 miles northeast of Ft. Worth.

Love Field is located in Dallas and serves Southwest Airlines,

FLYING TIMES (in hours)		
FROM Dallas-Ft. Worth		
TO		
Chicago:	**2**	
Los Angeles:	**3**	
New York:	**3½**	
Miami:	**3**	

214-263-1717. Redbird Airport, 214-670-7612, in southwestern Dallas, sees to the area's private air traffic. Addison Municipal Airport, 214-248-7733, is north of downtown Dallas.

Once you've landed: A cab ride to downtown Dallas takes about 35-40 minutes (during non-peak times) and costs about $25. A cab ride from Love Field to downtown takes about 15 minutes and costs about $10. Cab fare to Ft. Worth is about $20; the trip takes about 30 minutes. Cab companies include Yellow Cab: 214-426-6262; Ft. Worth, 817-534-5555; Terminal Cab, 214-350-4445.

Limousines (private): Services should be scheduled in advance; local firms include Carey Limousine, 214-263-7298, and Scripps Edward, Inc., 800-223-6710.

Directions Downtown: To Dallas: Take International Parkway south out of the airport complex, then take Route 183 (Airport Freeway) east to I-35E/U.S. 77 (Stemmons Freeway) south. Take Commerce St. exit to downtown.

To Ft. Worth: Take International Parkway south out of airport complex, then take Route 183/Route 121 (Airport Freeway) west to I-35W to Route 280 downtown.

Overland Adventures: *Route Map:* Dallas and Fort Worth are about 30 miles apart; they are linked by I-30. Two other interstates—I-35E and I-35W—cut through Dallas and Ft. Worth in a north-south direction; I-20 and I-30 are the major highways in and out of the city.

Driving Regulations: Seat belts required. Speed limit is 65 m.p.h. unless otherwise posted. Right turn on red permitted unless specifically prohibited.

Bottleneck Busters: The highways leading in and out of downtown Dallas are hopelessly clogged during rush hour. There are usually special problems on Interstate Routes 35, 75, 635, 30, and 20. Metrocell Traffic Central Hotline, 214-988-2060, is a telephone information line which has updated road conditions. Call 214-WIDEN 75 (214-943-3675) for information about I-75 (North Central Expressway) conditions. A local radio station, KLIF 1190 AM, has regular traffic reports.

Trains: Amtrak, Union Station, 400 S. Houston St., 214-653-1101; Amtrak Station, 1501 Jones St., Ft. Worth, 817-332-2931

Bus Service: Greyhound/Trailways Lines, 205 S. Lamar St., 214-655-7084; 901 Commerce St., Fort Worth, 817-429-3089. For general information at either station call 214-263-1181.

Public Transportation: The Dallas Area Rapid Transit (DART) operates a bus service, 214-979-1111. (There are better ways to get around.)

Road Service and Repairs: To reach AAA in Dallas: 214-526-7911; and in Fort Worth: 817-335-4871. AAA-approved Service Stations: Dallas: Lakewood Automotive Exxon, 214-823-1351 (for most American cars); Fischer's Foreign Car Service, 214-630-2807 (for most foreign cars). Ft. Worth: Pep Boys, 817-534-2227.

Parking Regulations: In both Dallas and Ft. Worth there is metered on-street parking. However, there is also ample space in parking lots around the city; costs ranges from $5-$10 a day. If you are going to use parking meters, be punctual: cars are ticketed and towed for abuses.
Towed? City of Dallas Transport: 214-670-3161; Ft. Worth Automotive Pound: 817-335-8247

International Travelers
Foreign Currency Exchange: BANK ONE: 1717 Main St., 214-290-2000; 777 Main St., Ft. Worth, 817-334-9000
Texas Commerce Bank, 2200 Ross Ave., 3rd floor, 214-922-2300
Translation Services: Berlitz Translation Services: 214-380-1693; Ft. Worth, 817-335-4393
Foreign Books and Periodicals: American News, 5155 E. Lancaster, Ft. Worth, 817-654-3810 (will deliver)

Business Visitor's Needs
Banking: BANK ONE: 1717 Main St., 214-290-2000; 777 Main St., Ft. Worth, 817-334-9000
NCNB Texas National Bank, 1401 Elm St., 214-988-6262; 500 W. 7th St., Ft. Worth, 817-390-6161
Team Bank, 500 Throckmorton St., Ft. Worth, 817-884-4000
Texas Commerce Bank, 2200 Ross Ave., 214-922-2300
Secretarial Services: Accountemps: 214-363-3300
Kelly Services (Ft. Worth): 817-332-7807
Manpower Temporary Services: 214-954-0085
Olsten Temporary Services (Ft. Worth): 817-336-9401
Copying and Printing: Alpha Graphics (Ft. Worth): 817-870-2660 (call for other locations)
Minuteman Press: 214-363-2876
Quik Print: 214-741-1425
Also: The Hyatt Regency (Ft. Worth), 817-870-1234, has copy service through the front desk
Fax and Telex Facilities: Virtually all major hotels have facsimile service available to guests.
Action Telex/Action Fax: 214-661-2913
Messengers: Metrocall Messengers (Ft. Worth): 817-572-4303
One Hour Delivery Service: 214-352-1732
Wingtip Couriers: 214-841-0801
Medical Needs: Doctor referral: Baylor University Doctor Referral: 214-820-3312
Dental referral: Dallas County Dental Society: 214-386-5741
Fort Worth District Dental Society: 817-923-9337
Weekend emergency: 817-924-7111
Pharmacies: Eckerd Drugstore: 214-827-9240
Hall's Pharmacy (Ft. Worth): 817-877-3677
Hospitals: Baylor University Medical Center: 214-820-2501
Presbyterian Hospital: 214-369-4111
All Saints Episcopal (Ft. Worth): 817-926-2544

Convention Centers
Dallas Convention Center, 650 S. Griffin, 214-658-7000.

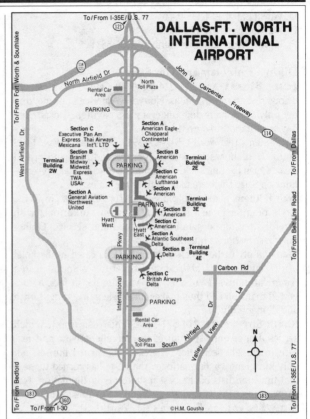

600,000 sq. feet of exhibition space.
INFOMART, 1950 Stemmons Freeway, 214-746-3500. A high-tech display mart for computer and office automation companies; 300,000 sq. feet available.
Dallas Market Center, 2100 Stemmons Freeway, 214-749-5455. Includes Market Hall, 202,000 sq. feet of convention space, and the Apparel Mart: glass-fronted showrooms with more than 110,000 sq. feet of exhibition space for fashion trade shows and conventions.
Ft. Worth-Tarrant County Convention Center, 1111 Houston St., Ft. Worth, 817-332-9222. 170,000 sq. feet.

Entertainment, Sports, and Culture
Sports: Baseball: Texas Rangers, Arlington Stadium, 817-273-5100
Basketball: Dallas Mavericks, Reunion Arena, 214-748-1808 and 214-988-0117; tickets 214-658-7068
Football: Dallas Cowboys, 214-556-9900; Texas Stadium, 214-438-7676; tickets 214-556-2500
Soccer: Dallas Sidekicks, Reunion Arena, 214-361-5425
The Arts: Dallas Opera: 214-443-1000
Dallas Repertory Theater: 214-369-8966
Dallas Symphony Orchestra: 214-692-0203
Dallas Theatre Center: 214-526-8857

Ft. Worth Ballet: 817-335-9000
Ft. Worth Opera: 817-731-0833
Ft. Worth Symphony Orchestra: 817-926-8831

Dining: Four Stars and Our Stars

Four Stars: Actuelle, 214-855-0440. One of the most luxurious restaurants in Dallas. Nouvelle American cuisine, dinner only. Customers dine under a glass pavilion. Closed Sunday; reservations required.

Cattlemen's (Ft. Worth), 817-624-3945. A classic Texas steakhouse, Cattlemen's specializes in barbecued beef, and grilled steak. Open for lunch and dinner daily; does not take reservations on Sats. There are usually lines for tables.

French Room, at the Adolphus hotel, 214-742-8200. This is the city's premier French restaurant; opulent, luxurious, with careful attention to detail in both food and service. Dinner only; reservations a must.

Mansion on Turtle Creek, 214-526-2121. Located in the hotel of the same name, this restaurant features a sophisticated American nouvelle cuisine. The Mansion is, in fact, a converted mansion and thus makes for an elegant setting. Lunch and dinner daily.

Routh Street Cafe, 214-871-7161. This restaurant, which serves dinner only, specializes in nouvelle cuisine and features regional specialities. The chef has earned himself not only local renown, but national: the place has turned up several times on lists of the best restaurants in the nation. Not surprisingly, reservations are essential; open Tues.-Sat.

Our Stars: Joe T. Garcia's (Ft. Worth), 817-626-4356. A local Tex-Mex favorite, this spot's specialties include chile relleno, quesadillas, and, of course, margaritas. Lunch weekdays, dinner daily. Reservations accepted for large groups only.

On the Border Cafe, 214-528-5900. Tex-Mex to the max. Try to get a table on the patio outside where you can enjoy the parade of passers-by. Open for lunch and dinner daily. No reservations.

Uncle Tai's, 214-934-9998. The city's finest Oriental restaurant, located in far north Dallas. Open for lunch and dinner daily. Reservations are a good idea.

Home Away from Home: Where to Stay

The Adolphus, 1321 Commerce St., 214-742-8200. One of the grand old ladies of Dallas hotels, this historic landmark has undergone extensive renovation lately, and has all the modern amenities a business traveler might require.

Loews Anatole of Dallas, 2201 Stemmons Freeway, (I-35E) in the Market Center area, 214-748-1200. With 1600 rooms (145 suites), 16 restaurants and bars, indoor/outdoor pool, indoor/outdoor jogging track, fully equipped health club, this is the city's largest hotel. A favorite convention spot.

Mansion on Turtle Creek, 2821 Turtle Creek Blvd., 214-559-2100. Located on 5 acres of landscaped park, this former villa has just 142 rooms. Affiliated with a golf course and tennis court 5 minutes away; the Mansion also offers a health club.

Four Seasons Resort and Club, 4150 N. MacArthur Blvd., Irving, 214-717-0700. Situated 10-15 minutes from the airport, this is locally noted for its conference facilities. As the name would suggest, the hotel has extensive recreational facilities.

Hyatt Regency Dallas, 300 Reunion Blvd., 214-651-1234. Located in southwest downtown, with 950 rooms (50 suites), this is a local businessman's favorite. The revolving restaurant at the top of the tower provides the city's best views.

Hyatt Regency Ft. Worth, 815 Main St., 817-870-1234. Formerly the Hotel Texas, this 500+ room hotel is smack in the center of downtown and convenient to the convention center.

Westin Hotel, 13340 Dallas Parkway, 214-934-9494. This 450-room hotel is attached to the Galleria, the huge shopping center in north Dallas. The location is convenient to the burgeoning north Dallas area.

Worthington Hotel, 200 Main St., Ft. Worth, 817-870-1000. Convenient to downtown Ft. Worth, this 500-room hotel (including a few luxury suites) is connected to Tandy Center shopping area. Full fitness facilities.

Keeping Your Tone Away from Home

Joggers and Bikers: Dallas has lovely trails for biking and running at Bachman Lake or White Rock Lake. For information call 214-670-4027. Ft. Worth has biking trails along the Trinity River through Forest Park.

Health Clubs: YMCA: 214-954-0500; Ft. Worth, 817-332-3281

Public Golf Courses: The following are among many public and municipal courses:
Cedar Crest: 214-670-7615
Grapevine Municipal Golf Course (Ft. Worth): 817-481-0421
L.B. Houston: 214-670-6322
Tenison: 214-670-1402

Shopping

Dallas: The original downtown location of Neiman Marcus can be found at 1618 Main Street. The Galleria is the area home to Macy's, Saks Fifth Avenue, Marshall Fields, Cartier, Mark Cross, Elizabeth Arden, and Brooks Brothers, as well as a year-round ice skating rink.

North Park Center, a centrally situated mall, includes stores like Neiman Marcus, Lord & Taylor, and Dillard's.

Ft. Worth: Shepler's, in Arlington, is a hot spot for Western wear and boots.

Ridgmar Mall is home to yet another Neiman Marcus branch, as well as an assortment of stores and restaurants.

Florists: Flowers on the Square (Ft. Worth): 817-870-2888
Petals, Etc. (Ft. Worth): 817-738-0934
Preston Flower Market: 214-386-2988

DENVER

Area Code: 303
Time Zone: Mountain
Weather: 398-3964
Police: 575-2011
Emergency: 911

Denver is the signpost for Pikes Peak (or Bust!), houses Buffalo Bill memorials, and is the first stop to a skier's paradise. But did you know the city itself is flat as a pancake, has more sunny days than either Miami or San Diego, and is home to the United States Mint? Denver's dynamic business district shed its desert dust long ago and has emerged as the Queen City of the Plains. When construction of Denver International Airport is finished, it will be the world's largest airport. A strong manufacturing base centered in microelectronics, computer peripherals, and defense augments Denver's oil industry, mining interests, and tourist industry. The area retains such major employers as Texaco, IBM, Honeywell Control and Test Instruments, Martin Marietta, AT&T, US WEST Communications, and Adolph Coors Company.

Business Profile
Population: 492,365
Population Growth (1980-1989): 1.6%
Unemployment Rate: 5.3%
Fortune 500 Corporate Headquarters: 7

General Information Sources
Denver Chamber of Commerce: 894-8500
Greater Denver Metro Convention And Visitors Bureau: 892-1505 or 892-1112

Getting There
By Air: Stapleton International Airport information, ground transportation, and flying weather: 800-AIR-2-DEN (800-247-2336)

Once you've landed: Taxis from the airport to downtown hotels are the quickest transportation. The ride takes 15-20 minutes, 30 minutes in the morning or afternoon rush, and costs about $9.50 including the airport gate fee. Metro Taxi Inc., 333-3333; Yellow Cab Cooperative Association, 777-7777; Zone Cabs, 861-2323.

Airporter vans leave Stapleton every 15 minutes for Denver hotels. The ride takes about 25 minutes and costs $5. Purchase tickets at the Airporter counter in the Ground Transportation Center, lower level opposite door 6, 321-3222.

Public bus transportation is also available. Regional Transportation District (RTD) bus Nos. 32, 28, and 38, leave the airport for the downtown area every 30 minutes. Exact fare is required: $1 during peak hours and 50 cents during regular hours. The AB express bus leaves every 30 minutes, takes about 20 minutes, stops at the Denver Bus Center on 20th and Curtis, and costs $1.50. Customer service, 722-1411; route and schedule information, 778-6000.

Limousines (private): 24-hour notice is recommended. Prince Limousine, 451-6622

Directions Downtown: When leaving the airport you will be on a road called Martin Luther King. Stay on this road until you reach downtown Denver, about 2 miles. The business district begins at 18th St.

Overland Adventures: *Route Map:* Three major interstate highways converge in Denver: I-25 runs north and south; I-70 and I-76 run east and west. A new beltway, C-470, (slated for completion in 1990) is the southwestern quarter of a roadway that will eventually link up with eastern section E-470, the new airport (currently under construction), and downtown Denver.

Driving Regulations: Right turn on red is permitted unless otherwise indicated. Left turn on red is permitted from one-way to one-way. Seatbelts are mandatory.

Bottleneck Busters: Interstate rush hour traffic from 7:15am-8:15am and from 4:30pm-5:30pm can cause delays up to 30 minutes. Rush hour traffic within downtown Denver is manageable.

Trains: Amtrak, Union Station, 800-872-7245; passenger service 534-2812. The east-west route connects Denver with Los Angeles, San Francisco, Seattle, and Chicago.

Bus Service: Greyhound/Trailways Lines, 1055 19th St., 292-6111. Daily service in Colorado; also serves major ski resorts.

Public Transportation: Regional Transportation District (RTD), 778-6000 or 722-1411. Public bus transportation for metropolitan Denver/Boulder.

Road Service and Repairs: For 24-hour car repair and towing, call AAA Auto Club-Colorado, 753-8888

Parking Regulations: Limited metered and non-metered parking. Allright Parking has over 100 parking lots and garages in downtown Denver.

Towed? Call the City Pound, 295-4363

International Travelers
Foreign Currency Exchange: Deak International, 1580 Court Pl., 571-0808

Stapleton International Airport, 2nd level of Concourse C; open 6am-9pm

United Bank of Denver, 1700 Lincoln, 9th floor, 861-8811

Translation Services: Berlitz Translation Services, 100 Filmore St., 399-8686

Foreign Books and Periodicals: Johnny's Newsstand, 1555 Champa Ave., 825-6397

Tattered Cover Bookstore, 2955 East 1st Ave., 322-7727

FLYING TIMES (in hours)
FROM Denver **TO**
Chicago: 2½
Los Angeles: 2½
New York: 3½
Miami: 5

Business Visitor's Needs
Banking: Central Bank of Denver, 1515 Arapahoe St., 893-3456
Colorado National Bank of Denver, 17th and Champa, 893-1862
First Interstate Bank of Denver, 633 17th St., 293-2211
Secretarial Services: Kelly Services: 623-6262
Margaret Hook's Personnel: 770-2100
Copying and Printing: Kinko's: 623-3500 (open 24 hours)
Xerox Reproduction Center: 592-4500
Fax and Telex Facilities: Answer America: 800-255-8783
Western Union: 800-325-6000
Messengers: Speedy 292-6000
Medical Needs: Doctor referral: Med Search (St. Joseph Hospital's doctor referral): 866-8000
Dental referral: Center Dental Associates: 592-1133
Pharmacies: Medisave Pharmacy: 233-6701
Walgreen's: 571-5316
Hospitals: St. Joseph Hospital emergency room: 837-7240
Mercy Medical Center: 393-3000
Rose Medical Center: 320-2121
St. Anthony's emergency room: 629-3721

Convention Centers
Colorado Convention Center, located at 14th and Welton Sts., 640-8000. The Center provides 300,000 sq. feet of exhibition space on one level, and 100,000 sq. feet of meeting space on another level.
Currigan Exhibition Hall, 14th and Welton Sts., 575-5106, offers a hall that can be divided into two 50,000-sq.-foot exhibit halls. This facility also has up to 1,000 10' x 10' booths.
Denver Merchandise Mart, 451 E. 58th Ave., 292-6278. The mart has a 65,000-sq.-foot hall and individual showrooms.

Entertainment, Sports, and Culture
Ticket Services: Ticketmaster provides tickets and information to sporting and cultural events: 290-TIXS (290-8497)
Sports: Baseball: Zephyrs, Mile High Stadium, 433-8645
Basketball: Nuggets, McNichols Sports Arena, 893-6565
Football: Broncos, Mile High Stadium, 433-7466
The Arts: Colorado Ballet, 298-0677, is a classical ballet company. The Denver Center for the Performing Arts, 893-4100, is home to plays, Broadway shows, and the Colorado Symphony Orchestra.
Opera Colorado, 778-6464, performs in a symphony hall in-the-round.

Dining: Four Stars and Our Stars
In the absence of true Four Star restaurants, try these gems:
Wellshire Inn, 759-3333. Stately English Tudor mansion specializes in Continental and Far Eastern choices. Moderately expensive.
Normandy French, 321-3311. French dining in an old-world atmosphere.
Casa Bonita of Denver (Lakewood), 232-5115. Denver's most exciting restaurant—Mexican village atmosphere and Mexican food.

Home Away from Home: Where to Stay
Brown Palace Hotel, 321 17th St., 297-3111. Denver's most famous and showy hotel has a Victorian heritage reaching back to 1892. Most rooms open onto a court area; concierge service caters to the businessman's needs. Singles from $125-$205.
Leows Girogio Hotel, 4150 E. Mississippi Ave., 782-9300. Italian-style super deluxe hotel. Singles from $109-$124.
Oxford Alexis Hotel, 1600 17th St., 628-5400. Built in 1891, the Oxford Alexis was Denver's first hotel. It is an historic sight sporting many antiques, plus a health club and concierge service. Singles range from $110-$330.
Cambridge Club, 1560 Sherman St., 831-1252. offers reasonable rates; singles from $69-155. Valet service is provided to airport, railroad, and bus depots.

Keeping Your Tone Away from Home
Denver Parks and Recreation, 458-4800. Joggers can enjoy some 20 miles of paths that follow both Cherry Creek and the Platte River. This park system provides indoor and outdoor pools, fitness classes, weight rooms, and drop-in basketball. Colorado Division of Parks and Outdoor Recreation can provide information about activities for its 31 parks. Write to them at this address: 1313 Sherman St., #618, Denver, CO 80203.
Health Clubs: International Athletic Club: 623-2100
YMCA: 861-8300
YWCA: 825-7141
Public Golf Courses: Park Hill: 333-5411
Wellshire: 757-1352
Willis Case: 455-9801
Skiing: For information, contact Colorado Ski Country, 837-0793. Just an hour outside of Denver is a choice of over 20 ski resorts.

Shopping
For those designing shoppers, high fashion can be found in Montaldo's. Try Cherry Creek North for boutiquing. The Shops, at Tabor Center, provide 70 shops with Brooks Brothers among the list. Traditional department stores like May D&E and Montgomery Ward are located along the 16th Street Mall which provides free shuttles.
Florists: Alpha Floral Company: 623-3222
Lehrer's Flowers: 455-1234

DETROIT

Area Code: 313
Time Zone: Eastern
Weather: 976-1212
Police (information): 224-4400
Emergency: 911

It's not the only game in town, but the automotive industry is still the overwhelmingly dominant business in this business-minded city. General Motors, Chrysler, Ford, and American Motors are all in Detroit or its surrounding towns, as are a multitude of automotive suppliers. In recent years Detroit's drubbing at the hands of the Japanese has curbed the city's swagger somewhat; unemployment has hit the city especially hard. Adding to these economic woes, Detroit has seen a classic flight to the suburbs. But the city has been pursuing a policy of urban revitalization and has had some success with it. Renaissance Center is the most visible symbol of this: a cluster of glass silo-type towers housing a hotel, office buildings, shops, and restaurants.

The music of Motown is the other industry which has given Detroit its identity: musical treasures like Stevie Wonder, Diana Ross and the Supremes, Smokey Robinson, the Temptations, and Marvin Gaye all came out of Detroit.

Other companies headquartered in the Detroit area include K Mart, Stroh's Brewery, Freuhauf, and the Budd Company.

Business Profile
Population (metropolitan area): 4.4 million
Population Growth (1980-1989): -2.4%
Unemployment Rate: 7.6%
Fortune 500 Corporate Headquarters: 8

General Information Sources
Metropolitan Detroit Convention & Visitors Bureau: 259-4333
What's Happening Line: 298-6262
Visitor Information Center: 567-1170
Mayor's Information and Complaint Bureau: 224-2989
Chamber of Commerce: 964-4000

Getting There
By Air: Detroit Metropolitan Airport: 942-3550. Located about 26 miles from downtown Detroit.
Detroit City Airport: 267-6400. 9 flights daily to Chicago.
Oakland/Pontiac Airport: 666-3900
Once you've landed: Buses run from the airport to major downtown hotels regularly. Fare: $11 one way; $20 round trip. Commuter Transportation Company, 941-9391.

A cab ride to downtown from the airport costs about $25; the trip takes about 45 minutes. Taxis: Checker Cab, 963-7000; Detroit Metro Airport Taxicab, 942-4690; Lorraine Cab Co., 582-6900; Southfield Cab Co., 356-1090.
Limousines (private): AAA VIP Limousine Service, 476-3060; Continental Limousine, 626-8282; Michigan Limousine Service, 546-6112. Reservations are a must.
Directions Downtown: To travel downtown from the airport take Interstate 94 East to U.S. 10 South to downtown.
Overland Adventures: *Route Map:* I-75 leads into downtown Detroit from both the north and the south, while I-96, I-94, and I-696 come from the western suburbs of the city into downtown. I-94 also leads in from northeast of downtown.
Bottleneck Busters: Rush hour tends to be earlier here than in some cities: in the morning it ends by about 8:30am, and starts up again at 4pm in the afternoon. Expect slow going on I-75 and U.S. 10 (also called Lodge Freeway). Radio station WWJ-AM 950 has regular traffic updates.
Trains: Amtrak Dearborn, 16121 Michigan Ave., 336-5407; Amtrak Detroit, 2405 W. Vernor Hwy., 800-872-7245.
Bus Service: Greyhound/Trailways Lines, 130 E. Congress St., 963-9840; Michigan Trailways, 1833 E. Jefferson Ave., 963-9840.
Public Transportation: People Mover, 962-RAIL (962-7245), is a rail system that connects major downtown sites. Detroit Department of Transportation (DDOT) operates city buses; call 933-1300 for route and schedule information. Suburban Mobility Authority for Regional Transport (SMART) runs buses to the suburbs, 962-5515.

Road Service and Repairs: AAA Emergency Road Service, 336-1111; AAA Dearborn, 336-0990 (call for other locations)
Towed? Call Municipal Parking Department, 224-0300

International Travelers
Foreign Currency Exchange: Comerica Bank, 211 W. Fort St., windows 3 and 4 in main banking area, 222-3000
National Bank of Detroit, lower level of main branch, 611 Woodward Ave. at Fort St., 225-1000
Translation Services: AAA Language Services, 3250 W. Big Beaver, Suite 120, 649-5551
Berlitz Translation Services, 30700 Telegraph Rd., Bingham Farms, 642-4401
International Translating Bureau, 20505 W. 12 Mile Rd., Suite 103, Southfield, 353-0366
Japan Business Consultants Ltd., 1140 Morehead Ct., Ann Arbor, 995-0847
Foreign Books and Periodicals: Cuda's East Bookstore, 14310 Michigan Ave., Dearborn, 581-5486
Jim's Newsstand, Woodward at Monroe, 496-0625
News Break, 615 Griswold, 961-4777

FLYING TIMES	
(in hours)	
FROM	
Detroit	
TO	
Chicago:	1½
Los Angeles:	4
New York:	1½
Miami:	2¾

Business Visitor's Needs

Banking: Comerica Bank, 211 W. Fort St., 222-3000
Manufacturers Bank, 100 Renaissance Ctr., 222-4000
National Bank of Detroit, 611 Woodward Ave., 225-1000
Secretarial Services: Dearborn Business Center: 565-4300
HQ-Headquarters Companies: 259-5422 (call for other locations)
Practical Business Services: 965-3322
Copying and Printing: American Speedy: 963-3600; fax 963-6393
Kinko's: 832-1442 (call for other locations)
Sir Speedy: 965-4050; fax 965-5433 (call for other locations)
Fax and Telex Facilities: Kinko's and Sir Speedy, listed above, have facsimile services. Also try Western Union, 800-325-6000.
Messengers: Expeditors of Michigan: 535-9797
PDQ Courier: 965-9600
Medical Needs: Doctor referral: Many local hospitals have physician referral services.
Detroit Medical Society: 832-7800
Dental referral: Dental Referral Service: 559-7900
Pharmacies: Perry Drug Stores: 892-4600 (open 24 hours; call for other locations)
St. Johns Hospital and Medical Ctr. After Hrs. Pharmacy: 343-4720 (open until midnight 7 days a week)
Hospitals: Detroit Receiving Hospital: 745-3330
Henry Ford Hospital: 876-2600
Harper Grace Hospitals: 745-5111
Children's Hospital of Michigan: 745-0113

Convention Center

Cobo Conference/Exhibition Center, One Washington Blvd., 224-1010. 2.4 million sq. feet of exhibition space.

Entertainment, Sports, and Culture

Sports: Baseball: Detroit Tigers, Tigers Stadium, 963-9944
Basketball: Detroit Pistons, The Palace of Auburn Hills, 377-0100
Football: Detroit Lions, Pontiac Silverdome, 335-4151
Hockey: Detroit Red Wings, Joe Louis Arena, 567-6000
The Arts: Detroit Repertory Theatre: 868-1347
Detroit Symphony Orchestra: 567-1400
The Fisher Theatre: 872-1000
Fox Theatre: 567-6000

Dining: Four Stars and Our Stars

The Caucus Club, 965-4970. A favorite for business lunches, the Caucus Club is convenient to the city's financial district. Open for lunch and dinner daily except Sun.
Nippon Kai (Clawson), 288-3210. Japanese menu features tempura, sushi, sukiyaki. The decor is serenely Oriental. Open daily.
Summit Steak House and Lounge, 568-8600. You can see for miles from this revolving restaurant at the top of the 73-story Westin Hotel. American regional specialties like Pacific salmon, and Baltimore scallops imperial. Open daily.
The Whitney, 832-5700. A lavish oak and marble mansion converted into an equally posh restaurant. American traditional and nouvelle cuisine. Reservations are essential.

Home Away from Home: Where to Stay

Dearborn Inn, 20301 Oakwood Blvd., 271-2700; Marriott toll-free # 800-228-9290. An elegantly restored hotel situated on 23 acres; complex also includes 5 reproduction colonial homes for bed-and-breakfast-style accommodations. Nearby is the Henry Ford Museum and Ford headquarters. Rates: singles $134-$189, doubles $149-$205.
Guest Quarters Suite Hotel, 850 Tower Dr., Troy, 879-7500. An all-suite hotel, ideal for business travelers. Provisions include 3 phones, microwave, coffee maker, wet bar. Convenient to I-75. Rates: $120-$175.
St. Regis Hotel, 3071 W. Grand Blvd., 873-3000. Located across from GM World Headquarters, this lovely smaller hotel (202 rooms, 22 suites) is connected by skywalk to GM, Fisher Theatre, and the shops at New Center One and the Fisher buildings. Rates: $130 for a single, $155 for a double.
Westin Hotel, Renaissance Center, Jefferson Ave., near Woodward Ave., 568-8000. A towering 73 stories tall, this hotel holds 1400 rooms and 65 suites, and is a favorite of both business travelers and conventioneers. Rates: $116-$194.

Keeping Your Tone Away from Home

Joggers and Bikers: Belle Isle is a municipal park on an island in the Detroit River and is convenient to downtown. There are extensive recreational facilities, including tennis courts, a fitness course, a 9-hole golf course, bicycle trails, and playing fields. Bicycle rentals are available at Stony Creek Metropark.
Health Clubs: Dearborn Racquet and Health Club: 562-1296
YMCA: 962-6126
YWCA: 961-9220

Shopping

Renaissance Center has more than 90 stores and restaurants. Nearby is Millender Center which also boasts an array of luxury shops. Trappers Alley Marketplace, a 5-story mall in a renovated fur-and wool-processing plant, has an eclectic assortment of stores. In Dearborn, Fairlane Town Center is a huge mall anchored by department stores like Hudson's, Lord & Taylor and Saks Fifth Avenue.
For bargain-hunting shoppers, Windsor, Ontario, is just across the river from downtown. Windsor is known for its shops specializing in British imports. Make sure you understand whether the prices quoted are in American dollars or Canadian dollars—the difference can be substantial.
Detroit has a 4% sales tax.
Florists: Entertainment Designs: 884-4224

HOUSTON

Area Code: 713
Time Zone: Central
Weather: 228-8703
Police: 222-3131
Emergency: 911

Houston has learned to wear more than 10-gallon hats since the oil recession has begun. Once known as the fastest growing city in America and now the third largest seaport in the U.S., diversifying has become a necessity for Houston's oil-heavy economy. On the flip side, Texas's largest city has advantages that business people can't resist: low housing costs, lots of skilled labor, and currently no corporate or personal income tax. Eventually, the city's oil-related traumas will heal. In the meantime, be sure to enjoy such delights as Houston's new and world-acclaimed art museum, the de Menil Collection.

Business Profile
Population: 3,229,000
Population Growth (1980-1989): 18%
Unemployment Rate: 6.3%
Fortune 500 Corporate Headquarters: 23

General Information Sources
Greater Houston Convention and Visitors Bureau: 523-5050 or 800-231-7799
Greater Houston Partnership: 651-7200
One Stop Business Assistance Center: 663-7867

Getting There
By Air: Houston Intercontinental Airport (IAH) general information: 230-3000
William P. Hobby Airport general information: 643-4597
Once you've landed: Connections among Houston Intercontinental Airport's 3 terminals (A,B,C) are provided by a free 24-hour "people mover."
Air connections between IAH and Hobby Airport are via Continental Express/Emerald Air (airline). Flights take 10 minutes and leave at various times from IAH to Hobby Airport between 9:30am and 8:05pm. Seats cost $15; Continental's passengers making connections fly at no charge. Flights leaving from Hobby Airport to IAH leave at 7:05am and 10:10am, and at regular intervals between 12:25pm and 7:10pm.
Helicopter Service to and from IAH during the 2- to 3-hour rush hour periods is widely used. The cost is about $45. Pick up the service at Gate 17 in C Terminal every 30 minutes M-F and land at the West Chase Hilton or at the Park 10 complex

in West Houston. Tarlton Helicopters, Inc., 871-8010. No helicopters are needed at Hobby Airport since it's 9 miles from Houston.
Taxi rides during non-rush hour times at IAH take about 40 minutes and cost approximately $22. Shared rides lower prices. Liberty Cab, 695-6700 or Yellow Cab, 236-1111. Call these same taxis for Hobby Airport. The cost is $12 to $14 and takes 30 minutes.
The Airport Express at IAH, 523-8888, provides vans to 4 downtown locations. Service is available M-Sun. from 6:50am until 12:30am. The ride takes approximately 30 minutes and costs about $8.50. The Hobby Airport Limousine, 644-8359, costs $5; it leaves every 30 minutes between 7:30am and 11:30pm. Downtown drop-offs as follows: Hyatt Regency, S. Main St., Post Oak, and Greenway Plaza.
Metropolitan Transit Authority provides public transportation from Hobby Airport to downtown via No. 50 Heights or Downtown bus. The fare is 60 cents in exact change and takes 50 minutes. Buses leave about every 20 minutes, M-F, 4:17am-12:12am. On weekends buses leave every 30-35 minutes. No public transportation is available at IAH.

Limousines (private): 24-hour reservations are recommended. Houston Executive Limousine, 928-5511; VIP Limousine Service, 522-0861
Directions Downtown: From IAH, take JFK Blvd. After the 2nd light turn left onto Beltway 8. The beltway leads you to Highway 59 South. Houston is 22 miles south of the airport. When you see signs for Downtown Houston, take any one of the 4 possible exits.
From Hobby Airport, take the 610 Loop or I-45. The airport is 9 miles southeast of downtown Houston.

Overland Adventures: *Route Map:* Houston's beltway encircling the city is Loop 610; for efficient and hassle-free traveling choose the Loop. Highway 59 runs north to Arkansas as well as south to Laredo and the border; it intersects with the other interstates in the center of Houston. I-10 runs east to Louisiana and west through Texas. I-45 runs north to Dallas and south to Galveston.
Bottleneck Busters: Houston is a city of congested rush hours and constant construction. For current construction information, call 869-4571; do your best to avoid the freeways during the elongated rush hours.
Trains: Amtrak, 902 Washington, 224-1577. Serves Los Angeles and San Francisco to the west and New Orleans and Washington, D.C. to the east.
Bus Service: Greyhound/Trailways Lines, 2121 Main St., 759-6500
Public Transportation: Metropolitan Transit Authority, 635-4000, provides bus service throughout the city. Most buses run north and south along Main St. The fare is 70 cents for local buses, $1 for express service.

FLYING TIMES
(in hours)
FROM
Houston
TO
Chicago: 2½
Los Angeles: 3
New York: 3¾
Miami: 3½

Road Service and Repairs: For service call American Automobile Association, 521-0211; Exxon Auto Repair Services, 659-8817; Kurt's Automotive, 468-6539
Towed? Call 247-8000

International Travelers
Foreign Currency Exchange: At Houston Intercontinental Airport, currency exchange is possible in all 3 terminals. Hobby Airport does not have money changing facilities.
First International Bank of Texas, 1000 Louisiana, 224-6611
Translation Services: Berlitz Translation Services, 396 Alhambra Circle, 529-8110
International Language Service (ILS), 2650 Fountain View, Suite 120, 783-1035
Consulates: Mexico-Consulate General: 524-2300
Republic of China-Taiwan: 626-7445
Foreign Books and Periodicals: Books International, River Oaks Shopping Center, 523-5330
Fiesta, 4200 Sanjacinto, 529-0155

Business Visitor's Needs
Banking: American Bank, 1600 Smith, 951-9844
First City Bank, 6424 Fannin, 797-9333
University State Bank, 5615 Kirby Dr., 526-1211
Secretarial Services: Executive Business Services, Inc.: 789-6343
Kelly Services: 972-1151
Copying and Printing: First Stop Printing: 796-9255
Kinko's: 654-8161
Messengers: Air Courier Express: 987-9900
CBS Couriers: 977-8676
Telex Facilities: Western Union International: 626-0676
Medical Needs: Doctor referral: Physician Referral: GET-HELP (438-4357)
Dental referral: Greater Houston Dental Society: 961-4337
Pharmacies: Eckerd Drugs: 522-3983
Walgreen's: 223-4243
Hospitals: Ben Taub Hospital: 793-2000
Saint Joseph Hospital: 757-1000
Memorial City Medical Center: 932-3000

Convention Centers
Albert Thomas Convention and Exhibition Center, 612 Smith St., 853-8000.
George R. Brown Convention Center, 1001 Convention Center Blvd., 853-8000.
The Summit, 10 Greenway Plaza, 627-9470. With seating for 15,600, this facility also has 17,000 sq. feet of exhibit space.
Astrodomain, I-610 and Kirby, 799-9555. This complex includes the Astrohall and the AstroArena.

Entertainment, Sports, and Culture
Ticket Services: Ticketron, 526-1709; Rainbow Ticket Masters,

977-3333; Showtix, 785-2787
Sports Highlights: 878-8000
Sports: Baseball: Astros, Astrodome, 799-9555
Basketball: Rockets, Summit, 627-0600
Football: Oilers, Astrodome, 797-1000

Dining: Four Stars and Our Stars
La Reserve, 871-8181 or 8177. Elegant dining. Continental menu includes such delectables as terrine of partridge with foie gras. Expensive. Reservations required.
Tony's, 622-6778. Moderately expensive. French cuisine with such specialties as snapper Hemingway and linguine pescatore. Reservations required.
River Cafe, 529-0088. Moderately priced, quasi-Bohemian hangout for journalists and artists. Mesquite grill provides fish, steak, sausage, and sauces to top them off.

Home Away from Home: Where to Stay
Four Seasons Hotel, Houston Center, 1300 Lamar, 650-1300. All the modern conveniences like concierge, pool, and shopping arcade make this hotel with its art deco design a sure bet. Singles $120-$150.
La Colombe D'Or, 3410 Montrose Blvd., 524-7999. Built in 1923, this inn houses works of local and well-known artists. Suites only, $150-$600.
The Lancaster Hotel, 701 Texas, 228-9500. Located in the theater district, this wonderful older hotel retains its elegance and has been splendidly restored. Singles $125-$150.

Keeping Your Tone Away from Home
Joggers and Bikers: A popular 3-mile run can be found in Memorial Park. Bikers and joggers enjoy the track along Buffalo Bayou. A starting point might be the Sabine Bridge downtown. Watch out for heat and humidity; the Memorial Park track is your best choice for some shade. City of Houston Parks information, 845-1000.
Health Clubs: The Texas Club: 227-7000
YMCA: 659-5566
YWCA: 868-9922
Public Golf Course: Memorial Park: 862-4033

Shopping
The ritziest shopping can be found at the Galleria mall. Look there for designer labels in such stores as Saks Fifth Avenue. Boutiques can be found downtown at The Park at Houston Center. Malls rather than traditional department stores are shoppers' choices in Houston, but such stores as Montgomery Ward can be found on Spencer Highway. Baybrook Mall is also popular.
Florists: Brookhollow Florists: 683-6162
Kirby Glen Floral Studio: 521-2171
Tanglewood Flowers: 965-9810

KANSAS CITY

Area Code: Missouri, 816; Kansas, 913 (Telephone numbers in this section are within the 816 calling area unless otherwise noted.)
Time Zone: Central
Weather: 471-4840, 913-384-6600
Police: Missouri, 234-5000; Kansas, 913-573-6015
Emergency: 911

Kansas City's wild west heritage is still juxtaposed to its modern-day hustle and bustle; it is a reminder of cattle and grain and fur trading, of wagon trains and railroad empires, of infamous robbers like Jesse and Frank James, and of President Harry S. Truman. But you may not know these facts: Kansas City has more miles of boulevards than Paris and more fountains than any city except Rome. Some of the nation's best shopping is at Country Club Plaza.

There's Oceans of Fun, the Midwest's largest theme park. The city has hot jazz, cool museums, and plenty of ribs. K.C. ranks first nationally in greeting cards (thanks to Hallmark), second in wheat flour production, and third in automobile and truck production. Always America's transportation hub, Kansas City is a center for distribution and manufacturing. It's also home to the Board of Trade and the Kansas City Stockyards. In spite of all this metropolitan might, Kansas City has a small town friendliness.

Business Profile
Population: 1,586,000
Population Growth (1980-1989): 10.6%
Unemployment Rate: 5.5%
Fortune 500 Corporate Headquarters: 6

General Information Sources
Convention and Visitors Bureau of Greater Kansas City: 221-5242
Kansas City Chamber of Commerce of Greater Kansas City: 221-2424
Visitor Information Phone: 474-9600

Getting There
By Air: Kansas City International Airport (KCI) general information: 243-5237. Radio station 1610 AM provides close-range KCI information.
Once you've landed: KCI has 3 C-shaped terminals which offer parking in the center and aircraft loading along the outer edges. Getting baggage and finding transportation are simple—from aircraft to curbside is 75 feet.
A taxi ride takes about 25-40 minutes and should cost about $25-$27. Cabs are deregulated so fares can vary. Checker Cab

FLYING TIMES
(in hours)
FROM
Kansas City
TO
Chicago: 1½
Los Angeles: 3½
New York: 3
Miami: 3

of Kansas City, 474-TAXI (474-8294); Quicksilver Taxi and Airport Service, 913-262-0905; Yellow Cab, 471-5000.
The KCI Express bus to major hotels leaves daily every half hour, takes 25-40 minutes, and costs from $9-$11, 243-5950. Located at Gate 63 in Terminal C. A cautionary note: beware that the ride can be as long as 1 hour if your hotel happens to be at the end of the route.
Limousines (private): Service is available with 24-hour reservations recommended. American Limousine Service, 471-6050 and 800-553-TAXI (800-553-8294); KC Limo, 356-2400; Limousines Unlimited, 453-2938
Directions Downtown: When leaving the airport, take I-29 South. Kansas City is 18 miles southeast of the airport. To reach the major hotels at Crown Center, for example, take the Broadway exit, turn left onto 15th St. and turn south onto Main St.

Overland Adventures: *Route Map:* Metropolitan Kansas City extends across 2 states, 2 rivers, and 5 counties. Some 334 miles of interstates, freeways, and expressways provide efficient travel throughout this metropolis. Beltways I-435, with 3 sides in Missouri, and I-635 as a fourth side in Kansas, encircle the city. I-35 travels through Kansas City north to Des Moines, IA and south to Wichita, KS. I-70 also enters and exits Kansas City going west to Topeka, KS and east to St. Louis, MO. I-29 is the main north-south connection between the city and its airport. Perhaps all roads do lead to Kansas City.
The city is laid out in a grid pattern: numbered streets run east and west while named streets run north and south.
Bottleneck Busters: Expect significant traffic delays on I-35 south and I-70 to the west.
Trains: Amtrak has service to Independence, St. Louis, Chicago, Topeka, and Los Angeles. New facilities are on 23rd and Main, 800-872-7245.
Bus Service: Greyhound/Trailways Lines has a downtown terminal at 12th and Troost, 698-0080.
Public Transportation: The Metro is Kansas City's public bus system and serves 4 Missouri counties. The minimum fee is 75 cents; fares vary according to traveled distance. For schedule and fare information, call 221-0660 when Metro is open M-F from 6am to 6pm.
Road Service and Repairs: Highway patrol emergency, 524-9200; AAA, 421-7900; Chet's Tow Service, 252-3322 (open 24 hours); Northland Tow Service, 741-2525 (open 24 hours)
Towed? In Missouri call 221-3640; in Kansas call police information, 913-573-6015.

International Travelers
Foreign Currency Exchange: Commerce Bank, 1000 Walnut, 234-2000
Translation Services: Berlitz Translation Services: 800-523-7548
PTI-Technical League Translators & Interpreters: 800-443-2344

Language Link: 913-831-9844
Consulates and International Organizations: Coordination Council for North American Affairs in Kansas City (Taiwan): 531-1298
Japanese Consulate General: 471-0111
Korea Republic Honorary Council: 913-341-8221
Foreign Books and Periodicals: B. Dalton, 8600 Ward Pkwy., 333-2047
Bookstore, 52nd and Troost, 276-1401

Business Visitor's Needs
Banking: American Bank, 1 W. Armour Blvd., 931-1700
Shawnee State Bank, 11101 Johnson Dr., 913-631-6300
Union Bank, 12th and Wyandotte, 221-3600
Secretarial Services: Executive Suite: 913-345-0121
Personal Secretarial, Inc.: 913-345-2323
Copying and Printing: Kinko's: 913-432-4971 (open 24 hours)
Kwik-Kopy Printing: 913-888-0112
Sir Speedy: 421-7137
Messengers: AB Express Inc.: 931-3880
Central Delivery Service: 913-384-6055
Telex Facilities: Western Union: 800-325-6000
Medical Needs: Doctor and Dental referral: Dial 4-Doctor (436-2867)
Trinity Lutheran Hospital Healthline: 751-3000
Pharmacies: Drug Emporium: 941-7166
Hyde Park Pharmacy: 931-7700
Hospitals: Trinity Lutheran Hospital: 753-4600
Truman Medical Center: 556-3000
St. Luke's Hospital: 932-2000

Convention Centers
Convention Center/H. Roe Bartle Hall and Municipal Auditorium, 301 W. 13th St., 421-8000. H. Roe Bartle Hall and Municipal Auditorium are adjacent to each other. Together they provide 300,000 sq. feet of exhibition space, seating for up to 20,000 in 50 meeting rooms, a theater, a music hall, and registration and dining areas.
American Royal Center, 1701 American Royal Ct., 421-6460. The American Royal Theater has both indoor and outdoor exhibition space totaling 600,000 sq. feet. The main arena seats 6,140, and the sports arena seats 18,000.

Entertainment, Sports, and Culture
Ticket Services: Ticketmaster: 931-3330; Jones Stores (walk-in): 391-7000 for information
Sports Scores: 234-4350
Sports: Baseball: Kansas City Royals, Truman Sports Complex, 921-8000; 800-422-1969 to charge tickets
Football: Kansas City Chiefs, Truman Sports Complex, 924-9300
The Arts: Concertline: 968-4100
Jazz Hotline: 931-2888
Kansas City Jazz Festival occurs annually Labor Day Weekend.

Dining: Four Stars and Our Stars
Four Stars: La Méditérranée, 561-2916. Reservations required for this finest French restaurant. Dinners to $38 with specialties like veau grosielle and crêpes au raspberries.
Jasper's, 363-3003. Italian continental dining with such delights as capelli Angelina and scallopine Don Salvatore. Prices to $22.
Our Stars: Remington's, 737-0200. With southwestern decor including Hopi Indian dolls and an antique firearms collection, the Old West ambiance fits with the menu of prime beef, game, and seafood. Dinners to $29.

Home Away from Home: Where to Stay
Ritz-Carlton Kansas City, Wornall Rd. at Ward Pkwy., 756-1500. Beautiful grounds, a glass-enclosed elevator to rooftop dining and panoramic city views are a few of this hotel's attractions. Amenities include: poolside service, tennis, health club, and airport transportation. Singles cost $105-$120.
Allis Plaza Hotel, 200 W. 12th St., 421-6800. Single rooms run from $92-$121. Extensive privileges include pool, tennis, health club, concierge, shopping arcade, and airport transportation. The luxury level, Vista Executive Towers, has singles for $121.
The Westin Crown Center, 1 Pershing Rd. at Main St., 474-4400. Equipped with an indoor tropical waterfall and garden, this hotel also has patios and balconies. Singles are $98-$130 and include pool privileges, tennis, golf, health club, and lawn games.

Keeping Your Tone Away from Home
Joggers and Bikers: During the summer, Swope Park has bike rentals. Penn Valley Park and Jacob L. Loose Park have jogging tracks.
Health Clubs: Bally Health and Racquet Clubs: 373-1600
Dale's Athletic Club: 913-888-9247
YMCA: 561-9622
Shamrock Hills Golf Course: 537-6556

Shopping
Kansas City has 3 major shopping areas. Westport once outfitted western travelers and traded with Indians. Recently restored and now called Westport Square, it is both an historic and modern shopping center. Look especially at the boutiques. Crown Center, a Hallmark creation, sports all kinds of shops, and Halls department store is a strong attraction. Country Club Plaza has top-name stores.
Florists: Al Manning Florist: 333-2445
Crestwood Flowers: 444-7200
Ranchview Floral & Interiors: 913-649-7222

LAS VEGAS

Area Code: 702
Time Zone: Pacific
Weather: 734-2010
Police: 795-3111; Nevada Highway Patrol: 385-0311
Emergency: 911

Life in Las Vegas revolves around gambling and has ever since gambling was legalized in 1931. Today visitors can find slot machines at the airport, in rest rooms, and in supermarkets and convenience stores around town. Approximately 80% of the population is employed by the hospitality industry, which includes hotels and casinos. In recent years, this Mohave Desert oasis has also become a popular convention destination, drawing some 2 million conventioneers annually. For visitors, the city is a relative bargain. Hotel rooms and meals can be had here for much less than in other cities; they are subsidized in part by the hotels' gambling profits.

Although it is the dominant industry, gambling isn't the only one. With Nellis Air Force Base and the Nevada Test Site located here, the U.S. Department of Defense is a major employer. Las Vegas has also become an important distribution center; companies such as Levi Strauss have established operations in the area. Citibank and Montgomery Ward have financial service centers in Las Vegas, and the city has a growing reputation as an entrepreneurial boomtown.

Business Profile
Population: 770,000
Population Growth (1980-1990): 59%
Unemployment Rate: 3.5%
Fortune 500 Corporate Headquarters: 0

General Information Sources
Las Vegas Chamber of Commerce: 457-4664
Las Vegas Convention and Visitors Center: 733-2323
Las Vegas City Hall: 386-6011

Getting There
By Air: McCarran International Airport is 8 miles south of the city's downtown district. Information, 798-5410.
Once you've landed: A taxi to the Strip will cost about $10; to downtown will run $10-$15. Taxi companies include: ABC, 736-8444; Checker Cab, 873-2227; Desert, 386-4828; Western, 736-8000. The Gray Line Airport Express, 384-1234, offers service to major hotels downtown and the Strip. The trip costs $4.25 and takes about 30-35 minutes.
Limousines (private): Reserve 24 hours in advance. Bell Limousine, 739-7990; Las Vegas Limousine, 739-8414

Directions Downtown: To get downtown from the airport take Paradise Rd. to Main St. to Fremont. The airport is located near the southern edge of the Strip; Las Vegas Blvd. runs parallel to Paradise Rd.

Overland Adventures: *Route Map:* I-15 will take you south to Los Angeles and I-15 north to Salt Lake City. U.S. 95 leads to Reno and to points south such as Phoenix.
In the city proper, the main north-south road is Las Vegas Blvd.; a section of this is known as "The Strip," where many of the hotel/casinos are located.
Driving Regulations: Right turn on red permitted unless posted. Seat belts mandatory. Radar detectors permitted.
Bottleneck Busters: Traffic congestion is not much of a problem in Las Vegas. Driving along the Strip in the evening can be slow, particularly on Friday and Saturday nights. Information on highway conditions, 486-3116.
Trains: Amtrak—the train station is actually part of a casino (only in Las Vegas!)—the Union Plaza Hotel, 1 N. Main St., 386-6896
Bus Service: Greyhound/Trailways Lines, 200 S. Main, 384-9561
Public Transportation: Las Vegas Transit, 384-3540, operates bus service from the Hacienda—the southernmost hotel on the Strip—to downtown's "Glitter Gulch" district with frequent stops along the way. Buses run every 15 minutes from 7am to midnight, every 30 minutes until 3am, and every 60 minutes until 7am. Fare is $1. There is also a trolley car, 382-1404, which travels the Strip and stops at most hotels. The fare is $1; service runs every 30 minutes from 9:30am to 2am.
Road Service and Repairs: AAA, 870-9171; Emergency Road Service, 878-1822
Towed? Call Ewing Brothers Towing, 382-9261, or Quality Towing, 649-5711

International Travelers
Foreign Currency Exchange: American Foreign Exchange, Las Vegas Hilton, 3000 Paradise Rd., 737-1900
Foreign Money Exchange, 3025 S. Las Vegas Blvd., 791-3301
Nevada Coin Mart, 750 E. Sahara Ave., 369-0500
Nevada Foreign Exchange, Fashion Show Mall, 731-4155
Valley Bank of Nevada, 101 Convention Center Dr., 654-1417
Translation Services: Arriagas's Bilingual Services, 216 S. 7th, 382-5497
Japan Convention & Translating Services: 734-6757
Multi-Lingual Translation Services, 1111 S. Las Vegas Blvd., 382-1254
Foreign Books and Periodicals: Readmore Magazine & Book Store, 2560 S. Maryland Pkwy., 732-4453

Business Visitor's Needs
Banking: First Interstate Bank, 300 E. Carson Ave., 385-8011

FLYING TIMES
(in hours)
FROM
Las Vegas
TO
Chicago: 4
New York: 9½
Miami: 9½

Nevada State Bank, 201 S. 4th St., 383-4111
Valley Bank of Nevada, 300 S. 4th St., 386-1000
Secretarial Services: Action Business Services: 366-1510; fax 382-0020
The Branch Office: 365-1327
Manpower Secretarial Services: 386-2626
Copying and Printing: Copy Shoppe: 649-6031
Kinko's: 735-4402 (open 24 hours; call for other locations)
Kwik-Kopy Printing: 382-1838
Quik Print: 794-0688
Fax and Telex Facilities: Kinko's: 735-4402 (open 24 hours; call for other locations)
Mail Boxes Etc. USA: 732-0024 (call for other locations)
Messengers: Paragon Courier Services: 739-7711
Pony Express: 873-7669
Medical Needs: Doctor referral: Clark County Medical Society: 739-9989
Dental referral: Clark County Dental Society: 435-7767
Pharmacies: Village East Drugs: 736-7018 (open 24 hours; call for other locations)
White Cross Drug Store: 382-1733; prescription dept. 384-8075 (open 24 hours)
Hospitals: Humana Hospital Sunrise: 731-8000
University Medical Center of Southern Nevada: 383-2000

Convention Centers
Las Vegas Convention Center, 3150 Paradise Rd., 733-2323. Meeting and exhibition space: 970,000 sq. feet.
Cashman Field Center, 850 Las Vegas Blvd. N., 386-7100. Exhibition space: 98,100 sq. feet. Stadium seats 9,300.

Entertainment, Sports, and Culture
Sports: Baseball: Stars (San Diego Padres AAA Farm Club), Cashman Field, 386-7200
Basketball: (College) Top-ranked University of Nevada-Las Vegas, Silverdome. For tickets call the Thomas and Mack Center at University of Nevada, 739-3900.
The Arts: Let's face it. You don't go to Las Vegas to hear chamber music. The big-name performers that are booked at the hotel casinos provide the best entertainment in town (next to people-watching).

Dining: Four Stars and Our Stars
Las Vegas restaurants run the gamut. There are four-star restaurants, a few of which we've profiled below. But the city is also the home of the hotel buffet. The **Golden Nugget Hotel**'s (385-7111) buffet is considered the best in Las Vegas; the **Tropicana**'s (739-2222), and the **Dunes'** (737-4110) are also popular.
Andre's, 385-5016. Located near downtown, and mercifully removed from the action at the casinos and hotels, this is styled like a French country inn.
Le Montrachet, 732-5111. The Hilton's premiere restaurant serves a continental menu; prices are high and reservations

essential. Dinner only.
Palace Court, 731-7110. Luxurious ambiance, features a domed stained glass skylight. French/Continental fare; extensive wine cellar. Dinner daily, lunch served Thur.-Sun.
Chin's, 733-8899. The best Chinese food in town. Reservations recommended.

Home Away from Home: Where to Stay
Caesars Palace, 3570 Las Vegas Blvd., 731-7110. Caesar's is one of the city's most opulent hotels. Designed and decorated to mimic ancient Rome. The hotel books big-name entertainers and has a pool, jogging course, several tennis courts, and can arrange golf privileges for guests. Located on the Strip. 1,600 rooms. Rooms $95-$160, suites $170-$875.
Desert Inn and Country Club, 3145 Las Vegas Blvd. S., 733-4444. Terrific sports facilities. Rooms have refrigerators. 820 rooms, on the Strip. Rooms $85-$125, suites $150-$1,500.
Golden Nugget Hotel and Casino, 129 E. Fremont St., 385-7111. This hotel has a turn-of-the-century motif, although the tower that houses the suites is distinctly modern. Located downtown. Rooms $58-$90, suites $210-$1,500.
Las Vegas Hilton, 3000 Paradise Rd., 732-5111. With 3,174 rooms, the Hilton boasts it is the largest luxury resort hotel in the world. It is predictably popular for conventions. Rooms $65-$125, suites from $330.
Marriott Residence Inn, 3225 S. Paradise Rd., 796-9300. An all-suite hotel. There are 1- and 2-bedroom suites available; each is equipped with a kitchen. Convenient to the Convention Center. Complimentary continental breakfast. Swimming pool, whirlpool, racquetball. Rates for the suites: $89-$149. For longer stays, per-night rates drop.
Tropicana Ramada, 3801 Las Vegas Blvd. S., 739-2222. Luxurious decor, spacious rooms. Good fitness facilities. VIP accommodations with suites. Located on the Strip, convenient to the airport. Rooms $59-$115, suites $200-$600.

Keeping Your Tone Away from Home
Joggers and Bikers: There is a track at the University of Nevada-Las Vegas and a few hotels have jogging tracks on the premises. Bicyclists might want to try the University of Nevada campus; pedaling in the downtown or Strip traffic is a dicey proposition. Bike rentals: Bikes USA, 642-2453. And remember, this is the desert. Be careful not to over-exert yourself midday when temperatures can hit 100° and higher.
Health Clubs: Most hotels have extensive fitness facilities. Also, Sports Club-Las Vegas, 733-8999, is open to tourists.

Shopping
Several of the major casino hotels rent out space to luxury shops and boutiques. For a larger selection of stores, the Fashion Show Mall on the Strip is home to 140 stores, including Saks Fifth Avenue, Neiman Marcus, and Bullocks. Nevada sales tax is 6%.
Florists: A French Bouquet: 739-8484

LOS ANGELES

Area Code: Los Angeles: 213; Burbank, Pasadena, the San Fernando Valley, Sherman Oaks, Van Nuys, Toluca Lake, and Glendale: 818; Anaheim and Orange County, south of Los Angeles proper: 714. (Telephone numbers in this section are within the 213 calling area unless noted otherwise.)
Time Zone: Pacific
Weather: 554-1212
Police: Metro: 626-5273
Emergency: 911

To understand Los Angeles, it's important to comprehend its size. At 464 square miles, it's half the size of the state of Rhode Island. In population, it is the nation's second largest city, and by the year 2000 Los Angeles will be the largest. And as if that weren't enough, it is surrounded by communities that are widely considered to be part of the LA metropolitan area, and which are a pretty good size themselves—like Pasadena, Santa Monica, Anaheim, Long Beach and Glendale. All of this helps explain the incredible diversity that can be found in Los Angeles.

Founded originally as an agricultural community, Los Angeles was forever changed when the film industry discovered that Southern California's sunny climate made it possible to shoot movies all year long. Today Los Angeles remains the entertainment capital of the world. Other key businesses include the defense and aerospace industry, oil, real estate, and tourism. The city is the banking and finance capital of the West Coast, and serves as the U.S. gateway to the Pacific Rim countries. A steady flow of immigrants to Los Angeles has fueled its growth and helped ensure a growing labor pool.

Some of the major corporations which call Los Angeles and environs home are Occidental Petroleum, Atlantic Richfield, Rockwell International, Unocal, Litton Industries, Wickes, Times Mirror, and Avery International.

Business Profile
Population (includes Los Angeles County): 8.8 million
Population Growth (1980-1989): 17.7%
Unemployment Rate: 5%
Fortune 500 Corporate Headquarters: 26

General Information Sources
Visitor Information Centers: downtown, 689-8822; Hollywood, 461-4213
Los Angeles Chamber of Commerce: 629-0602
Hollywood Chamber of Commerce: 469-8311

Los Angeles Convention and Visitors Bureau: 624-7300

Getting There
By Air: Los Angeles International Airport is located 17 miles southwest of downtown Los Angeles. For information call 646-5252; for parking information, 646-2911.

Los Angeles airport has a unique service, Skytel, 417-0200. It is in the Tom Bradley International Terminal and is a small hotel which rents out very small cabins to travelers on an hourly basis. Here solo travelers (one person per room) can nap, shower, make telephone calls, and do work. Rates starts at $8.75 per half-hour. The airport also has business service centers located in Terminals 1, 4 and 7, which offer travelers secretarial services, fax machines, and small conference rooms for a fee.

Once you've landed: The average taxi fare between the airport and downtown runs about $25-$27; between Beverly Hills and the airport, about $18-$20. The drive downtown can take anywhere from a half-hour to an hour or more. Taxis can easily be hailed at the airport or on downtown streets. In other locations, you may need to call a cab. Bell Cab, 221-1112; Independent Cab Co., 385-8294; L.A. Taxi, 627-7000; United Independent Taxi, 653-5050. Try to arrange a flat fee with your cab driver before leaving the airport.

There are also several airport transportation companies that offer bus or van service to the downtown district and local hotels. Super Shuttle, 338-1111, travels from the airport to downtown for $11 and to the hotels along Wilshire for $10. There are several other companies which offer a similar service, including Airport Flyer Express, 216-1006; and Amtrans Airport Shuttle, 532-5999 or 800-356-8671.

Limousines (private): In most cases, advance reservations are required. Carey Limousine, 275-4153; Liberty Limousine Service, 464-2456; Pacific Limousine Services, 649-5466 or 800-426-4007. The typical limousine fee to drive downtown is $65-$70.

Also, many hotels have complimentary airport shuttle or limousine service.

Overland Adventures: *Route Map:* In other large cities, a car is a hassle. In Los Angeles it is a necessity. Be sure to pick up maps when you rent a car. Also: *Thomas' Road Guide* has detailed maps of the entire area and is an excellent resource for drivers. It is available at bookstores, and on newsstands around the city and at the airport. Los Angeles has more than 30 freeways and several highways that crisscross the city. Some of the larger ones include the San Diego Freeway (I-405), the Harbor Freeway (I-110), the Long Beach Freeway (I-710), the Santa Monica Freeway, and the San Bernadino Freeway (both I-10, heading in opposite directions), the Hollywood Freeway (U.S. 101), and the Golden State Freeway (I-5). Generally freeways are named for the

FLYING TIMES
(in hours)
FROM
Los Angeles
TO
Chicago: 4
New York: 5
Miami: 5

area they lead to, coming from the downtown area; for example the Santa Monica Freeway (I-10) leads from the LA business district west to Santa Monica.

Directions Downtown: Follow airport exit signs leading to I-405 (San Diego Freeway). Take I-405 North; several exits lead to downtown, including those for the Santa Monica Freeway and Wilshire Blvd. Take either east to downtown.

Bottleneck Busters: LA's rush hour is infamous. The same freeways which can be efficient traffic-movers during off hours jam up twice daily (or more—in some cases the morning rush hour tends to drag on until it's time for evening rush hour!). I-405 (San Diego Freeway) and I-10 (Santa Monica Freeway) and U.S. 10 (Hollywood Freeway) tend to be especially bad.

Trains: Amtrak, Union Station, 800 N. Alameda St., 624-0171

Bus Service: Greyhound/Trailways Lines Terminal, 208 E. 6th St., 620-1200

Public Transportation: Southern California Rapid Transit District operates an extensive network of buses; there are more than 250 designated bus routes. Call 626-4455 for information; to receive maps and schedules by mail write to 419 S. Main St., Los Angeles, CA 90001. If you visit in 1992, the RTD is scheduled to have a light rail transportation system serving metropolitan Los Angeles by then.

Downtown Los Angeles has DASH, short for Downtown Area Short Hop, a short distance shuttle service that operates 2 routes. DASH makes stops at several popular downtown destinations, including some of the large office buildings. The fare is 25 cents. For information, call 800-874-8885.

Road Service and Repairs: AAA, 741-3111; Emergency Roadside Service, 747-6800

Towed? Central Enforcement Office: 485-3117

International Travelers

Foreign Currency Exchange: AFEX-Associated Foreign Exchange, 433 N. Beverly Dr., Beverly Hills, 274-7610

Amforex Foreign Currency Exchange, Bonaventure Hotel, 404 S. Figueroa St., #604, 622-1219

Bank of America, 525 S. Flower St., 228-2721 or 800-468-4546; and LA International Airport, Tom Bradley Terminal, 291-0530

Deak International, Los Angeles Hilton, 911 Wilshire Blvd., 624-4221

LA Currency Exchange, LA Airport, Terminals 2, 5, and Tom Bradley International Terminal, 417-0364; and 531 W. 6th St., 488-0144

Translation Services: Allied Interpreting and Translating Services, 7471 Melrose Ave., Suite 9, 653-8020

Amerikanji Communications C.C., 23018 Ventura Blvd., #108, Woodland Hills, 818-704-7199. Specializes in Asian languages.

Berlitz Translation Services, 6415 Independence Ave., Woodland Hills, 818-347-8282

DLI, Diversified Language Institute, 1670 Wilshire Blvd., 484-8710. Specializes in Japanese.

Intex Translations, 9021 Melrose Ave., Suite 205, 275-9571; 714-751-1302 from outside Los Angeles

Consulates: There are some 45 foreign consulates in Los Angeles. Some of the larger ones are listed below. Check the Yellow Pages for others.

Australia: 469-4300

Canada: 687-7432

Japan: 624-8305

France: 653-3120

United Kingdom: 385-7381

Israel: 651-5700

Italy: 820-0622

Fed. Rep. of Germany: 930-2703

Republic of Korea: 385-9300

Foreign Books and Periodicals: Book Soup, 8818 W. Sunset Blvd., 659-3110

Business Visitor's Needs

Banking: First Interstate Bank of California, 707 Wilshire Blvd., 239-4000

Mercantile National Bank, 1840 Century Park East, 277-2265

Security Pacific National Bank, 333 S. Hope St., 345-6211

Union Bank, 445 S. Figueroa St., 236-5000

Full Service Assistance: HQ-Headquarters Companies: Burbank, 818-845-3422; Century City, 551-6666 or 277-6660; Glendale, 818-507-1199; Woodland Hills, 818-710-7787

Secretarial Services: American Business Center: 623-8894

Modern Secretarial Service: 870-5882

Office Support Centers: 683-1631
Copying and Printing: Copy Mat: 461-1222 (open 24 hours; call for other locations)
Kinko's: 747-8341 (open 24 hours; call for other locations)
Fax and Telex Facilities: HQ, Copy Mat, and Kinko's, listed above, have fax and telex services, as well as:
Mail Boxes Etc. USA: 274-7721
Mister Mail: 874-2910
Messengers: Executive Express: 558-0800
Red Arrow Messenger: Los Angeles, 626-6881; Beverly Hills and Century City, 276-2388
United Couriers (Burbank): 818-845-8883
Medical Needs: Doctor referral: Los Angeles County Medical Association: 483-6122
Dental referral: Los Angeles Dental Society: 380-7669
Pharmacy: Horton & Converse Pharmacy: 818-782-6251 (open 24 hours; call for other locations)
Hospitals: Cedars-Sinai Medical Center: 855-5000; 24-hour emergency, 855-6517
Hospital of the Good Samaritan: 977-2121; 24-hour emergency, 977-2420
Queen of Angels Hollywood Presbyterian Medical Center: 413-3000
UCLA Medical Center 825-9111: 24-hour emergency, 825-2111

Convention Center
Los Angeles Convention Center, 1201 S. Figueroa St., 748-8531. 234,000-sq.-foot exhibition space. The center is undergoing an expansion which will add another 350,000 sq. feet of exhibition space. It is due to be completed in 1993.

Entertainment, Sports, and Culture
Sports: Baseball: LA Dodgers, Dodger Stadium, 224-1400
California Angels, Anaheim Stadium, 714-634-2000
Basketball: LA Lakers, Great Western Forum, 419-3182
LA Clippers, Los Angeles Sports Arena, 748-8000, ext. 339
Football: LA Raiders, Los Angeles Coliseum, 322-5901
LA Rams, Anaheim Stadium, 277-4700 or 714-937-6767
Hockey: LA Kings, Great Western Forum, 673-6003
The Arts: Ticket Services: Ticketmaster: 480-3232 or 381-5447
Ahmanson Theater, 972-7211. Part of the Music Center complex, hosts comedies and dramas, classics and new plays.
Center Theatre Group/Mark Taper Forum, 972-7373. Part of Music Center complex, a small intimate theater; host to many new plays.
Dorothy Chandler Pavilion, 972-7200. Winter home to Los Angeles Philharmonic.
Hollywood Bowl, 850-2000. Outdoor amphitheater featuring pop and classical music stars. Summer home of the Los Angeles Philharmonic.
Shrine Auditorium, 749-5123. American Ballet Theatre performs here, as do touring musicians.
Schubert Theatre, 800-233-3123. Features Broadway musicals.

Museums: J. Paul Getty Museum (Malibu): 458-2003. First-rate, reservations required.
Los Angeles County Museum of Art: 857-6211
Museum of Contemporary Art: 621-2766
Norton Simon Museum (Pasadena): 818-449-3730

Dining: Four Stars and Our Stars
Bistro Garden, 550-3900. With the California cuisine menu (which relies heavily on fresh produce) and the outdoor dining patio, a meal at the Bistro Garden seems to personify all the best of California. (The indoor customers also get to enjoy a garden-like atmosphere.) A popular lunch spot. Lunch and dinner M-Sat., dinner only Sun.
Chasen's, 271-2168. Chasen's is "old" Hollywood; it's where the movie stars of yesteryear gathered. While that title has passed, it is still a terrific place to eat steaks, lamb chops, and chili. The decor is comfortable and club-like. Open for dinner, closed Mon.
La Chaumière (Century City), 551-3360. This luxurious restaurant is located on the 5th floor of the Century Plaza Hotel Tower, and has the ambiance of a French country house. The food is a blend of French and California cuisine, and the restaurant has a quiet elegance that encourages conversation. Lunch weekdays, dinner daily.
L'Ermitage, 652-5840. This is considered one of the city's (and the country's) finest French restaurants. Not connected with the hotel by the same name, although both enjoy a first-rate reputation. Dinner only.
Pacific Dining Car, 483-6000. This downtown eatery is a Los Angeles tradition. It is located in an old railroad car, but has been expanded over the years. It specializes in steaks and is open 24 hours. Good wine list.
Rex il Ristorante, 627-2300. Two floors of an Art Deco building in the middle of LA's downtown were rebuilt to look like the dining room of an Italian luxury ocean liner. Excellent Italian cuisine. Open for lunch and dinner weekdays, dinner on Sat., closed Sun.
Spago, 652-4025. This is the hottest restaurant in Los Angeles; reservations must be made several weeks in advance. Owner-chef Wolfgang Puck was a pioneer of California cuisine and continues to delight guests with his inventions. The pizza is famous here, and with toppings like duck sausage, goat cheese, tomatoes and mozzarella, it's an experience not to be missed. Open for dinner nightly.

Home Away from Home: Where to Stay
Because the distances you may have to travel in Los Angeles are vast, business travelers in Los Angeles often prefer to stay at a hotel located near where they will be doing business. That way traffic delays and irritations will be kept at a minimum. Hotels are listed below by location.
Downtown: The Biltmore Hotel, 506 S. Grand Ave., 624-1011. A $40-million restoration was completed a few years

ago, and this 67-year-old grand old dame of LA hotels shines more brightly than ever. Complimentary airport transportation, pool, Jacuzzi, foreign exchange services. Rates: rooms $140-$220, suites $355-$1,100.

Checkers, 535 South Grand St., 624-0000. A new small luxury hotel, which prides itself on service. Only 190 rooms, 15 suites. Checkers has extensive services for the business traveler, including multi-telephone-line rooms, secretarial and courier services, and meeting room facilities. The hotel has a health club, lap pool, and foreign exchange services. The rooms have mini-bars and spacious writing tables. Rates: rooms $190-$285, suites $450-$975.

The New Otani and Garden, 120 S. Los Angeles St., 629-1200 or 800-421-8795. A touch of the Orient in downtown LA, this hotel caters to Japanese business travelers, as well as American travelers who want to try something serenely different. The hotel has a Japanese garden, several Japanese suites with futons on the floor to sleep on, and a Japanese health club that features baths and massage in addition to the usual amenities. Hotel also has airport bus service, kitchen units, foreign exchange. Rates: rooms $110-$157, suites $375-$700.

Westin Bonaventure, 404 S. Figueroa St. (main entrance and valet parking on Flower), 624-1000. With its 35-story reflective glass silo towers, the Westin Bonaventure is easy to pick out on the LA skyline. This is a popular convention hotel, thanks to its 1500-odd rooms, its several restaurants, and the 5-story mall it sits atop. The hotel has a pool, and guests have use of the fitness facilities adjacent to the hotel. Rates: rooms $130-$215, suites $250-$2,010.

Beverly Hills: **Beverly Hills Hotel**, 9641 Sunset Blvd., Beverly Hills, 276-2251. This pink-stucco palace is a legendary hotel, and is a favorite with celebrities and tourists alike. It is set in 12 acres of lush, beautifully landscaped grounds. The most desirable accommodations are the bungalows by the pool; if you're dying to impress somebody have yourself paged by the pool or in the world famous Polo Lounge. Rates: rooms $150-$250, suites $350-$1,000.

Beverly Wilshire, 9500 Wilshire Blvd., 275-5200. Well located, at the intersection of Wilshire Blvd. and Rodeo Drive, and convenient to Beverly Hill's business addresses. The hotel has pool and fitness facilities, some kitchen units, and limo service to the airport. Rates: rooms $190-$275, suites $275-$2,500.

Four Seasons Hotel Los Angeles, 300 S. Doheny Dr., 273-2222 or 800-332-3442. An elegant new hotel in Beverly Hills, The Four Seasons is located in a quiet residential area. The hotel has a large number of suites, a pool, Jacuzzi, and weight room, and foreign exchange service. Rates: rooms $215-$280, suites $330-$1,700.

L'Ermitage Hotel, 9291 Burton Way, 278-3344 or 800-424-4443. This small all-suite hotel has a European ambiance and American amenities. Rates: $255-$1,500.

Century City: **Century Plaza Hotel & Tower**, 2055 Ave. of the Stars, Century City, 277-2000. The Century Plaza Hotel

has 1,072 rooms, including its Tower rooms, which offer upgraded rooms and services to travelers. Each room has a refrigerator and a balcony. The Century Plaza also has an International Business Center, and offers full business services to guests. Complimentary shuttle service to and from Beverly Hills for shopping. Pool, fitness facilities. Rates: rooms $150-$190, suites $375-$1,400. Tower: rooms $195-$250, suites $875-$3,000.

JW Marriott Hotel at Century City, 2151 Ave. of the Stars, Century City, 201-0440. This elegant hotel is the company's West Coast flagship. Convenient to the ABC Entertainment Center, the hotel has a spa, fitness complex, and indoor and outdoor pools. Used to be a favorite with Ronald Reagan. Rates: rooms $155-$275, suites $375-$3,000.

Keeping Your Tone Away from Home

Joggers and Bikers: Griffith Park is the country's largest city park. Its miles of roadways are excellent for biking; its paths are good for jogging. Echo Park Lake is also popular with runners.

There probably is no better way to take in the California beach than by bicycling or jogging along it. In Santa Monica, San Vicente Blvd. has a cycling lane adjacent to the sidewalk. There is also a bike path that goes from Santa Monica to Palos Verde along the beach. Bicycle rentals available from Spokes 'N Stuff, 650-1076. They also have rentals at Venice and Marina Del Ray.

Shopping

Some of the major department stores in Los Angeles include I. Magnin (formerly Bullock's) and Robinsons's.

For many visitors, shopping in Los Angeles means one thing: Beverly Hills's Rodeo Dr. For a few blocks off Wilshire Blvd., Rodeo Dr. is lined on either side with high-priced exclusive stores: Cartier, Hermès, Gucci, Bijan (by appointment only), Fred Hayman and others.

The shops along Melrose Ave., in West Hollywood, are cheaper, funkier, and just as fashionable. The area is filled with offbeat boutiques, antique stores, and good little restaurants. A good starting place is Melrose Ave. between La Cienega Blvd. and La Brea Ave.

Malls are found everywhere in Southern California. In downtown LA, Seventh Street Marketplace is a fun, urban vertical mall, with an attractive courtyard for dining. The Beverly Center is a 200-plus store upscale mall located in Beverly Hills. Its stores include Rodier, Conran's, and Bullocks.

Sales tax is 7%.

Florists: Bloomsbury Floral Design: 855-1001
Flourish and Garlande, Ltd. (Beverly Hills): 271-5030
Pete's Flowers: 466-4060

MEMPHIS

Area Code: 901
Time Zone: Central
Weather: 756-4141
Police: 528-2222

Memphis's history and economic health are tied to its location overlooking the mighty Mississippi River. From its beginnings as a busy port, the city has grown into a major distribution center in America. Although Memphis's largest corporations today include firms as varied as Holiday Inns, Federal Express, Schering-Plough, and International Paper, much of the city's economy is still tied to agriculture. The days of King Cotton are not so far gone: half of the U.S. cotton crop still goes through Memphis and the city remains the largest spot cotton market in the world.

A modern city, but still thoroughly Southern, with an appreciation of gracious (read: slower-paced) living, Memphis also takes pride in its musical heritage: it is the home of the blues and Elvis Presley.

Business Profile
Population: 820,000
Population Growth (1980-1987): 6.5%
Unemployment Rate: 4.1%
Fortune 500 Corporate Headquarters: 1

General Information Sources
Memphis Visitor Information Center: 526-4880
Memphis Convention and Visitors Bureau:
576-8181
Memphis Area Chamber of Commerce: 575-3500

Getting There
By Air: Memphis International Airport: 922-8000. Served by American, Delta, Piedmont, Northwest, TWA, United, USAir, and Northwest Airlink regional commuter carriers. Charter flights: AMR Combs, 345-4720.

Once you've landed: The airport is about 10 miles southeast of the city, about a 30-minute drive from downtown. A taxi ride to downtown costs about $13. The Airport Limousine Service costs $6. There is public bus transportation, but it is not recommended, since the route involves changing buses and takes well over an hour.

Taxis and Limousines (private): Yellow Cab Co.: 577-7777 and 577-7700

Directions downtown: Take Route 240 West heading downtown; the highway has several downtown exits, including Union Ave. and Linden Ave.

Overland Adventures: *Route Map:* I-240 surrounds the city; Route 40 is the main route to Little Rock to the west and Nashville to the east. Route 55 leads to St. Louis to the north and to Jackson, MS to the south. A second business district, in East Memphis, is located around the area where Poplar Avenue meets I-240.

Driving Regulations: Seat belts required. Right turn on red unless specifically prohibited.

Bottleneck Busters: Traffic frequently ties up I-240, the expressway around the city. The Mississippi River bridges on I-40 and I-55 can also be traffic choke points. In downtown Memphis, beware of the Poplar Ave. corridor; it can be slow going. WHBQ-AM 560 is a local talk radio station which broadcasts regular traffic reports.

Trains: Amtrak Station, 545 S. Main St., 526-0052

Bus Service: Greyhound/Trailways Lines, 203 Union Ave., 523-7676

Road Service and Repairs: AAA Mid South Auto Club: 761-5371

Parking Regulations: Downtown streets have parking meters; there are also numerous private parking lots and garages. Prices range anywhere from 50 cents an hour to $3-$5 a day.

Towed? "Towed?," said the woman at the Convention and Visitors Bureau, "gee I've never heard of anybody who ever had their car towed. Mostly they just give you a ticket if the meter runs out." (However, if you park in a restricted zone — i.e., "No Parking Anytime"—you *will* be towed. Call the Vehicle Storage office, 528-2018.)

FLYING TIMES
(in hours)
FROM
Memphis
TO
Chicago: 1½
Los Angeles: 4
New York: 2½
Miami: 2

International Travelers
Foreign Currency Exchange: Union Planters National Bank, 67 Madison Ave., mezzanine level, 523-6753.

Translation Services: International Enterprises, 417 Fleda Rd., 683-3575

Foreign Books and Periodicals: Tobacco Corner Newsroom, 669 Mendenhall Rd. S., 682-3326 and 1803 Union Ave., 726-1622

World News Co., 124 Monroe Ave., 523-9970

Business Visitor's Needs
Banking: A + I Travel Service, 8 S. Third St., 525-0151
Boatmen's Bank of Tennessee, 6060 Poplar Ave., 529-5900
Union Planters National Bank, 67 Madison Ave., 523-6000

Secretarial Services: BBS Office Service: 767-8015
Clark Tower Executive Suites: 767-1601
Manpower Temporary Services: 576-8282
Norrell Services: 527-7777

Copying and Printing: Kinko's: 683-8300 (open 24 hours)
Pip Printing: 725-9314

Fax and Telex Facilities: Kinko's: 683-8300
Western Union: 800-325-6000

Messengers: Above Average Express: 763-3306

Financial Courier Services: 761-4555
Medical Needs: Doctor referral: Memphis & Shelby County
Medical Society: 761-0200
Dental referral: Memphis Dental Society Referral Service:
682-4928
Pharmacy: Walgreen's: 754-1470 (24-hour prescription service; call for other locations)
Hospitals: Baptist Memorial Hospital: 522-5252
Methodist Central: 726-7000

Convention Centers

The phone numbers given for each facility should be able to tell you if special transportation arrangements have been made to the major hotels.
Memphis Cook Convention Center, 1 Convention Plaza, 255 North Main St., 576-1206. 150,000 sq. feet of convention space.
Agricenter International, 7777 Walnut Grove Rd., 757-7777. A marketing center for agriculture; 140,000-sq.-foot exhibition pavilion; 1,000-acre demonstration farm.

Entertainment, Sports, and Culture

Sports: Baseball: Memphis Chicks (the class AA team of the Kansas City Royals), Tim McCarver Stadium, 272-1687
Football: Memphis State University Tigers, Liberty Bowl Memorial Stadium, 678-2337
The Arts: Memphis Symphony Orchestra, 324-3627, performs October-May.
Orpheum Theatre, 525-3000. Home to touring Broadway shows, as well as the local opera and ballet companies.
Entertainment: Graceland, Elvis Presley's home, has become something of a shrine; it is now the city's biggest tourist attraction, 332-3322.
Beale Street. Considered the birthplace of the blues, Beale St., is a collection of restaurants, shops, and nightclubs.

Dining: Four Stars and Our Stars

Chez Philippe, 529-4188. Located in the Peabody Hotel, this is Memphis's premier French restaurant. The atmosphere is formal and luxurious; the food is excellent French nouvelle cuisine. Open for dinner only; M-Sat.
Dux, also in the Peabody Hotel, 529-4199. This is a local favorite for business lunches, although breakfast and dinner are also served. The menu, which changes frequently, usually features seafood and steak.
Justine's, 527-3815. Classic French cuisine served in a showplace of a French colonial home. Considered one of the finest restaurants in the South, in good weather patrons can dine outside in the lush gardens. Dinner only.
Rendezvous, 523-2746. Memphis prides itself on its pork barbecue; Rendezvous is one of several local favorites. Quaint basement restaurant decorated with area artifacts.

Home Away from Home: Where to Stay

Peabody, 149 Union Ave., 529-4000. For many Memphis visitors the list of preferred hotels begins and ends with the Peabody. It is an elegantly restored grand hotel with an entrance lobby that features marble columns and a marble fountain. Twice a day trained ducks march to and from the marble fountain in the lobby where they swim. The hotel has all modern business conveniences, including 24-hour concierge and health club.
Holiday Inn Crowne Plaza, 250 North Main St., 527-7300. Connected to the Memphis Cook Convention Center, this is Holiday Inn's flagship hotel. The hotel has a health club and pool, and an executive floor with upgraded services and accommodations for the business traveler.
French Quarter Inn, 2144 Madison Ave., 728-4000. A small all-suite luxury hotel. It is convenient to downtown, and has a pool and exercise equipment.
Bed and Breakfast in Memphis, 726-5920. This organization can arrange weekly or monthly executive accommodations in furnished condominiums on the river, carriage houses or fully equipped apartments.

Keeping Your Tone Away from Home

Joggers and Bikers: Overton Park has hiking and bicycle trails
Health Clubs: Most hotels have their own health clubs.
Peabody Athletic Club: 529-4161
Public Golf Courses: For courses run by Memphis Park Commission call 325-5759
Audubon Golf Course: 683-6941 (18-hole course)
Overton Park Golf Course: 725-9905 (9-hole course)
Stonebridge Golf Course: 382-1886 (18-hole course)

Shopping

Downtown, the leading department stores include Goldsmith's and Dillard's. In East Memphis, Oak Court Mall has a variety of upscale stores, including Lord & Taylor.
The sales tax in Memphis is 7 1/2%.
Florists: John Hoover Flowers: 274-1851

MIAMI

Area Code: 305
Time Zone: Eastern
Weather: 661-5065
Police: Metro: Miami, 579-6111; Miami Beach, 673-7900; State: Florida Highway Patrol, 470-2510
Emergency: 911

It used to be that people pegged Miami as the haven for retirees and snowbirds, those northerners who migrate south every winter to flee the cold. Then, in the 1980s, the city's image was shaped by the hit television series "Miami Vice;" both the show and the city were seen as stylish, fast-moving, vivid and violent. City boosters protested both of these characterizations, however if truth be told, they are not inaccurate. What they are is incomplete. Miami is much more than these one-dimensional stereotypes.

It is a young city; for all purposes not yet a hundred years old. Until 1896 when railroad tycoon Henry Flager extended the rail line south from Palm Beach to Miami, it was a tiny community. Today the waves of immigrants, mostly from Latin America, that continue to pour into southern Florida keep the city young and vigorous. It is one of American's most ethnic cities; the primary language of some 50% of the population is Spanish, not English.

Miami has become a center for international banking, and a major import-export port. It is the place for doing business with South and Central America. And blessed by its location along the water and its tropical weather, Miami remains a major tourist destination. The Port of Miami is the world's busiest cruise port. Among the major U.S. companies located here: media giant Knight-Ridder.

Business Profile
Population: 1.8 million
Population Growth (1980-1989): 12.4%
Unemployment Rate: 6.7%
Fortune 500 Corporate Headquarters: 8

General Information Sources
Greater Miami Chamber of Commerce: 350-7700
Greater Miami Convention and Visitor's Bureau: 539-3000
Miami Beach Chamber of Commerce: 672-1270

Getting There
By Air: Miami International Airport general information: 876-7515
Once you've landed: The airport is 7 miles northwest of downtown.

A taxi to downtown Miami takes about 20 minutes and costs about $15; to Miami Beach the fare is about $22, and riding time will usually run 25-30 minutes. Taxis can be easily hailed at the airport. Central Cab, 532-5555; Metro Taxi, 888-8888; Yellow Cab, 444-4444

SuperShuttle, 871-2000, has vans that provide transportation from the airport. Fares range from $5 to $25. The service is located outside the airport baggage claim area; reservations are required for service to the airport.

The city-run Metrobus, 638-6700, travels to and from the airport. The fare is cheap ($1), but it's a long ride—45-50 minutes.
Limousines (private): ABC Limo, 888-4407; American Sightseeing Tours/Red Top Luxury Limousine Service, 688-7700, 800-367-5149; Regal Limousines/Carey Systems, 945-5553, 800-262-9299
Directions Downtown: Take Route 953 South to Route 836 (East West Expressway) East to downtown exits. Or take Route 953 (NW 42nd Ave.) north to Airport Expressway East to downtown exits.

Overland Adventures: *Route Map:* I-95, the main north-south route along the eastern seaboard, passes right through Miami. I-75 and U.S. 41 both enter the city from the west. In downtown Miami, the intersection of Miami Ave. and Flagler St. divides the city into quadrants. (Miami Ave. is the east-west dividing line; Flagler is the north-south division.) Streets run east-west; avenues run north-south. And, just to confuse matters, many named streets in Miami are also numbered.
Driving Regulations: Radar detectors permitted. Right turn on red allowed unless forbidden by sign. Seat belts mandatory.
Bottleneck Busters: Miami's rush hour traffic is heavy. I-95 is always congested (in both directions, but it is particularly bad southbound in the morning; northbound in the afternoon.) The intersection of I-95 and the Palmetto Expressway (Route 826) is usually backed up. The causeways to Miami Beach—particularly the Julia Tuttle Causeway—are also a commuter's headache. They're clogged going east in the morning and west in the afternoon. Radio Station WINZ-AM 940 broadcasts a news/talk format and has frequent traffic updates.
Trains: Amtrak, Liberty Station, 8303 N.W. 37th Ave., 800-872-7245
Bus Service: Greyhound/Trailways Lines Bus Terminal, 99 N.E. 4th St., 374-7222. There are also bus terminals in Coral Gables, Miami Beach, North Miami Beach, and Hialeah-Miami Springs.
Public Transportation: Metrobus has an extensive network of routes. The city's Metrorail system is an elevated rail that serves downtown Miami, and then travels west to Hialeah, and south to Kendall. Miami also has the Metromover system; individual motorized cars which ride on top of a 1.9 mile elevated track that loops around downtown Miami and connects to the Metrorail. For information on all of these call

FLYING TIMES
(in hours)
FROM
Miami
TO
Chicago: 3¾
Los Angeles: 4½
New York: 3

638-6700. Tri-Rail is a new train system which serves 3 counties along a 67-mile route. Tri-Rail links with Metrorail at 1149 E. 21st Rd. in Hialeah. For information call 800-TRI-RAIL (800-874-7245) or 728-8445 (in Broward and Palm Beach Counties).

Road Service and Repairs: AAA Emergency Road Service, 592-2525

Towed? Call Auto Pound, 579-6455

International Travelers

Foreign Currency Exchange: BankAmerica International, currency exchange locations at Miami International Airport, 526-5677; and 1000 Brickell Ave., 9th floor, 377-6600

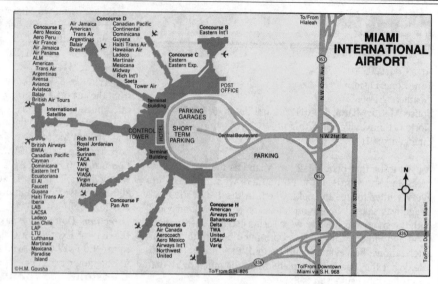

Barnett Bank of South Florida, currency exchange at airport and all branches, 825-5900

Deak International, 155 SE 3rd Ave., 381-9252; and at Fontainebleau Hilton, 4441 Collins Ave., Miami Beach, 674-1907

Translation Services: Berlitz Language Center, 100 N. Biscayne Blvd., 371-3686

Certified Translating Services, 1150 N.W. 14th St., Suite 211, 325-9955

Consulates: For a more complete listing check the Yellow Pages.

Argentina: 373-7794	France: 372-9541
Bahamas: 373-6295	Germany: 358-0290
Brazil: 377-1734	Great Britain: 374-1522
Chile: 373-8623	Japan: 445-1477
Venezuela: 577-3834	

Foreign Books and Periodicals: Bus Terminal Newsstand, 2320 Salzedo St., Coral Gables, 443-7979

Joe's News, 1549 Sunset Dr., Coral Gables, 661-2020

Plaza News, 7900 Biscayne Blvd., 754-6397

Business Visitor's Needs

Banking: Ocean Bank of Miami, 780 NW 42nd Ave., 442-2660

Southeast Bank, 200 S. Biscayne Blvd., 375-7500

SunBank Miami, 777 Brickell Ave., 577-5115

Full Service Assistance: Abacus Secretarial Center: 576-8310

Secretarial Services: A Wizard Word Processing Services: 893-7500

Brickell Executive Colony: 358-3554

Coral Gables Secretarial Services: 443-8973

The Word Processing Center: 591-8365 (airport)

Copying and Printing: Kinko's (Coral Gables): 662-6716 (open 24 hours; call for other locations)

Pip Printing: 372-9400 (call for other locations)

Sir Speedy: 633-9059 (call for other locations)

Messengers: ASAP Courier Corp.: 591-2727

Bayside Express: 551-8788, 279-9066

Sunshine State Messenger: 944-6363 (call for other locations)

Fax and Telex Facilities: Most photocopying stores also have fax service, see "Copying and Printing," above, as well as;

Mail Boxes Etc. USA: 594-1190; fax 594-4458

Telex Fax Service Co.: 223-3333

Medical Needs: Doctor referral: Dade County Medical Association: 324-8717

Dental Referral: East Coast District Dental Society: 667-3647

Pharmacies: Eckerd Drugs (North Miami Beach): 932-5740 (open 24 hours; call for other locations)

Terminal Rexall Pharmacy: 876-0556 (open 24 hours)

Hospitals: Baptist Hospital of Miami: 596-1960

Cedars Medical Center: 325-5511, 800-327-7386

University of Miami/Jackson Memorial Medical Center: 325-7429

Mt. Sinai Medical Center (Miami Beach): 674-2121

Convention Centers

Miami Convention Center, 400 S.E. 2nd Ave., 372-0277. Available space: 70,000 sq. feet.

Miami Beach Convention Center, 1901 Convention Center Dr., Miami Beach, 673-7311. Exhibition space: 1.1 million sq. feet.

Entertainment, Sports, and Culture

Sports: Basketball: Miami Heat, Miami Arena, 577-HEAT (577-4328)

Football: Miami Dolphins, Joe Robbie Stadium, 620-2578

University of Miami Hurricanes, Orange Bowl, 643-7100

The Arts: Coconut Grove Playhouse, 442-4000. Modern and classical theater.

Greater Miami Opera Association, Dade County Auditorium: 854-7890
Miami Ballet Company, Dade County Auditorium: 667-5985
Miami Chamber Symphony, Maurice Gussman Concert Hall: 662-6600
Miami City Ballet, Gussman Center for the Performing Arts: 532-7713

Dining: Four Stars and Our Stars

Cafe Chauveron (Miami Beach), 866-8779. Classic French cuisine, acknowledged as the best in the city. Soufflés are a specialty here. Dinner only, nightly. Reservations required.

Joe's Stone Crab (Miami Beach), 673-0365. A local institution, this is a seafood lover's heaven. Order the stone crabs and the Key Lime pie. Unfortunately, this popular place doesn't take reservations. The result: there's usually a line, although the food is well worth a wait. Dinner nightly, lunch Tues.-Sun. (Open October-May only.)

Pavillon Grill, 372-4494. Nouvelle American cuisine in a luxurious setting. Extensive wine list. Lunch weekdays, dinner nightly, closed Sun. Reservations.

Reflections on the Bay, 371-6433. The setting and the views here are breathtaking; the Caribbean-influenced cuisine is a treat. Dinner daily, Sun. brunch. Reservations.

Home Away from Home: Where to Stay

Fontainebleau Hilton, 4441 Collins Ave., 538-2000, 800-345-6565, 800-445-8667. The Fontainebleau has long been a Miami Beach landmark. It is huge: the hotel has some 1,200 rooms and 12 restaurants. Popular for conventions, this hotel boasts lighted tennis courts, whirlpools, health club, windsurfing, and parasailing. Don't miss the lagoon-like pool with the waterfall. Rooms have terraces and refrigerators. Rates: rooms $150 and up.

Alexander, 5225 Collins Ave., 865-6500, 800-327-6121. This elegant all-suite hotel is located in Miami Beach, and features water views—of either the bay or the ocean—from every room. Rooms are tastefully decorated with antiques; fitness and recreational facilities include 2 outdoor heated pools, Jacuzzi, a private marina, and nearby golf and tennis facilities. Rates start at $175.

Hotel Inter-Continental, 100 Chopin Plaza, 577-1000, 800-327-0200. This modern 34-story, 645-room hotel has a 5-story atrium that is filled with marble and palm trees. Located in downtown Miami and convenient to nearby office towers, there are outdoor tennis courts, indoor racquetball courts, an outdoor pool by the bay, and a jogging track. Rooms have refrigerators. Rates: rooms $120-$170, suites $400-$2,000.

Mayfair House, 3000 Florida Ave., 441-0000, 800-433-4555. This all-suite hotel is located in Coconut Grove in a stylish open-air shopping mall. Suites are individually designed and decorated with hot tubs and terraces. Rates: $210-$375.

Omni International, 1601 Biscayne Blvd. at 16th St., 374-0000, 800-843-6664. The hotel begins on the 5th floor, atop shops and restaurants; rooms have gorgeous views. There is a luxury level that provides upgraded rooms and amenities. Outdoor heated pool, tennis courts, access to health club. Rates: rooms $110-$145, suites $165-$550. Luxury level: $145-$160, suites $195.

Art Deco Hotels: Hotel Cardozo/Hotel Leslie/Hotel Cavalier, Miami Beach, 534-2135, 800-338-9076. These 3 are Miami's famed art deco hotels. Ignored for years, they were rediscovered in the 70s and early 80s and were lovingly restored to their 1930s grandeur. They are now owned and run by the same owner. Rooms here tend to be small, and amenities are limited, but these are a slice of Miami Beach history. Rates at the 3 range from $85-$140.

Keeping Your Tone Away from Home

Joggers and Bikers: There are popular jogging trails at David T. Kennedy Park as well as at Margaret Pace Park.
With the city's warm weather and flat terrain, Miami is a bicyclist's dream. There are more than 100 miles of local bike trails; the city's Convention and Visitor's Bureau has information on them, 539-3000. The trails in Crandon Park on Key Biscayne and in Tropical Park are some of the nicest. Bike rentals available from: Dade Cycle (Coconut Grove), 443-6075; Gary's Megacycle (North Miami Beach), 940-2912; Key Biscayne Bicycle Rentals (Key Biscayne), 361-5555; Miami Beach Bicycle Center (Miami Beach), 531-4161.

Health Clubs: YMCA: 576-9622; YWCA: 377-8161

Public Golf Courses: During winter months, we advise you to call the golf courses for reservations. For more information on other public courses call the Parks and Recreation Dept.: Miami, 575-5256; Miami Beach, 673-7730; Metro-Dade County, 579-2968.
Bayshore Golf Course (Miami Beach): 673-7705
Greynolds Park (North Miami Beach): 945-3425
Haulover Park (Miami Beach): 940-6719 (par 3, 9-hole course)
Palmetto Golf Course (Greater Miami South): 238-2922

Shopping

Burdine's is a large Florida department store chain. Bal Harbour Shops has the largest list of exclusive stores in the area. They include Martha, Gucci, Fendi, Cartier, Neiman Marcus, Bonwit Teller, and Saks Fifth Avenue.
In Miami proper, Bayside Marketplace is a new, lively shopping center featuring 120 shops, restaurants, and a special market that showcases local artisans. Omni International Mall is also a popular shopping spot. It houses J.C.Penney, Maas Brothers/Jordan Marsh, Saks Fifth Avenue, and Lord & Taylor. In Coconut Grove, the Mayfair Shops in the Grove is a sophisticated mix of shops, art galleries, and restaurants.
State sales tax is 6%.

Florists: Brickell Worldwide: 374-8471

MILWAUKEE

Area Code: 414
Time Zone: Central
Weather: 936-1212
Police: 933-4444

Milwaukee is a city of many names. The Indians christened it Millioki (the gathering place by the waters) and German settlers called it Gemutlichkeit (conviviality). By the turn of the century Milwaukee was labeled the Machine Shop of America and Cream City for the yellow brick homes made from local clay. More recently the city has been dubbed A Great Place on a Great Lake (courtesy of the Metropolitan Milwaukee Association of Commerce). Milwaukee's civic tradition should bear a title too, that of Enlightened Leadership. Milwaukee possesses the assets of a strong industrial and agricultural economy, and is the brewing capital of the U.S. In addition to the richness of its multi-ethnic heritage, Milwaukee has led the fight for women's rights and fair labor laws, has a low crime rate, diverse employment, and a lower than national average of unemployed minorities.

Business Profile
Population: 1,404,000
Population Growth (1980-1989): 0.5%
Unemployment Rate: 4.4%
Fortune 500 Corporate headquarters: 2

General Information Sources
The Greater Milwaukee Convention and Visitors Bureau: 273-7222 or 273-3950
The Metropolitan Milwaukee Association of Commerce: 273-3000

Getting There
By Air: General Mitchell International Airport: 747-5245
Once you've landed: General Mitchell International Airport is comprised of 2 terminals, the Main Building houses domestic flights and the International Building houses international flights. Within the Main Building are 3 concourses (C, D, E) and within walking distance downstairs are both the baggage claim and Ground Transportation Services. AAA Airport Limousine, Inc., 272-1955, provides van service to and from most major downtown hotels. There are departures every 30 minutes, M-F; the cost is about $6.50.
Taxi rides from the airport to downtown take about 20 minutes and cost about $15. City Veteran Taxi, 643-4433; Yellow Cab, 271-1800.
Bus No. 80 of the Milwaukee County Transit System, 344-

6711, has an airport-to-downtown service that takes 35 minutes and costs $1. The bus picks up passengers at the airport shelter at the far right (north) end of the ramp outside the terminal and deposits them at 6th St. and Wisconsin Ave. Buses depart every 15-50 minutes M-F hours are 5:50am to 9:58pm; Sat., buses leave every 30 minutes between the hours of 7:09am to 6:13pm; Sun. the bus leaves at 11:50am, 12:41pm, and then every 30 minutes until 5:45pm.
Limousines (private): Service is provided with 24-hour reservations. Carey Limousine-Milwaukee, 271-5466.
Directions Downtown: Take I-94 North spur. Milwaukee is 7 miles north of the airport. To get to the downtown area, take the exit for I-43 North and the Convention Center.
Overland Adventures: *Route Map:* Two major interstates travel through Milwaukee, I-94 and I-43. I-94 is the major east-west route enabling a traveler to reach Madison, west of Milwaukee. I-94 also continues south to Chicago. I-43 goes north linking Milwaukee with Green Bay, or it travels south-west to Beloit. In the downtown area, streets run north and south while avenues run east and west.
Bottleneck Busters: Be aware of 30-minute rush hour delays in the morning from 6:30am to 9am, and in the afternoon from 4:30pm to 6pm.
Trains: Amtrak Station, 433 W. St. Paul Ave., 800-872-7245
Bus Service: Greyhound/Trailways Lines Bus Station, 606 N. 7th St., 272-8900. Greyhound service includes Eau Claire, Green Bay, Chicago, IL, and Minneapolis-St. Paul, MN.
Public Transportation: Milwaukee County Transit System, 344-6711. 24-hour bus route and schedule information is available daily.
Road Service and Repairs: AAA, 464-1212; A-1 Towing Company, 445-6001
Towed? Call the Milwaukee police department Tow Desk, 935-7445

International Travelers
International Agencies: Mitchell International Visitor Information Center, 5300 S. Howell Ave., 747-4808
JForeign Currency Exchange: First Wisconsin, 777 E. Wisconsin Ave., main floor, 765-4321
Translation Services: Berlitz Translation Services, 257 Park Ave. S., 276-4944
International Institute of Wisconsin, Inc., 2810 W. Highland Blvd., 933-0521
Consulates: Norwegian Vice Consulate: 271-7271
Swedish Consulate: 273-3393
Foreign Books and Periodicals: Websters Books, 2559 N. Downer Ave., 332-9560

Business Visitor's Needs
Banking: Bank One Milwaukee, 111 E. Wisconsin Ave., 765-3000

FLYING TIMES		
(in hours)		
FROM		
Milwaukee		
TO		
Chicago: **1**		
Los Angeles: **5**		
New York: **2**		
Miami: **1½**		

First Interstate Bank of Wisconsin, 735 W. Wisconsin Ave., 224-4000

First Wisconsin, 777 E. Wisconsin Ave., 765-4321

Marshall & Isley Bank, 770 N. Water St., 765-7700

Secretarial Services: Kelly Services: 277-9900

The Last Word: 272-3787

Copying and Printing: Kinko's: 344-3506 (open 24 hours)

Speedy Print: 257-1565

Messengers: Action Express, Inc.: 549-3300

Time Courier: 797-7948

Telex Facilities: Western Union: 800-325-6000

Medical Needs: Doctor referral: Call-A-Nurse of Sinai Samaritan Medical Center Physician Referral and Health Information: 342-7676

Dental referral: Greater Milwaukee Dental Association: 461-0230

Pharmacies: Prescription Center: 272-2815

Walgreen's: 276-2622

Hospitals: Sinai Samaritan Medical Center: 283-7111

St. Luke's Medical Center: 649-7062

Columbia Hospital: 961-3500 (emergency room)

Convention Centers

Milwaukee Exposition Convention Center and Arena (MECCA), 500 W. Kilbourn Ave., 271-4000. Covering 4 city blocks and composed of 3 buildings, this very up-to-date convention center has room for 750 booths, several multi-level halls, an arena, and an auditorium.

Wisconsin State Fair Park, West Allis, 257-8800. This facility has the versatility to be a large exhibit hall with 3 separate wings or the Family Living Center, which includes a stage, outdoor possibilities at the Grandstand, and the Coliseum. The Wisconsin State Fair Park is easy to find 10 minutes from downtown, just off I-94.

Entertainment, Sports, and Culture

Ticket Services: Ticketron, 273-6400; Quick Tix, 271-3335

Sports: Baseball: Milwaukee Brewers, County Stadium, 933-9000

Basketball: Milwaukee Bucks, Bradley Center, 227-0500

Football: Green Bay Packers, County Stadium, 494-2351

Hockey: Milwaukee Admirals, Bradley Center, 227-0550

Indoor Soccer: Milwaukee Wave, Bradley Center, 962-WAVE (962-9283)

Winter Sports: Milwaukee County Parks Hotline: 257-5100

The Arts: Funline: 799-1177

Arts Information: 789-5000

Performing Arts Center, 273-7206. Home to the Bell Canto Chorus, the Repertory Theater, the Florintine Opera Company, the Ballet Company and the nationally-acclaimed Symphony Orchestra.

Dining: Four Stars and Our Stars

Grenadier's, 276-0747. With a continental menu and specialties like Dover sole or lamb curry Calcutta, Grenadier's offers some of the finest dining in Milwaukee. Reservations recommended; prices to $26.

Boulevard Inn, 445-4221. This restaurant has a local reputation of providing the best seafood and German dishes available. A pianist plays nightly. The cost is moderate and some tableside preparation is practiced.

Boder's On-The-River (Mequon), 242-0335. This delightful restaurant, although a bit out of the way, has a charming country riverside presence. The chef has owned Boder's since 1929. Such specialties as continental veal and whitefish are expensively delicious.

Home Away from Home: Where to Stay

Marc Plaza, 509 W. Wisconsin Ave., 271-7250. This hotel's indoor/outdoor pool has poolside service. Other extras include a concierge, health club, and shopping arcade. Single rooms cost $65-$85, Luxury level singles are $85-$100.

Pfister, 424 E. Wisconsin Ave., 273-8222. This hotel has a turn-of-the-century elegance with the modern comforts of pool, health club, concierge, and nightly entertainment. Don't miss the collection of original oil paintings from the 18th and 19th centuries located on the 7th floor. Single rooms are $85-$110.

Keeping Your Tone Away from Home

Bikers: A scenic 76-mile loop follows Lake Michigan's shoreline and the banks of the Milwaukee and Menomonee Rivers. Call Milwaukee County Department of Parks, Recreation and Culture, 257-6100 .

Health Clubs: The Downtown Club, Ltd.: 291-0444

Vic Tanny Health Clubs: 421-9250

YMCA: 291-5960

SHOPPING

Probably the most convenient and spectacular shopping is at The Grand Avenue. Scads of shops and restaurants are connected by glass skywalks, including Boston Store and Marshall Field's. Don't miss Old World Third Street: take a walking tour through this historic district, check out Green Dolphin Antiques and end up at either of these famous landmarks—Usinger's Sausage and Mader's Restaurant. East Town, located near the Performing Arts Center, is the most historic area in Milwaukee; it offers art galleries and terrific shops among its attractions. The Milwaukee Antique Center has 75 antique dealers. Discover service, charm, and ethnic diversity on Mitchell Street, one of Milwaukee's oldest Southside neighborhoods. Shopping centers and malls include Bayshore, Brookfield Fashion Center, Greenfield Fashion Center, Mayfair, and Southgate Mall Merchants Association.

Florists: Flower Hut: 342-6859

Klose Flowers: 223-4500

MINNEAPOLIS – ST. PAUL

Area Code: 612
Time Zone: Central
Weather: 725-6090
Police: Metro: Minneapolis, 348-2345; St. Paul, 291-1111; State: Minnesota State Patrol: East Metro, 297-3934; West Metro, 541-9411

In years past, it was easy to pin labels on Minneapolis and St. Paul, the Twin Cities which are separated by the Mississippi River. Minneapolis is the larger city and has long been considered the more urbane, more sophisticated, and more aggressive of the two. St. Paul, which is the state capital, has always been thought of as the more conservative twin, the metropolitan area's small town. There is still a lot of truth to those stereotypes, but in recent times, these two fraternal twins have become increasingly similar.

At the southern edge of the metropolitan area is Bloomington, a suburb which has grown rapidly in the last decade to become the state's third-largest city and an increasingly important place to do business.

Historically, Minneapolis-St. Paul's economy was linked to flour milling and lumber. Those industries are still vital to the area's health, but so are the high-technology, electronics, and communications businesses that now call Minneapolis-St. Paul home. Corporations located here include General Mills, Pillsbury, 3M, Honeywell, Control Data, and Land O'Lakes. Note: All addresses in this section are in Minneapolis unless otherwise stated.

Business Profile:
Population: 2.4 million
Population Growth (1980-1989): 13.%
Unemployment Rate: 4.4%
Fortune 500 Corporate Headquarters: 27

General Information Sources
CityLine: 645-6060 (city information)
The Connection: 922-9000 (Metro area activities information)
Greater Minneapolis Convention and Visitors Association: 348-4313
Minneapolis Chamber of Commerce: 370-9132
Minneapolis City Hall: 673-3000
St. Paul Chamber of Commerce: 222-5561
St. Paul City Hall: 298-4012
St. Paul Convention and Visitors Bureau: 297-6985

Getting There
By Air: Minneapolis-St. Paul International Airport is located 10 miles southeast of Minneapolis, and 9 miles southwest of St. Paul. Airport information: 726-5555.

Once you've landed: A cab ride to the downtown district of either city takes about 30 minutes and costs about $15-$20. Taxis: Airport Taxi, 721-6566; Blue & White, 333-3331; Metro Yellow Cab, 824-4444; Suburban Yellow Cab, 824-4000.

The Minneapolis Airport Limousine, 726-6400, offers transportation to downtown hotels. The fare is $7.50 one way, $10 round trip; the limos leave every half-hour from the lower level of the airport, and the trip takes about 45 minutes. St. Paul & Suburban Limousine Service, 726-5479, has the same service to St. Paul hotels.

Limousines (private): Premier Limousine, 722-4467; Twin City Limousine, 641-1108; Twin Star Limousine, 641-1385. Advance reservations are essential.

Directions Downtown: To Minneapolis: Take Route 62 West to I-35W to downtown, or take Route 55 North to downtown. To St. Paul: Take Shepard Road or W. 7th St. to downtown.

Overland Adventures: *Route Map:* I-94, a major coast-to-coast east-west highway meets I-35, a major north-south highway in downtown Minneapolis. I-494 and I-694 form a belt looping around the Twin Cities. There has been significant commercial and residential development along both highways.

Driving Regulations: Seat belts mandatory. Right turn on red permitted unless posted. Radar detectors permitted.

Bottleneck Busters: Avoid I-394 (also known as Highway 12), which is currently under construction. Radio station WCCO-AM 830 has frequent and thorough traffic updates.

Trains: Amtrak, Midway Station, 730 Transfer Rd., St. Paul, 800-872-7245

Bus Service: Greyhound/Trailways Lines Station, 29 N. 9th St., 371-3311; 9th and St. Peter Sts., St. Paul, 371-3311

Public Transportation: Metropolitan Transit Commission, 827-7733. The cities' bus service is clean and efficient.

Road Service and Repairs: AAA 24-hour Emergency Service, 927-2727; Auto Travel Tips, 927-2626; general information, 927-2600

Parking Regulations: We recommend using the cities' downtown lots and garages; open on-street metered parking is tough to find. During winter, check for parking restrictions on streets; during snow emergencies, take care not to park along a snow emergency route.

Towed? Call 348-2991

International Travelers
Foreign Currency Exchange: First Bank of Minneapolis, 120 S. 6th St., 370-4141. Currency exchange is handled by tellers 7-13 on the bank's main floor.

FLYING TIMES
(in hours)
FROM
Minneapolis-St. Paul
TO
Chicago: 2
Los Angeles: 4
New York: 3
Miami: 3

Mutual of Omaha Tele-Trip Co., Minneapolis-St. Paul Airport, 726-5848

Norwest Bank Minnesota, 6th and Marquette Sts., 667-1234. Currency exchange is located on the second floor, Special Sections, tellers 22-28.

Translation Services: AAA Worldwide Translation, 7800 Olson Memorial Hwy., Golden Valley, 377-7989

Berlitz Translation Services: 920-0939 Garden Associates, 6225 Virgina Ave. S., Edina, 920-6160

University Language Center Inc., 1313 5th St. S.E., 379-3823

Foreign Books and Periodicals: The Conservatory News, 800 Nicollet Mall, 338-2111

Shinder's, 912 Nicollet Mall, 333-6942; 733 Hennepin Ave., 333-3628; 389 Wabash, St. Paul, 227-4344

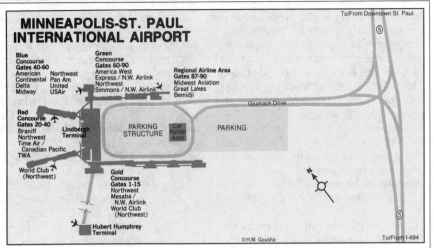

MINNEAPOLIS-ST. PAUL INTERNATIONAL AIRPORT

Business Visitor's Needs

Banking: American National Bank & Trust, 5th and Minnesota Sts., St. Paul, 298-6000

First Bank of Minneapolis, 120 S. 6th St., 370-4141

First Bank of St. Paul, 332 Minnesota St., St. Paul, 291-5000

Marquette Bank Minneapolis, 6th and Marquette Sts., 341-5600

Midway National Bank of St. Paul, 1578 University Ave. W., St. Paul, 646-2661

Norwest Bank Minnesota, 6th & Marquette Sts., 667-1234

Full Service Assistance: Colwell Executive Center: 333-6000

Janal Business Center: 349-5200

Office Plus: Bloomington, 921-2300; Minnetonka, 449-5100

Secretarial Services: Kelly Temporary Services: 339-7154

L & M Secretarial Services: 888-4477

Twin City Executive Suites: 337-9503; St. Paul, 297-6400

Copying and Printing: Kinko's, 24-hour locations: 822-7700; St. Paul, 699-9671

Sir Speedy: 339-1610 (call for other locations)

Fax Facilities: Try firms listed under "Copying and Printing," above, as well as:

Insty-Prints Printing Center: 332-8669 (call for other locations)

My Office: 823-4140; fax 823-6873

Messengers: Action Messenger Inc.: 881-5100

Data Dispatch: 546-8610

Dependable Courier: 338-5088

Quicksilver Express Courier: 339-2244

Medical Needs: Doctor referral: Hennepin County Medical Association: 623-9555

Dental referral: Minnesota Dental Association (St. Paul): 646-7454

Pharmacies: Snyder Brothers Drug Stores and Walgreen's have many metro locations. Walgreen's, 861-7276, has a 24-hour prescription service.

Hospitals: Abbott Northwestern Hospital: 863-4234

Hennepin County Medical Center: 347-3131

St. Paul-Ramsey Medical Center (St. Paul): 221-2121 (emergency room)

Convention Centers:

Minneapolis Convention Center, 1301 2nd Ave. S., 335-6000. This center is scheduled to open in the fall of 1990.

St. Paul Civic Center, 2004 Randolph Ave, 224-7361. Exhibition space: 180,000 sq. feet.

Entertainment, Sports, and Culture:

Sports: Baseball: Minnesota Twins, Hubert H. Humphrey (HHH) Metrodome, information 375-7444; tickets 800-843-8946

Basketball: Minnesota Timberwolves, The Arena, 337-3865

Football: Minnesota Vikings, HHH Metrodome, 333-8828

Hockey: Minnesota North Stars, Met Center, 853-9420

The Arts: The Guthrie Theater, 377-2224. Classical repertory theater.

Minneapolis Chamber Symphony, 339-0235. Performs at World Theater in St. Paul and Willey Hall, University of Minnesota.

Minnesota Opera, St. Paul, 221-0256 and 221-0122. Performs at Ordway Music Theatre.

Minnesota Orchestra, 371-5656, at Orchestra Hall in Minneapolis, Ordway Theatre in St. Paul.

St. Paul Chamber Orchestra, St. Paul, 291-1144. Performs at 20 locations.

Dining: Four Stars and Our Stars

510, 874-6440. One of the Twin Cities' most elegant French restaurants. Terrific wine list. Reservations essential. Lunch M-F, dinner M-Sat.

Blue Horse (St. Paul), 645-8101. The pasta and seafood are both highly recommended. Lunch and dinner weekdays, dinner only Sat., closed Sunday. Reservations.

Forepaugh's (St. Paul), 224-5606. Joseph Forepaugh's 1870 Victorian mansion has been converted to a first-rate French restaurant. Open for lunch and dinner daily. Call for reservations.

Murray's, 339-0909. Specializing in American cuisine. Try their trademark "butterknife" steaks. Open for lunch M-Sat., dinner nightly. Reservations.

New French Café, 338-3790. Nouvelle French cuisine reigns here; the menu changes regularly as different ingredients are "in season." Open for breakfast, lunch and dinner daily. Reservations recommended.

Windows on Minnesota, 349-6250. Gracious continental dining 50 stories in the sky. Open daily.

Home Away from Home: Where to Stay

Embassy Suites-Airport, 7901 34th Ave. S., 854-1000. Convenient to the airport, this all-suite hotel is decorated in an art deco motif. The price of your room includes a free full breakfast and 2 hours of complimentary cocktails in the evening. Indoor swimming pool, sauna, and steam room. Free shuttle to the airport. Rooms $100-$110.

Hyatt Regency, 1300 Nicollet Mall, 370-1234. Located in the middle of downtown, this 540-room (and 20-suite) hotel is a favorite with conventioneers and business travelers. The VIP floor is called the Regency Club; it offers upgraded rooms and amenities. Full health club facilities. Rooms $100-$140; Regency Club rooms $140-$160.

Marriott City Center, 30 S. 7th St., 349-4000. At 32 stories tall, with 582 rooms, this hotel is located within the City Center shopping mall and extremely convenient to the downtown business district. It hooks up to the city's Skyway. Health club. Rooms $120-$134, suites $300-$600.

Radisson St. Paul, 11 E. Kellogg Blvd., St. Paul, 292-1900. This 23-story hotel was recently renovated. It has 423 rooms, 52 suites, and is popular for conventions. Rooms $85-$105. Luxury level suites $95-$105.

St. Paul, 350 Market St., St. Paul, 292-9292. The city's grand old lady of a hotel, now 80 years old, was redone beautifully about 10 years ago. It now has 253 rooms, 30 suites. Guests have privileges at a nearby health club. Rooms $89-$119, suites run $240-$495.

Marquette, 7th and Marquette Aves., 332-2351. The hotel occupies 19 floors in the the IDS Tower, which makes it a favorite with business travelers. The service here is highly touted. Rooms $88-$110; Executive Floor rates $135-$150.

The Whitney Hotel, 150 Portland Ave., 339-9300. This all-suite hotel (97 suites) is a converted flour mill. It has all the conveniences of a modern hotel and all the charm of an older one. Suites $125-$175.

Keeping Your Tone Away from Home

Joggers and Bikers: Loring Park is a favorite with joggers in Minneapolis, as is the Minnehaha Parkway, which goes from Minnehaha Park to Lake Harriet. In St. Paul a popular jogging route is Summit Avenue. There are lovely bike trails around several of the Twin Cities' lakes: in Minneapolis try the one around Lake Harriet or Lake Calhoun. In St. Paul try Lake Como or Lake Phalen.

Bicycle Rentals: The Bike Shop, 331-3442; Calhoun Cycle Center, 827-8231; Cycle Goods, 872-7600.

Health Clubs: YMCA: 371-8700
YWCA: 332-0501

Public Golf Courses: The following are all 18-hole courses:
Como Park (St. Paul): 488-9673
Francis A. Gross Golf Course: 789-2542
Hiawatha Golf Course: 724-7715
Meadowbrook Golf Course: 929-2077
Phalen Park (St. Paul): 778-0413

Shopping

Sales tax in Minneapolis is 6%, in St. Paul it is 5%.

Nicollet Mall is a 13-block-long pedestrian mall which is the middle of downtown Minneapolis's shopping district. Located along this avenue are the city's 2 large department stores: Dayton's and Carson Pirie Scott.

The biggest concentration of shops occurs at the intersection of Nicollet Mall and 7th. There are shopping centers on 3 of the 4 corners: City Center (which contains 70 stores and Carson Pirie Scott), Gaviidae Common (Saks Fifth Avenue and 70 other stores) and The Crystal Court, located in the IDS Center (30 shops). The Conservatory is also not to be missed.

Across the river in St. Paul, in the Minnesota World Trade Center, is Saint Paul Center. This shopping center has Dayton's Carson Pirie Scott and 100 more stores and restaurants.

Florists: Larkspur, 332-2140

NEW ORLEANS

Area Code: 504
Time Zone: Central
Weather: 465-9212
Police: Metro: 821-2222; State: 483-4830
Emergency: 911

At the mouth of America's mighty Mississippi River is a city that is like no other in the country. New Orleans was founded by the French, then taken over by the Spanish before being bought by the United States. Irish, Italian, German, and Greek immigrants brought their traditions to New Orleans's melting pot. Consequently, the city's culture is a mix of all these, with a strong portion of Caribbean tradition thrown in. It all makes for a town with a delightfully foreign accent.

Tourism is big business here. Visitors head for the French Quarter, or the Vieux Carre, and Bourbon Street, where nightlife is a way of life. Jazz was born, and still thrives, in New Orleans.

The petrochemical industry is pre-eminent in New Orleans, and the economic problems that the industry has had have been felt in this city. Similarly, while New Orleans's port, 90 miles from the Gulf of Mexico, is still a busy and important one, traffic has declined in recent years.

Business Profile
Population: 1.3 million
Population Growth (1980-1989): 3.7%
Unemployment Rate: 8.6%
Fortune 500 Corporate Headquarters: 5

General Information Sources
New Orleans Chamber of Commerce: 527-6900
New Orleans Tourist & Convention Commission: 566-5011
Visitor Information Center: 566-5031

Getting There
By Air: New Orleans International Airport (or Mouissant Airport) is located 14 miles northwest of the city. For information call 464-0831.

Once you've landed: The airport is a 45-minute drive from downtown; allow an hour during rush hour. Taxi fare is $18 for up to 3 people; $6 for each additional passenger. Taxis: Morrison's Cab Service, 891-5818; Service Cab of Metairie, 834-1400; United Cab, 522-9771; Yellow Check Cab, 525-3311. Rhodes Airport Transportation, 469-4555, provides transportation to downtown and French Quarter hotels. The fare is $7. Public buses depart from the airport and go downtown to Tulane St. between Elks Pl. and South Saratoga St. Fare is $1.10.

For more information call 737-9611.
Limousines (private): Carey Limousine of New Orleans, 523-5466; Landry's Limousine Service, 244-0127; New Orleans Limousine Service, 529-5226
Directions Downtown: To get downtown from the airport, take I-10 east to the Poydras St. exit.

Overland Adventures: *Route Map:* I-10 is the main interstate highway in and out of the city; there are several downtown exits. Poydras St. is the main boulevard in downtown New Orleans.

Bottleneck Busters: Rush hour traffic jams are common on I-10, both east- and westbound, and downtown on Poydras St. Radio station WWL-AM 870 runs frequent traffic reports.
Trains: Amtrak, Union Passenger Terminal, 1001 Loyola Ave., 800-872-7245
Bus Service: Greyhound/Trailways Lines, 1001 Loyola Ave., 525-6075
Public Transportation: New Orleans's RTA (Regional Transit Authority), 569-2700, operates a public bus system. Fare is 60 cents plus 5 cents for transfers. There is also the St. Charles Streetcar, a historic attraction which travels a 5-mile route from downtown to Carrollton along St. Charles Ave. Fare is the same as for the bus. The Riverfront Streetcar covers 2 miles along the river and stops at several major tourist attractions. Cost: 60 cents. A VisiTour pass entitles one to unlimited ridership on all streetcar and bus lines. The cost is $2 for 1 day; $5 for 3 days.

Road Service and Repairs: AAA Emergency Road Services, 837-1080; AAA Travel Services, 838-7500
Towed? Call The Auto Pound, 528-3993

International Travelers
Foreign Currency Exchange: Deak International, 111 St. Charles Ave., 524-0700
Whitney National Bank, main office at 228 St. Charles Ave., 586-7272; and New Orleans International Airport, lobby level, 838-6490
Translation Services: Modern Language Institute, 1208 St. Charles Ave., 529-4121
Professional Translators & Interpreters, World Trade Ctr., Suite 1042, 581-3122
Foreign Books and Periodicals: Octave's Newsstand, 112 University Pl., 525-5774
Veterans Newsstand, 2307 Veterans Blvd., Metairie, 835-6988

Business Visitor's Needs
Banking: First National Bank of Commerce, 210 Baronne St., 561-8500
Hibernia National Bank, 313 Carondelet St., 586-5552
Whitney National Bank, 228 St. Charles Ave., 586-7272
Full Service Assistance: HQ-Headquarters Companies: 525-1175
Secretarial Services: Executive Secretarial Services: 837-7998
First Choice Secretarial Services (Metairie): 836-5272

FLYING TIMES
(in hours)
FROM
New Orleans
TO
Chicago: 3¼
Los Angeles: 4½
New York: 3
Miami: 1½

Workload, Inc.: 522-7171
Copying and Printing: Kinko's: 581-2541 (open 24 hours; call for other locations)
Kwik-Kopy Printing: 827-5358 (call for other locations)
Quik Print: 581-7262 (call for other locations)
Fax and Telex Facilities: Try the firms listed under "Copying and Printing," above, as well as:
The Business Center: 584-3939
HQ-Headquarters Companies: 525-1175
Messengers: Barnett Services Inc.: 734-0580
Express Courier (Metairie): 733-3933
New Orleans Messenger Service: 586-0036
Reliable Ron: 525-9269
Medical Needs: Doctor referral: Orleans Parish Medical Society: 523-2474
Jefferson Parish Medical Society: 455-8282
Dental referral: New Orleans Dental Assoc.: 834-6449
Pharmacies: Eckerd Drugs: 488-6661 (open 24 hours)
K&B: 947-6611 (open 24 hours)
Walgreen's: 523-7201 (call for other locations)
Hospitals: Charity Hospital: 568-2311
Tulane University Medical Center: 588-5711
Touro Infirmary: 897-8250

Convention Centers
New Orleans Convention & Exhibition Center, 900 Convention Center Blvd., 582-3000. Has 350,000 sq. feet of exhibition space and 100,000 sq. feet of meeting rooms.
Rivergate Exhibition Center, 4 Canal St., 592-2000. 130,000 sq. feet of exhibition space.
Louisiana Superdome, 1500 Poydras St., 587-3663. Seats 80,000. Has 167,000 sq. feet of exhibition space on 4 levels.

Entertainment, Sports, and Culture
Sports: Baseball: No professional team calls New Orleans home. Two local universities, Tulane (865-5000) and University of New Orleans (286-6000), play first-rate collegiate ball.
Basketball: University of New Orleans is a NCAA Division I team, 286-6000.
Football: New Orleans Saints, Superdome, 522-2600. Also the Sugar Bowl is held annually in the Superdome.
The Arts: Preservation Hall, 522-2841 during the daytime; 523-8939 at night. A shrine to New Orleans jazz; performances nightly.

Dining: Four Stars and Our Stars
Antoine's, 581-4422. This French Quarter landmark has been serving up creole cooking since 1840. Lunch and dinner M-Sat. Reservations.
Arnaud's, 523-5433. Classic creole food in an elegant, romantic setting, complete with beveled glass and crystal chandeliers. Open for lunch weekdays, brunch on Sun., dinner nightly. Sun. jazz brunch is an experience.

Commander's Palace, 899-8221. Cited by restaurant critics as one of the best in the country, this elegant restaurant is located in a gracious old Victorian house in the city's garden district. The menu features Creole cooking with an American and a French accent. Open daily for lunch and dinner; Sun. brunch. Reservations are a must.
K-Paul's Louisiana Kitchen, 942-7500. This small restaurant (seating for 65) has been made famous by its owner-chef Paul Prudhomme. No reservations are taken.

Home Away from Home: Where to Stay
Hotel Maison de Ville, 727 Toulouse St., 561-5858. An architectural gem, this small Vieux Carre hotel has just 14 rooms, 2 suites and 7 cottages (former slave quarters). Accommodations and service are top-notch. Rooms are furnished with antiques, stocked mini-bars. Complimentary continental breakfast. Rooms $100-$155, suites $185, cottages $275-$300.
Hotel Meridien New Orleans, 614 Canal St., 525-6500. A masterpiece of modern elegance. Located on the edge of the French Quarter and in the central business district. 497 rooms, 5 suites. Health club, pool, and business center with multilingual service for executives. Rooms $115-$155, suites $275-$1,200.
New Orleans Hilton Riverside & Towers, Poydras at Mississippi River, 561-0500. 1602 rooms, 86 suites. Two pools, 11 tennis courts, 5 restaurants—the multitude of facilities that are common in a hotel this size. Comfortable, efficient service. VIP floors available. Popular for conventions and meetings. Rooms $120-$175, suites $290-$475. Luxury floors: rooms $160-$185, suites $375-$1,300.

Keeping Your Tone Away from Home
Joggers and Bikers: Audubon Park has a jogging path with fitness stations along the way. City Park is also popular with both bicyclists and joggers. Bicycle rentals: Bicycle Michael's, 945-9505; and Joe's Bicycle, 821-2350.

Shopping
In New Orleans the sales tax is 9%—it is slightly less outside of the city. However, for international visitors, there is a program called Louisiana Tax Free Shopping (LTFS). For information call 527-6958.
Major department stores in downtown include Maison Blanche. Canal Place Shopping Center offers Saks Fifth Avenue, Brooks Brothers, and Guy Laroche. The recently opened New Orleans Centre houses Macy's and Lord & Taylor. Jackson Brewery (also called Jax Brewery), located in the French Quarter, is a brewery which has been renovated and holds interesting shops, galleries, and restaurants.
Florists: Flowers Unlimited by Jesse: 524-6567
The French Quarter Florist: 523-5476

NEW YORK

Area Code: Manhattan and Bronx: 212 (the Bronx is slated for area code 917 by 1992); Brooklyn, Queens, Staten Island: 718. (Telephone numbers in this section are in the 212 calling area code unless noted otherwise.)
Time Zone: Eastern
Weather: 976-1616
Police: Metro: 374-5000
Emergency: 911

All of the cliches, and all of the hackneyed phrases used to describe New York are true. It is the city that never sleeps. Life seems to move to a faster pulse in New York. It is a place of enormous contradictions; unimaginable wealth and unbearable poverty exist side by side. It is the melting pot of America, and a place where creativity and ambition are celebrated as they are nowhere else. New York has well publicized drawbacks—the high cost of living, the grime and the crime are all problems. But for the millions of residents and visitors, these are balanced by the sheer excitement of the city. Most important to the business traveler: New York is still the business capital of the country. In some industries, like finance, communications, the arts, it's the center of the universe. The city has lost much of its manufacturing industry base in recent decades, and several major companies have relocated in search of cheaper labor and operating costs. But the New York area remains home to the largest concentration of Fortune 500 companies.
True, New York City isn't just Manhattan, as any citizen of Brooklyn, Queens, the Bronx, or Staten Island will tell you. But since Manhattan is the center of the city's business world, as well as its tourist trade, we will discuss only Manhattan here.

Business Profile
Population: 8.6 million
Population Growth (1980-1989): 4.2%
Unemployment Rate: 5%
Fortune 500 Corporate Headquarters: 110

General Information Sources
Chamber of Commerce: 561-2020
Convention & Visitors Bureau: 397-8222
NYC/On Stage Hotline: 587-1111 (Music, dance, theater)
Mayor's Office: 566-5700

Getting There
By Air: JFK International Airport is 15 miles SE of the city. General information 718-656-4520; parking information 718-656-5699.

LaGuardia Airport is 8 miles NE of the city. General information 718-476-5000; current parking status 718-476-5072.
Newark Airport is 16 miles SW of the city. General information 201-961-2000; current parking status 201-961-2012.
Once You've Landed: Landing at JFK: A taxi ride to midtown will cost about $30-$35 and take about 45 minutes to an hour. A cab can easily be hailed at the terminals. Budget-minded cab riders are encouraged to share taxis with other passengers. Carey Transportation, 718-632-0500, provides bus services that leaves every 30 minutes and stops at Grand Central Terminal (E. 42nd St. and Park Ave.), and the Port Authority Bus Terminal (W. 42nd St. and 8th Ave.). A transfer for major hotels is available at Grand Central Terminal. The fare is $9.50 and the trip takes an hour to an hour and a quarter.
New York Helicopter, 800-645-3494, offers service to the Manhattan heliport at E. 34th St. from the TWA Terminal at JFK. Fare is $61; the trip takes about 10 minutes. Some airlines offer a free or reduced price connection.
Landing at LaGuardia: A cab ride will cost $17-$20 plus tolls; the trip will take about 40 minutes. There is a Share-A-Ride service that can reduce taxi costs. Carey Transportation, 718-632-0500, departs every 20 minutes to Grand Central Terminal and major hotels. A transfer to Port Authority Bus Terminal is available at Grand Central Terminal. Fare: $7.50. To Wall St.: Pan Am Water Shuttle, 800-54-FERRY (800-543-3779), runs weekdays. Take the shuttle bus to the boat dock at Marine Air Terminal. It's a 40-minute trip by water to Pier 11, corner Wall St. and South St. Fare: $20 one way.
Landing at Newark: A taxi ride to or from midtown Manhattan will cost about $40 and take about 45 minutes. New Jersey Transit, 201-460-8444, has bus service between Newark Airport and Port Authority Bus Terminal every half-hour. Fare is $7 one way, $12 round trip; the ride takes about 30 minutes.
Olympia Trails, 964-6233, has regular buses from Newark to the World Trade Center, Penn Station, and Grand Central Terminal. Cost: $7; the ride takes about 35 minutes.
Limousines (private): 24-hour advance reservations are usually required. Carey Limousines, 599-1122; Carmel Car & Limousine, 662-9300; Fugazy Limousine, 661-0100
Overland Adventures: *Route Map:* I-95 connects to New York from points north and south on the eastern seaboard; I-80 approaches from the west.

For the most part, streets and addresses in Manhattan follow an orderly pattern. The avenues run north and south, and are numbered from 12th (the western-most avenue) to 1st (the avenue farthest east). Numbered streets run in an east-west direction. Fifth Ave. is the dividing line between west and east addresses.
This logical system breaks down once you travel south of 14th St., and particularly in the Wall St. district. This is New York's

FLYING TIMES
(in hours)
FROM
New York
TO
Chicago: 3
Los Angeles: 5½
Miami: 3

earliest settled area and the named streets were probably once cow-paths. If you are going to spend any time in this area, buy a map at a bookstore or pick up a free one from the Convention & Visitors Bureau.

Bottleneck Busters: This is the city where the term "gridlock" was coined. That's when traffic is so thoroughly clogged in an intersection that it doesn't matter which direction has a green light—no one can move anyway. Any vehicle caught standing in an intersection when the signal changes runs the risk of being ticketed.

The West Side Highway is under repair south of 72nd St., and the FDR Drive (which is the East River Dr. expressway) is perpetually being rebuilt. The FDR is also subject to frequent flooding in rainstorms.

The tunnels and bridges that connect the island of Manhattan with New Jersey, Brooklyn, Queens and the Bronx are frequently clogged—a 45-minute wait is standard at rush hour.

Trains: Amtrak has 2 stations in New York: at Pennsylvania Station (7th Ave. and 33rd St.) and Grand Central Terminal (Park Ave. and 42nd St.) Trains depart from Grand Central heading north and west of the city. Routes from Penn Station run along the East Coast and through the Midwest. The Metroliner to Washington, D.C. leaves from Penn Station. Amtrak information: 800-872-7245.

Lost articles: Penn Station, 560-7388; Grand Central, 560-7534.

The PATH train system, 466-7649,

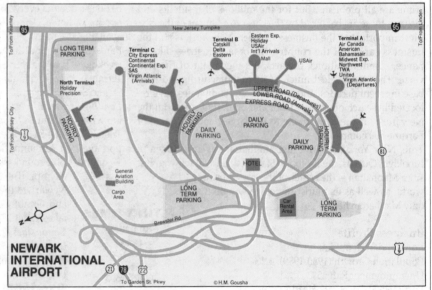

is a line which connects the World Trade Center and Penn Station with Jersey City, Newark, and Hoboken, NJ.

Bus Service: Some 3 dozen different bus lines operate from the Port Authority Bus Terminal (8th Ave. and 42nd St., 564-8484). The George Washington Bridge Bus Terminal (Fort Washington Ave. between 178th and 179th Sts., 564-1114) services about 6 bus lines, mostly for commuters from Rockland County, NY and Bergen and Passaic Counties in northern NJ.

Taxis: They can easily be hailed on most city streets (with an aggressive hand up in the air), but during off-hours or in residential neighborhoods you may need to telephone for one or

walk to a major street or avenue.

Public Transportation: Yes, New York subways are grimy and dangerous to ride late at night. But they can't be beat for getting from point A to point B in a hurry. Tokens are $1.15. Study a subway map carefully before you descend into a subway station—the system can be a bit confusing. (A free map is available at token booths—sometimes, and you can easily purchase a pocket-sized map at newsstands, bookstores, and stationery shops.) Buses are slower than subways, but will take you across town, which subways generally won't do. There is a bus line that runs on nearly every avenue. Exact change ($1.15 in coins) or a subway token is required on buses. The New York City Transit Travel Information Bureau number is 718-330-1234.

Road Service and Repairs: AAA, 586-1166; Emergency Road Service, 757-3356

Parking Regulations: In Manhattan there is no on-street parking from 23rd St. to 72nd St. except where there are meters. Check street signs for alternate side of the street parking schedules.

Towed? Call Violations and Towing, 971-0770

International Travelers

Foreign Currency Exchange: BankAmerica International, 335 Madison Ave., 503-7441

ChequePoint, 551 Madison Ave., 980-6443 (open 7 days: M-F 8am-6pm, Sat. and Sun. 10am-6pm)

Deak International, 630 5th Ave., 757-6915; 41 E. 42nd St., 883-0400; Herald Center, 1 Herald Square, 736-9790; 29 Broadway, 820-2470

Translation Services: Berlitz Translation Services, 257 Park Ave. S., 777-7878 or 785-0943; 61 Broadway, 425-3866

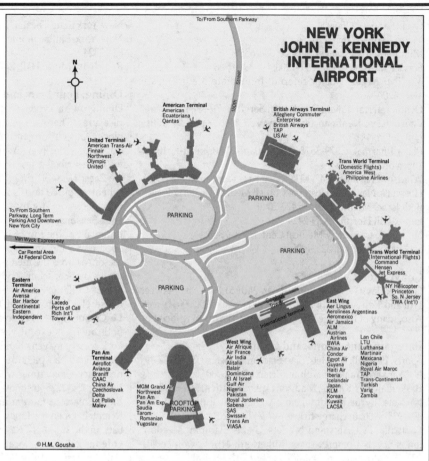

NEW YORK
JOHN F. KENNEDY
INTERNATIONAL
AIRPORT

© H.M. Gousha

Inlingua School of Languages Translation Service, 551 5th Ave., 682-8585

Japan Services Co., 1 Union Sq. West, Suite 304, 929-6022; fax 929-6255

The Language Lab, 211 E. 43rd St., 697-2020; fax 697-2891

Consulates: Nearly every country maintains a consulate and/or a chamber of commerce in New York. Some of the larger consulates are listed below. Check the Yellow Pages for more.

Australia: 245-4000	Israel: 351-5200
Canada: 768-2400	Italy: 737-9100
Fed. Rep. of Germany: 308-8700	Japan: 371-8222
People's Rep. of China: 868-7752	France: 606-3600
Republic of Korea: 752-1700	India: 879-7800
United Kingdom: 752-8400	Ireland: 319-2555

Foreign Books and Periodicals: Hotaling's News Agency, 142 W. 42nd, between Broadway and 6th Ave., 840-1868

Rizzoli Bookstore, 31 W. 57th, 759-2424; 3 World Financial Center, 385-1400; 454 W. Broadway, 674-1616

Business Visitor's Needs

Banking: Bankers Trust, 280 Park Ave., 250-2500

Chase Manhattan Bank, 1 Chase Manhattan Plaza, 552-2222

Chemical Bank, 277 Park Ave., 310-6161

Citibank, 399 Park Ave., 559-1000

Manufacturers Hanover Trust Co., 270 Park Ave., 286-6000

Morgan Guaranty Trust Co. of New York, 23 Wall St., 483-2323

Full Service Assistance: Adia Personnel Services: 682-3438

IFD Secretarial and Printing Services: 308-0049

Secretarial Services: Accountemps: 221-6500

Kelly Services: 949-8555

Manpower Temporary Services: 557-9110

Copying and Printing: CopyCats Inc.: 734-6236 (open 7 days, M-F until 11pm)

The Copy Exchange: 785-1610 (open 24 hours)

Graybar Copier: 599-3344 (M-F 8am-8pm)

Kinko's: 924-0802 (open 24 hours; call for other locations)

Mid-City Duplicating: 687-6699 (open 24 hours M-F, weekends 9am-5pm; call for other locations)

Fax and Telex Facilities: Most hotels have fax transmission service. Kinko's and Mid-City Duplicating, listed above in "Copying and Printing," also have such services.

Messengers: Choice Courier Systems: 683-6411

Cycle Service: 925-5900
Metro Express: 765-2720
Minute Men Messenger Service: 354-6555
Service Messenger Co.: 391-1900; fax 398-0968
Medical Needs: Doctor referral: Immediate Medical Care: 496-9620
Dental referral: Emergency Dental Service: 679-3966
Pharmacies: Kaufman Pharmacy: 755-2266 (open 24 hours; will deliver)
Plaza Pharmacy: 879-3878 (open 10am-10:30pm M-F, 10am-10pm on weekends)
Windsor Pharmacy: 247-1538 (open 8am to midnight, 7 days)
Hospitals: New York Hospital/Cornell Medical Center: 746-5454
Beth Israel Medical Center: 420-2000
Lenox Hill Hospital: 439-2424
New York University Medical Center: 340-7300
St. Luke's Hospital: 523-4000

Convention Centers

Jacob K. Javits Convention Center, 34th to 39th Sts. between 11th and 12th Aves., 216-2000. Exhibition space: 900,000 sq. feet. Also, many of the large hotels have extensive meeting facilities.

Entertainment, Sports, and Culture

Sports: Baseball: NY Mets, Shea Stadium (Queens), 718-507-8499
NY Yankees, Yankee Stadium (Bronx), 293-6000
Basketball: NY Knicks, Madison Square Garden, 563-8300
NJ Nets, Byrne Meadowlands Arena (East Rutherford, NJ), 201-935-3900; to charge tickets 307-7171 or 201-507-8900
Football: NY Giants and NY Jets, Giants Stadium, Meadowlands Sports Complex (East Rutherford, NJ), box office 201-935-3900; to charge tickets 307-7171 or 201-507-8900
Hockey: NY Rangers, Madison Square Garden, 563-8300
NY Islanders, Nassau Coliseum (Uniondale), 516-794-9300; to charge tickets 307-7171 or 516-888-9000
Museums: American Museum of Natural History: 769-5100
Frick Collection: 288-0700
Solomon R. Guggenheim Museum: 360-3500
Metropolitan Museum of Art: 535-7710
Museum of Modern Art: 708-9480
Whitney Museum of American Art: 570-3676
The Arts: For half-price day of performance tickets for music and dance events, try the Music & Dance Booth, on 42nd St. just east of 6th Ave., 382-2323. Cash or travelers checks only.
For half-price day of performance tickets for Broadway and Off-Broadway shows, try the TKTS Booth, 47th St. and Broadway, 354-5800. Open after 3pm for evening performances, after 10am for matinees. Be prepared to wait in line. Also try the TKTS Booth at the mezzanine of 2 World Trade Center, M-F 11am-5:30pm; Sat. 11am-3:30pm. Cash or travelers checks only.
Carnegie Hall: 247-7800
Metropolitan Opera, Lincoln Center: 362-6000
New York City Ballet, Lincoln Center: 870-5570

New York State Theater, Lincoln Center: 870-5570
New York Philharmonic, Avery Fisher Hall, Lincoln Center: 874-2424
Radio City Music Hall: 247-4777

Dining: Four Stars and Our Stars

Dining on an expense account is one of New York's great pleasures. There are first-class restaurants on almost every block. Any visitor can probably tick off the names of a half dozen or so of New York's most beloved eateries. Below we've described a few. For more guidance on which ones to try, *Zagat New York City Restaurant Survey* (about $10) is an excellent resource and is available on many newsstands and most bookstores (or by calling 302-0505).

Four Seasons, 754-9494. For decades, this place has managed to remain at the top of lists of New York's great restaurants. Food and wine are spectacular. The decor changes with the season, as does the menu. A special "Spa cuisine" is available for the diet-conscious. Closed Sundays. Reservations.

Christ Cella, 697-2479. The quintessential New York steakhouse. (Try the roast beef, too.) Closed Sundays.

Le Cirque, 794-9292. Posh, glamorous, and a favorite with both business executives looking to impress and the New York society mavens looking for the latest gossip. French cuisine with a passion for perfection. Reservations necessary—sometimes weeks in advance.

Lutèce, 752-2225. Intimate, and considered by many to be the finest French restaurant in the city. Haute cuisine, and prices to match. Open for lunch Tues.-Sat., dinner M-Sat. (closed on Sats. in the summer). Reservations.

Odeon, 233-0507. Located in a gray cast-iron building in TriBeCa, just north of Wall St. Nouvelle cuisine in an offbeat art deco atmosphere. Open daily, Sun. brunch.

Harry's at Hanover Square, 425-3412. A legendary Wall Street hang-out, Harry's is especially convenient and popular for business lunches.

The Post House, 935-2888. The menu features continental cuisine; the restaurant's steaks are excellent. Well-stocked wine cellar.

Seryna, 980-9393. Japanese food; steak and seafood are both featured in this Upper East Side eatery. Open weekdays for lunch and dinner; dinner only Sat.; closed Sundays.

"21" Club, 582-7200. Frequented by the city's high society and business moguls alike, this landmark restaurant has recently been renovated and reinvigorated by a first-rate new chef. Continental food; long-time favorites on the menu include Maryland crab cakes and 21's chicken hash. Lunch and dinner daily; closed Sundays.

Carnegie Delicatessen, 757-2245. When Woody Allen wanted to depict a New York deli in his movie *Broadway Danny Rose*, this is the one he filmed. Enormous, delicious, jaw-wrenching sandwiches are featured. The atmosphere is crowded, confused, and delightful. Open 6:30am to 4am for late-night noshing.

Home Away from Home: Where to Stay

Sheratons, Hiltons, and Holiday Inns are in the phone book. The following hotels were selected to give excellent choices in each business neighborhood of Manhattan.

Algonquin, 59 W. 49th St. between 5th and 6th Aves., 840-6800. A terrific midtown location, and a theatrical and literary landmark. Comfortable and rates are reasonable. Rooms $140-$160, suites $280-$300.

Beverly, 125 E. 50th St., at Lexington Ave., 753-2700. In a town that loves a deal, a room or suite here is a great one. Multilingual concierge. All rooms have refrigerators; suites with kitchenettes and terraces are available. Ideal for a business traveler watching the budget. Rooms $109-$150, suites $160-$245.

Carlyle, Madison Ave. at E. 76th St., 744-1600. Known for its posh upper east-side neighborhood, aristocratic atmosphere, and attentive service. The Carlyle has attracted an extremely loyal clientele: some 80% of its rooms are permanently rented. Rooms $215-290, suites $450-$1,000.

Gramercy Park, 2 Lexington Ave. at E. 21st St., 475-4320. A quiet, comfortable hotel overlooking one of New York's small gems, Gramercy Park (the Park is private; residents of the Square and guests of the hotel have keys to the gates). Popular with Europeans. Rooms $115-$130, suites from $150.

Grand Hyatt, Park Ave. at Grand Central on 42nd St., 883-1234. The old Commodore hotel was transformed with a modern, mirrored glass exterior and a dramatic 4-story greenery-filled atrium with a waterfall. Convenient location next to Grand Central Terminal. Rooms in the Hyatt Regency Club on the 31st and 32nd floor offer extra amenities. Rooms $210-$275, suites $350-$2,500.

Helmsley Palace, 455 Madison Ave. between 50th and 51st Sts., 888-7000. Luxury on a grand scale. The Helmsley Palace is an ultra-modern tower which is grafted onto an elegant 19th-century mansion. All modern conveniences; guests can make health club arrangements. Rooms $210-$285, suites $550-$2,000.

Morgan's, 237 Madison Ave., 686-0300. Sophisticated, trendy, urbane and innovative. Rooms have high tech stereo and television systems, some have VCRs. Rooms $155-$205, suites $270-$380.

Parker Meridien, 118 W. 57th St., 245-5000. The fitness facilities are among the best in New York. Owned and run by Air France, the hotel itself has an atmosphere of refined elegance. Rooms $190-$270, suites $280-$650.

Pierre, 5th Ave. at E. 61st. St., 838-8000. Across from Central Park, this hotel has traditionally defined elegance. It prides itself on first-rate service. Rooms $250-$370, suites $475-$1,100.

Regency, 540 Park Ave. at E. 61st St., 759-4000. A lavish Louis XVI decor reigns here. Rooms have mini-bars, as well as desks you can actually work on. The hotel has terrific health club facilities. Looking for the legendary New York power breakfast? This is where it takes place. Rooms $185-$265; suites $390-$950.

United Nations Plaza, 1 UN Plaza at E. 44th St. and 1st Ave., 355-3400. Across the street from the United Nations, and favored by the international diplomatic corps. Rooms begin on the 28th floor so street noise is almost non-existent. Health club with glass-enclosed swimming pool. Complimentary weekday limo service to Wall St. and the Garment District. Rooms $190-$245, suites $400-$750.

Vista International, 3 World Trade Center at West and Liberty Sts., 938-9100. For all purposes, this is Wall St.'s only hotel. It offers a full range of business services, and a health club. There is also free nightly transportation to the theater district. The Vista Executive Floors have even more amenities. Rooms $200-$305, suites $390-$1,425.

Keeping Your Tone Away from Home

Joggers and Bikers: A favorite route of runners is the circle around the reservoir in Central Park. The New York Road Runners Club can suggest other routes, 860-4455.

Bicyclists will have the most room riding on the roads in Central Park, which are often closed to traffic. Bicycle rentals are available at Metro Bicycles, 427-4450, or at the Loeb Boathouse in Central Park near the 72nd St. lake., 861-4137.

Health Clubs: There are facilities at the YMCAs and YMHAs around town. Call the Y general information office at 564-1300.

Public Golf Courses: There are no public golf courses in Manhattan.

Shopping

Major department stores include: Bloomingdale's, Macy's Herald Square, Lord & Taylor, Saks Fifth Avenue, Bergdorf Goodman.

The city's most famous shopping strip is upper Fifth Ave., home to shops like Cartier, Tiffany's, FAO Schwartz, Bijan, Van Cleef & Arpels, and Gucci. Shops on 57th St. and Madison Ave. are no less chic or exclusive.

New York City's sales tax is 8 1/4%.

Florists: Les Fleurs de Maxim's: 752-9889
Mädderlake: 941-7770
Ronaldo Maia: 288-1049
Twigs: 620-8188

NORFOLK

Area Code: 804
Time Zone: Eastern
Weather: 666-1212
Police: 441-5610
Emergency: 911

Norfolk has always been an important seaport and a coastal community, but now with recent downtown and waterfront renovations, this city has capitalized on its resorts attractions. With the help of such well-known and respected institutions as the Chrysler Museum, Norfolk has been able to redo its historic Ghent neighborhood. In the next few years, Ocean View Beach will be redeveloped. The United States Armed Forces have naval, air force, army, and coast guard installations in and around Norfolk, and so along with shipping and seafood harvesting industries, the city's economy thrives. Norfolk is an East Coast diamond in the rough—living costs are low, yet expensive and important cities like Washington, D.C. and New York are only hours away.

Business Profile
Population: 1,403,000
Population Growth (1980-1989): 21.0%
Unemployment Rate: 4.3%
Fortune 500 Corporate Headquarters: 2

General Information Sources
Norfolk Convention and Visitors Bureau:
441-5266 or 800-368-3097
Chamber of Commerce of Hampton Roads,
Norfolk Office: 622-2312

Getting There
By Air: Norfolk International Airport: 857-3351 or 857-3200
Once you've landed: Norfolk International Airport has 2 concourses within the Main Terminal; services like baggage claim, taxis, and limos are an easy walk.
The Airport Limousine Service to Norfolk costs $5.25; cars leave every hour daily through the last flight of the day.
Taxi rides cost $15 and take 20-25 minutes. Norfolk Checker Cab, 855-3333; Yellow Cab, 622-3232
Limousines (private): Service can be arranged with 24-hour advance reservations. VIP and Celebrity Limousine, 853-5466
Directions Downtown: When leaving the airport take I-64 East. Then pick up I-264 West which travels through Norfolk. The city is 6 miles southwest of the airport.
Overland Adventures: *Route Map:* Norfolk-by-the-Sea is an appropriate title for this city, with Chesapeake Bay to the north, the Atlantic Ocean to the east, and the James

River, Hampton Roads, and the Elizabeth River to the west. (Hampton Roads is a term which describes the important waterways around Norfolk.)

Surrounded by water on 3 sides, Norfolk is linked to Hampton and Portsmouth via tunnels and bridges. To the north is the Hampton Roads Bridge Tunnel which crosses the Chesapeake and connects Norfolk to Hampton. To the west are 2 tunnels which cross the Elizabeth River and connect Norfolk to Portsmouth. Called the largest bridge-tunnel in the world, the Chesapeake Bay Bridge-Tunnel spans the Chesapeake Bay and connects Virginia's eastern shore with the mainland.

Highway 13 comes from the northeast across the Chesapeake Bay Bridge-Tunnel and hooks up with I-64 in Norfolk. Norfolk is served by I-64 which comes from the north in Hampton (where such locations as Langley Air Force Base, Jamestown, Yorktown, and Williamsburg are found). I-64 continues southwest to Portsmouth. I-264 is linked to I-64 and runs east and west through the city.

Bottleneck Busters: Minor traffic delays of about 10 minutes can be expected during rush hours: 7:30am to 9am and 4:30pm to 6pm.

Trains: Amtrak, 9304 Warwick Blvd., Newport News, 245-3589 or 800-287-7245 (Newport News is north of Norfolk next to Hampton.)

Bus Service: Greyhound/Trailways Lines, 701 Monticello Ave., 627-5641

Public Transportation: Tidewater Regional Transit (TRT), 623-3222, provides bus service in Norfolk and the surrounding communities. TRT also provides trolley service within Norfolk and to Virginia Beach just east of the city. The Elizabeth River Ferry between Norfolk and Portsmouth is also operated by TRT. The ferry leaves Norfolk from Waterside (the recently completed harborside marketplace) and docks in Portsmouth at Portside. A TRT information kiosk is located outside The Waterside at 333 Waterside Dr.

Road Service and Repairs: American Automobile Association, 622-4321; Wards Corner Exxon Servicenter, 588-7416

Parking Regulations: Parking is plentiful in Norfolk. Parking garage costs run from 50 cents to $1 per hour.

Towed? Call 441-5610

International Travelers
Foreign Currency Exchange: Crestar Bank, 5 Main Plaza E., 858-3000
Sovran Bank NA, Norfolk Center Office, 1 Commercial Place, 441-4000
Translation Services: The American Red Cross Language Bank, 611 Brambleton Ave., 446-7749
Foreign Books and Periodicals: Ghent News, 807 Shirley Ave., 623-0607

FLYING TIMES (in hours)	
FROM	
Norfolk	
TO	
Boston:	2
Los Angeles:	5½
New York:	1
Houston:	1½

Business Visitor's Needs

Banking: Dominion Bank, 999 Waterside Dr., 628-0458
First Virginia Bank of Tidewater, 101 St. Paul's Blvd., 628-6600
Secretarial Services: Added Touch Business Services: 499-3721
Kelly Services: 461-5435
Copying and Printing: Kinko's: 461-7136 (open 24 hours)
Kopy Kat Instant Printing: 626-1998
Fax and Telex Facilities: Western Union: 800-325-6000
Messengers: Cycle Express: 523-0200
Envoy Couriers: 622-3530
Medical Needs: Doctor referral: Physician Referral Service: 628-3677
Dental referral: Dental Referral Service: 627-6457
Pharmacies: Peoples Drug Store: 461-7977
Phar-Mor Discounts: 461-2605
Hospitals: DePaul Medical Center: 489-5000
Norfolk Community Hospital: 628-1400
Sentara Leigh Memorial Hospital: 466-6000

Convention Centers

Norfolk Scope, Scope Plaza, corner of Brambleton and St. Paul Sts., 441-2764, is a multi-structured complex which includes Convention Hall, Chrysler Hall, Exhibit Hall, and 20 smaller meeting rooms. This facility can seat 12,000 people and the Exhibit Hall has 85,000 sq. feet of available space.
Norfolk Centre is in the planning and will add 49,000 more sq. feet for meeting needs. This waterfront facility, which will be attached to the Marriott Hotel via glass walkways, is due to open in the spring of 1991.

Entertainment, Sports, and Culture

Ticket Services: Ticketron: 499-0597
Sports and Entertainment Information: 431-8800
Sports: Baseball: Tidewater Tides, Metropolitan Park (Northampton), 461-5600
Hockey: Hampton Roads Admirals, Scope Arena, 640-1212
The Arts: The Virginia Opera performs at Norfolk Center Theater from October through March. This company performs both traditional and new operas. Call 623-1223 for information.
Virginia Stage Company, 627-1234, performs at Wells Theatre. This resident theater company has performances October through May.
The Virginia Symphony, 623-2310, has both classical and pops programs. Peanut Butter and Jam Sessions Family Concerts are also included in this remarkable symphony's repertoire. The season runs from September to May.
Chrysler Hall, 441-2163, presents Broadway shows and entertainers.

Dining: Four Stars and Our Stars

Four Stars: Le Charlieu, 623-7202. European dining, salmon and veal specialties, and a restored location are a few of the fine points of this restaurant. Reservations are required and prices are very reasonable.
Lockhart's Seafood Restaurant, 588-0405. Sailing motif, antiques, and background music greet you at Lockhart's. Besides the pleasures of home-baked bread and home-grown herbs, poach-broiled seafood platter and Paris bouillabaisse are on the menu. Reservations are required and the dinners are moderately expensive.
Our Stars: Riverwalk Cafe, 622-2868. Harbor views and outdoor dining always make the food taste best. The cafe's specialties include char-grilled fish and mesquite-grilled steak. Make your reservation because the price is right.

Home Away from Home: Where to Stay

Omni International Hotel, 777 Waterside Dr., 622-6664. Single rooms are $69-$129. The luxury level has single rooms for $109-$119. Located on the harbor, the Omni has a pretty lobby which resembles an atrium, and balconies overlooking the harbor view. Pool and poolside service, valet parking, dockage, and a gift shop are a few special amenities.
Hilton Airport, 1500 N. Military Highway at Lansdale Circle, 466-8000. Single rooms are $55-$90; the luxury level Concierge Tower offers single rooms from $90. Amenities include pool and poolside service, lighted tennis, health club, free valet parking, and free airport transportation.

Keeping Your Tone Away from Home

Health Clubs: Downtown Athletic Club: 625-2222
YMCA of South Hampton Roads: 622-6328
Public Golf Courses: Bow Creek Municipal Golf Course (Virginia Beach): 431-3763
City Park Golf Course (Portsmouth): 393-8005
Lake Wright: 461-2246
Ocean View Golf Course: 480-2094

Shopping

The most extravagant shopping experience in Norfolk has to be The Waterside and the soon-to-be-completed Waterside II which is scheduled to open in the fall of 1990. Norfolk operates a Shopper's Shuttle Trolley from downtown Norfolk to The Waterside (fare: 50 cents).
At the d'Art Center find an unusual collection of artists creating, displaying, and selling their work. The savvy shopper will find jewelry, pottery, photographs, and paintings.
Specialty shops are located in Ghent. Department-store types should try Military Circle Mall.
The sales tax in Norfolk is 4 1/2%
Florists: Norfolk Florist and Gifts: 627-1616
The Sunflower Florist: 625-2041

ORLANDO

Area Code: 407
Time Zone: Eastern
Weather: 851-7510
Police: 849-2414

Orlando was a sort of "Sleepy Hollow" until Walt Disney World (WDW) began in the early 1970s. Called The City Beautiful, Orlando has almost doubled its size in the last 20 years. The delicious orange blossoms and beautiful springs and lakes remain undisturbed by urban sprawl, and the winter climate is pleasant. Twenty miles away, WDW is the most popular tourist attraction in the world, and Orlando is becoming the transportation hub of central Florida. Big-name firms like Harcourt Brace Jovanovich and Universal Studios are headquartered here, and it has become a service center for nearby Kennedy Space Center.

Business Profile
Population: 1,019,045
Population Growth (1980-1988): 45%
Unemployment Rate: 4.6%
Fortune 500 Corporate Headquarters: 1

General Information Sources
Greater Orlando Chamber of Commerce: 425-1234
Orlando/Orange County Convention and Visitors Bureau: 363-5871

Getting There
By Air: Orlando International Airport general information: 825-2001
Once you've landed: Orlando International Airport is currently undergoing major renovations. Besides the existing 3 terminals, a new international arrivals terminal should be ready in 1990. Elevated trains take passengers from the plane to the terminals.
Taxi cab rides to downtown Orlando take about 25 minutes and cost about $20. Cab rides to Walt Disney World (WDW) take about 35 minutes and cost about $32. Even though most cabs are metered, ask drivers about prices and if necessary negotiate a price before leaving. Ace Metro, 855-1111; City Cab, 422-4561 (after hours call 699-9999); Yellow Cab, 425-3111.
Airport Limousine, 423-5566, has van service to Orlando. After landing, be sure to reserve space; vans depart about every 20 minutes. The cost one way to Orlando is $9, round trip is $16. The cost to WDW is $11 one way, $20 round trip.
City bus No. 11 leaves hourly for Orlando, takes 40 minutes, costs 75 cents, and debarks at the Pine St. Terminal. Daily operating hours are 5:45am until 9:20pm, 841-8240.

Gray Line, 422-0744, and Rabbit, 291-2424, are services that cater to groups. They provide transportation to hotels and major attractions. Most hotel desks would have more information.
Limousines (private): Service is available with 24-hour reservations. American Limousine, 859-2250; Carey Limousine, 352-6700; Dav-El Limousines, 800-922-0343
Directions Downtown: Orlando is 12 miles northwest of the airport. Take Route 436 North and turn left onto Highway 50 North. To reach downtown, exit at any of the Orlando signs.

Overland Adventures: *Route Map:* Although Orlando has grown rapidly, its size is manageable and car travel is aided by a good road system. The major interstate, I-4, passes through Orlando, travels northeast to Daytona and then southwest to Tampa. The East-West Expressway is a handy route for Highway 50 traffic to pass through the city while avoiding city traffic. The Beeline Expressway, located south near the airport, makes a beeline between I-4 and east coast spots like Cocoa Beach. The important Florida Parkway is a link between Central Florida (Orlando) and points northwest, southwest and Miami. Finally, The Spacecoast Highway, U.S. 192, skirts WDW and passes the Magic Kingdom's main entrance. Continuing east through neighboring Kissimmee, U.S. 192 eventually reaches Florida's Atlantic coast.
WDW can be reached from Orlando via I-4 South and then a short jog west on U.S. 192. This adventure park has its 28,000 acres divided into 3 sections which are linked by monorail. Everyone knows about The Magic Kingdom, but just as exciting are EPCOT Center and Vacation Kingdom.
Bottleneck Busters: Be aware of heavier traffic during the rush hours of 7:30am-9:30am and 4:30pm-6:30pm.
Trains: Amtrak, 1400 Sligh Blvd., 800-USA-RAIL (800-872-7245). Amtrak has very good service to east coast cities like Washington, D.C. and New York, or to southern Florida's cities like Tampa and Miami.
Bus Service: Greyhound/Trailways Lines, 300 W. Amelia St., 843-7720
Public Transportation: Tri County Transit, 841-8240. This public transportation bus system encompasses the counties of Orange, Seminole, and Osceola. Local fares are 75 cents with 10 cent transfers. Express fares are $1.25. The Metereater Trolley, which runs from Orange Ave. to Magnolia St., accommodates Orlando's business district. Departing every 10 minutes, the fare is 25 cents and free from 9:30pm-2am.
Road Service and Repairs: AAA Emergency Road Service, 896-1166
Towed? Call Orlando City Police Information at 849-2414

International Travelers
International Services: International Guide Book available through the Orlando/Orange County Convention and Visi-

---

FLYING TIMES
(in hours)
FROM
Orlando
TO
Chicago: 2¾
Los Angeles: 5
New York: 2¾
Miami: 1

tors Bureau, 7208 Sandlake Rd., Suite 300, 363-5871
Foreign Currency Exchange: Americash, 6227 International Dr., 351-3363
Translation Services: Berlitz Translation Services: 800-523-7548
Translation and Interpretation Institute, 227 N. Magnolia, 422-8458
Foreign Books and Periodicals: Book Stop, 4924 E. Colonial Dr., 894-6024
Canterbury Books, Florida Mall, 8001 S. Orange Blossom Trail, 855-9313

Business Visitor's Needs

Banking: Bank of Central Florida, 1401 Lee Rd., 298-6600
Citizens and Southern National Bank of Florida, 1118 S. Orange Ave., 628-1924
First Union National Bank of Florida, Orange Tower, 20 N. Orange St., 649-2265
Secretarial Services: Executive Support Centers, Inc.: 275-6455
HQ-Headquarters Companies: 425-5600
Copying and Printing: Kinko's: 658-9518
Triangle Reprographics, Inc.: 843-1492
Messengers: Ace Courier Express: 256-9453
Medical Needs: Doctor referral: Ask-A-Nurse Physician Referral Service: 897-1700
Dental referral: Dental Society of Greater Orlando: 331-2526
Pharmacies: Eckerd Drugs: 351-0160
Leggett-Rexall Drug Stores: 422-4438
Hospitals: Florida Hospital Medical Center: 896-6611
Orlando Regional Medical Center: 841-5111
Winter Park Memorial Hospital: 646-7000

Convention Centers

Orange County Convention/Civic Center, 9800 International Dr., 345-9800. The convention center has 173,000 sq. feet of exhibition space, 22 meeting rooms, and seating for up to 2,500.
Expo Center, 500 W. Livingston St., 849-2562. Located in downtown Orlando, the Expo Center has 130,000 sq. feet of exhibition space.
Tupperware Convention Center, Orange Blossom Trail, 847-1800. Tupperware has 25,000 sq. feet of exhibit space, 2,000 auditorium seats, and a 2,000-seat dining area.
Walt Disney World Hotel and Convention Complex, Swan and Dolphin Hotels. WDW central reservations, 934-7639.

Entertainment, Sports, and Culture

Ticket Services: Ticketmaster: 839-3900
Sports: Baseball: Osceola Astros (A-Club Houston affiliate), Osceola Stadium (Kissimmee), 933-5500
Basketball: Orlando Magic, Orlando Arena, 649-3290
Jai-Alai: Orlando Seminole Jai-Alai (Fern Park), 339-6221
The Arts: Zev Bufman Broadway Series appears at the Bob Carr Performing Arts Center, 849-2020, as do the Florida Symphony Orchestra, 894-2011, the Orlando Opera Company,

896-7664, and the Southern Ballet Theater, 628-0133.

Dining: Four Stars and Our Stars

Four Stars: Cafe on the Park, 841-3220. Overlooking Eola Park and Lake, and offering a continental menu of seafood and prime rib. This moderately expensive restaurant is a good choice.
Lili Marlene's Aviators Restaurant and Pub, 422-2434. Located in the shopper's delight called Church Street Station, this restaurant offers steak, seafood, nightly entertainment, and attractive moderate prices.
Our Stars: Top of the World, 934-7639 for groups under 6 people; 824-3950 for groups of 6 or more. Expect rooftop dining and a view of the Magic Kingdom. The dinner and show are $35. Specialties such as prawns and stuffed veal chops are featured. Reservations are required.

Home Away from Home: Where to Stay

Contemporary Resort, WDW, 824-1000. Singles cost $120-$180; luxury level suites cost $300-$500. Balconies, huge lobby and a convenient monorail stop plus all the amenities make this hotel very comfortable. To stay fit try these privileges: 2 pools, lighted tennis, golf, and health club. The hotel has an up-to-date shopping arcade and provides airport transportation.
Peabody Orlando, 9801 International Dr., 352-4000. Single rooms are $125-$170; luxury level singles are $195. Beautiful grounds, lavish water fountains and private patios greet you at the Peabody. Pool, tennis, golf, and health club.
Harley Hotel of Orlando, 151 E. Washington St., 841-3220. Single rooms are $75-$95. Free transportation to the airport and WDW. Amenities include pool, exercise room, and restaurant.

Keeping Your Tone Away from Home

Joggers: A good jogging route is around Lake Eola in downtown Orlando. Also, any of the roads in WDW can be used as jogging routes since cars are banned.
Health Clubs: Contemporary Resort Health Club (WDW): 824-1000
YMCA: 896-6901

Shopping

A variety of choices exists for shoppers. The new Florida Mall has many shops. Nearby Winter Park, known as Central Florida's Little Europe, has quaint boutiques, antiques, fine men's and women's clothing stores, and art galleries. Walt Disney World Village has unique and worldwide selections. Church Street Station has pleasing stores and lots to see.
Florists: College Park Florist: 422-0894
Flowerama, Inc.: 843-3561

PHILADELPHIA

Area Code: 215
Time Zone: Eastern
Weather: 936-1212
Police: 683-3090
Emergency: 911

As every U.S. schoolchild knows, Philadelphia was the "cradle of democracy" during colonial times. It was here that the Declaration of Independence was signed, the Liberty Bell was rung, and Betsy Ross's flag was sewn. But the area's vibrant economy prevents the city from being merely a museum piece. It is a regional center of insurance and finance, and has a strong health care and pharmaceutical industry. Major corporations such as SmithKline Beckman, Scott Paper, and CIGNA are headquartered in Philly. In addition, companies like Campbell Soup, Sun Oil, and Unisys are located within the larger metropolitan area. The city also has a major and thriving port.

Business Profile
Population: 4.9 million
Population Growth (1980-1989): -4.5%
Unemployment Rate (1989): 4%
Fortune 500 Corporate Headquarters: 15

General Information Sources
Philadelphia Convention and Visitors Bureau: 636-3300
Mayor's Office Information: 686-2250
Chamber of Commerce of Greater Philadelphia: 545-1234

Getting There
By Air: Philadelphia International Airport general information: 492-3333
Once you've landed: South-Eastern Pennsylvania Transit Authority (SEPTA), 580-7800, has an airport rail line that links the domestic terminals with 30th Street Station, 16th St., and Market Street East. Fare: $4 at ticket booth, $5 if ticket is bought on train. Frequency: leaves every half-hour. Time: 25 minutes.
A taxi ride between Center City and the airport costs $15 to $20. Allow 30 minutes for the trip, 45-60 minutes during rush hour. Quaker City Cab, 728-8000; Yellow Cab, 922-8400.
Hotel van service to downtown Philadelphia is about $6 per person. Call 463-8787.
Limousines (private): 24-hour reservations are recommended. Carey Limousine, 492-8402; Royal Limo & Coach, 800-248-7557.
Directions Downtown: Take Route 291 North to I-76 West to Vine Street.

FLYING TIMES
(in hours)
FROM
Philadelphia
TO
Chicago: 2
Los Angeles: 4¾
New York: ½
Miami: 3

Overland Adventures: *Route Map:* I-95 is the main north-south route. From points west, the Pennsylvania Turnpike comes into the Schuylkill Expressway (I-76). The Schuylkill has several exits downtown.
In Center City, numbered streets run north and south, named streets run east and west.
Driving Regulations: Seat belts required. Right turn on red permitted except where a sign specifically prohibits it.
Bottleneck Busters: The Schuylkill has legendary delays. KYW-AM News Radio (1060) has frequent traffic reports. I-95 slows to a crawl during rush hour, particularly approaching the Center City exits.
Trains: Amtrak serves 30th Street Station and provides convenient links with New York, Baltimore, Washington, D.C. Call 824-1600 for information. SEPTA, 574-7800, operates an extensive commuter rail network which serves surrounding suburbs.
Bus Service: Greyhound/Trailways Lines Terminal, 1001 Filbert St., 931-4000
Public Transportation: SEPTA, 580-7800, runs subways, trolleys, and buses. Information centers underground at Market and 15th Sts., and Market and 10th Sts.
Road Service and Repairs: For car repair, call Center City Service, 985-9535; Keystone AAA, 864-5000
Parking Regulations: Off-street parking lots are in abundance; prices range from $3.50 an hour to about $12-$15 for all day parking. Parking meters generally limit parking to 2 hours. Be careful if you park on the street—they tow in Philadelphia. Frequently.
Towed? Call Philadelphia Parking Authority, 574-3636

International Travelers
Foreign Currency Exchange: Deak International, 16 N. 17th St., 563-5544
First Pennsylvania Bank, Market and 15th, 786-8880
Philadelphia National Bank, Market and 5th St., 973-4402
Translation Services: Berlitz Translation Services, 1608 Walnut St., 735-8500
Nationalitics Service Center, 1300 Spruce St., 893-8400
Foreign Books and Periodicals: Afterwards, 218 S. 12th St., 735-2393 (M-F 11am-11pm, weekends 11am-3am)

Business Visitor's Needs
Banking: Large full service banks, in addition to those mentioned In "Foreign Currency Exchange," above, include:
Fidelity Bank, Broad & Walnut Sts., 985-6200
Mellon Bank, Broad & Chestnut, 553-3000
Provident National Bank, Broad & Chestnut, 585-5000
Secretarial Services: Accountemps: 568-4580
CPS Services: 985-9535
Kelly Services: 564-3110

Copying and Printing: Kinko's: 386-5679 (open 24 hours)
Minuteman Press: 925-5858 (call for other locations)
Fax and Telex Facilities: Western Union: 800-325-6000
Messengers: Kangaroo Couriers: 561-5132
Philadelphia Express Couriers: 627-6700
Quick Courier Service: 592-9933
Medical Needs: Doctor referral: Philadelphia County Medical Society: 563-5343
Dental referral: Philadelphia County Dental Society: 925-6050
Pharmacies: Haussman's Pharmacy: 627-2143 (open 365 days a year; specializes in foreign and unusual prescriptions)
Leof's Pharmacy: 877-0235 (open 7 days, 9am-midnight)
Also: CVS and RiteAid are 2 pharmacy chains with several local outlets.
Hospitals: All have very fine reputations: Hahnemann University Hospital: 448-7000
Thomas Jefferson University Hospital: 955-6000
University of Pennsylvania Hospital: 662-4000

Convention Centers
Philadelphia Civic Center, 34th and Civic Center Blvd., 823-5600. The Center has a convention hall with a 36,000 sq.-foot exhibition space, a center hall with 50,000 sq. feet available, and 2 plazas with a total of 190,000 sq. feet of space.
Some of the major hotels have special transportation arrangements with the Civic Center.

Entertainment, Sports, and Culture
Ticket Services: Central City Ticket Office, 735-1350
Sports: Baseball: Phillies, Veterans Stadium, 463-1000
Basketball: 76ers, Spectrum Arena, 339-7676; Ticketron 800-233-4050; Ticketmaster 215-574-1200
Football: Eagles, Veterans Stadium, 463-5500
Hockey: Flyers, Spectrum Arena, 755-9700
The Arts: Academy of Music, 893-1930. Home to Philly's orchestra, opera and ballet companies.
Annenberg Center, University of Pennsylvania, 898-6791. Multi-purpose performing arts center.
Forrest Theater, 923-1515. Home to touring Broadway shows.
Mann Music Center, 567-0707. Summertime concerts.
Walnut Street Theater, 574-3586. Classic, contemporary, and experimental plays and musicals.

Dining: Four Stars and Our Stars
Four Stars: Le Bec Fin, 567-1000. The city's best and most luxurious French restaurant. Reservations necessary; weekend dinner reservations should be made a few weeks in advance. Lunch weekdays only. Very expensive.
The Fountain, 963-1500. This restaurant's modern American/French cuisine is touted as imaginative and elegant. Expensive.
Our Stars: Bookbinders Seafood House, 545-1137. A Philadelphia tradition, this seafood restaurant is often con-

fused with Old Original Bookbinders. This is the better, less-touristy version. Moderate to expensive.
DiLullo Centro, 546-2000. This restaurant is located in a luxuriously renovated Center City theater. North Italian cuisine is the specialty here.

Home Away from Home: Where to Stay
The Barclay Hotel, Rittenhouse Sq. and 18th St., 545-0300. 244 rooms, exemplifies quiet elegance. Guests have use of adjacent Rittenhouse Fitness Center. Double rooms run $145 a night and up.
Latham Hotel, 135 S. 17th St., 563-7474. Smaller hotel (139 rooms); newly redone, each room boasts 2 phones with call waiting and computer hook-ups. Guests have privileges at a nearby health club. Rooms $145 a night and up.
Four Seasons, 1 Logan Sq., 963-1500. Modern with all attendant conveniences: pool, health club, sauna. Impressive and prestigious. Rooms $205 nightly and up.
Wyndham Franklin Plaza, 17th and Race, 448-2000. 26-floor modern hotel with city's most complete convention facilities. Double rooms start at $160.

Keeping Your Tone Away from Home
Joggers and Bikers: Joggers can replicate boxer Rocky Balboa's inspirational movie run up JFK Parkway and on up the steps of the art museum. Upon reaching the top, don't forget to raise hands above head in triumphant fashion and turn around for a glorious view of Center City. More circumspect joggers might want to try Kelly Dr. and West River Dr. in Fairmount Park. Bicycle rentals: Fairmount Park Bike Rental, 236-4359.
Health Club: YMCA: 557-0082
Public Golf Course: John F. Byrne: 632-8666

Shopping
Sales tax is 6% on most purchases, excluding many apparel items.
The Gallery at Market East is the city's biggest shopping center with 230 stores and restaurants. Large department stores in Philly include John Wanamaker's, Jeweler Baily Banks and Biddle, and the old standard, Brooks Brothers.
Florists: Center City Flowers: 592-4333
Society Hill Florist: 925-5715
Balloon Deliveries: Balloons Magnifiques: 483-6880

PHOENIX

Area Code: 602
Time Zone: Mountain
Weather: 957-8700
Police: 262-6151
Emergency: 911

Phoenix had its second rising after the second World War when the city's manufacturing and tourism trade began flourishing. Known as the Valley of the Sun and claiming 300 sunny days yearly, Phoenix's low cost of living and lovely climate have made it a popular city for both the business person and retiree. Such industries as Phelps Dodge, Honeywell Information Systems, and Western Electric coexist with Luke Air Force Base and Williams Air Force Base. Phoenix's burgeoning city limits are not designed in the spirit of Frank Lloyd Wright; for that inspiration seek out his historically famous Taliesin.

Business Profile
Population: 789,704
Population Growth (1988-1989): 2.3%
Unemployment Rate: 3.9%
Fortune 500 Headquarters: 7

General Information Sources
City of Phoenix Public Information: 262-7176
Phoenix Chamber of Commerce: 254-5521
Phoenix and Valley of the Sun Convention and Visitors Bureau: 254-6500

Getting There
By Air: Sky Harbor International Airport general information: 273-3300. Inter-Airport Transportation offers shuttle bus service at no charge 24 hours daily among the 3 terminals, executive terminal, and parking lots C and D.
Once you've landed: Car rental is your best bet for getting around the sprawling city of Phoenix. The major agencies are located at all 3 terminals.
A taxi cab ride between the airport and Phoenix takes about 12 minutes; the rates differ—be sure to talk with the driver. Checker Cab, 257-1818; Yellow Cab, 252-5252.
24-hour shared van rides are provided by Super Shuttle, 244-9000. Rates differ, but start at $5 to downtown Phoenix. Locations: terminal 3 and executive terminal outside baggage claim; between terminal 2 and international terminal at ground transportation building.
City of Phoenix Transit System, 257-8426, runs the No. 2E bus from terminal 3, M-F 6am-6:40pm. Cost: 75 cents; count on a 25-minute ride to downtown.

Limousines (private): Require 24-hour notice. Valley Limousine, 254-1955.
Directions Downtown: Take the 24th St. exit right from the airport. After one mile, turn left onto Washington St. Go about 3 miles and turn right onto Central Ave.
Overland Adventures: *Route Map:* I-17 and I-10 are the main routes intersecting downtown Phoenix. I-17 goes north to the Grand Canyon. I-10 continues west to Los Angeles, or both south and east to Tucson and New Mexico. Within Phoenix, streets are east of Central Avenue while avenues are west.
Driving Regulations: Seat belts not required. Right turn on red permitted unless indicated. Left turn on red from one-way to one-way.
Bottleneck Busters: Avoid freeways during rush hours.
Trains: Amtrak, 401 W. Harrison St., 800-872-7245. Provides links to New York and Washington.
Bus Service: Greyhound/Trailways Lines, 5th St. and Washington. Suburban bus station, 2647 W. Glendale Ave., Glendale 246-4341. Fare and information for both stations, 248-4040.
Public Transportation: Phoenix Rapid Transit System Valley-wide Bus System, 253-5000. Provides local and express bus service.
Road Service and Repairs: If an emergency arises on a highway, raise the car hood and, if possible, call the Department of Public Safety, 800-525-5555—identify the nearest milepost number. For 24-hour car repair or towing call Arizona Automobile Association, 274-1116, or Park Central Mobil, 274-9429.
Parking Regulations: Plenty of metered parking is available.
Towed? Call the Phoenix Police Dept., 262-6151

FLYING TIMES
(in hours)
FROM
Phoenix
TO
Chicago: 3½
Los Angeles: 1¼
New York: **5**
Miami: **5-6**

International Travelers
Foreign Currency Exchange: Valley Center, 241 N. Central Ave., 261-1255
Translation Services: Berlitz Translation Services, 6415 Independence Ave., Woodland Hills, 265-4368
Consulate: Mexican Consulate: 242-7398
Foreign Books and Periodicals: Shakespeare Beethoven & Co., 6166 N. Scottsdale, Scottsdale, 991-1966

Business Visitor's Needs
Banking: Citibank, 3300 N. Central Ave., 248-2223
First National Bank of Arizona, 1001 N. Central Ave., 258-2265
Secretarial Services: Addtemps: 224-5625
Kelly Services: 264-0717
Copying and Printing: Kinko's Copies: 241-9440
Sir Speedy: 264-3990
Messengers: Dial-A-Messenger: 240-6060
Telex Facilities: Western Union: 800-325-6000
Medical Needs: Doctor referral: Physician Referral Service at Humana Hospital: 279-9800

Pharmacies: Lahr's Pharmacy: 944-3326 (open 365 days a year, 7am-midnight)
Walgreen's: 247-1014
Hospitals: Humana Hospital: 241-7600
Arizona State Hospital: 244-1331
Phoenix Memorial Hospital: 258-5111

Convention Centers
Arizona Veterans Memorial Coliseum & Exposition Center, 1826 McDowell Rd., 258-6711. The Arena, 30,000 sq. feet, holds 14,000 seats.
The Phoenix Civic Plaza Convention Center, 225 E. Adams Ave., 262-7272. Has 330,000 sq. feet of exhibit space plus an expansion of 3 extra exhibit halls. The center also has 4 large meeting rooms that can make 43 smaller rooms seating between 75 to 150.

Entertainment, Sports, and Culture
Ticket Services: Dillard's Charge Line: 829-5555
Sports: Baseball: Phoenix Firebirds, Phoenix Municipal Stadium, 275-4488
Basketball: Phoenix Suns, Veterans Memorial Coliseum, 263-SUNS (263-7867)
The Arts: Ballet West Arizona: 381-0184
Grady Gammage Center for the Performing Arts (Tempe): 965-3434
Phoenix Little Theatre: 254-2151
Scottsdale Center for the Arts: 994-ARTS (994-2787)
Symphony Hall: 262-7272

Dining: Four Stars and Our Stars
Four Stars: Mr. Louie's Cafe de Perouges, 263-8000. Surrounded by water pools, this restaurant features live piano music, a continental menu, and is moderately expensive.
La Fontanella, 955-1213. Reservations recommended. Italian menu; chef-owned.
Our Stars: Pointe In Tyme, 866-7500. Specializes in famous recipes from well-known U.S. restaurants.

Home Away from Home: Where to Stay
Arizona Biltmore , 24th St. and Missouri Ave., 955-6600. Architecture inspired by Frank Lloyd Wright; this luxurious resort rests on 250 acres of golf course, palms, cactus and gardens. Singles $185-$305.
The Pointe at Squaw Peak, 7677 N. 16th St., 800-528-0428. Southwestern flavor with tiled courtyards, balconies, and fountains; 280 acres including golf and tennis. Ask for the corporate discount.
Executive Park, 1100 N. Central Ave., 252-2100. Small hotel (105 rooms) in downtown with pool, Jacuzzi, sauna. Peak season corporate rates, $75.
Ritz-Carlton Phoenix Hotel, 2401 E. Camelback Rd., 468-0700. Luxury hotel with fitness center, tennis, 2 restaurants, lounge. Singles $89-$209.

Keeping Your Tone Away from Home
Health Clubs: Center Court: 230-1759
Valley Fitness Center: 245-9312
YWCA: 258-0990
Public Golf Courses: Paradise Valley Golf Course: 992-7190
Papago Golf Course: 495-0555

Shopping
Designer labels can be found in the Biltmore Fashion Park in such stores as I. Magnin and Saks Fifth Avenue. The open-air Park Central Mall located in midtown has been recently renovated. Further from downtown Phoenix, in Scottsdale, the Borgata has 50 boutiques. In Mesa, the Fiesta Mall is the most popular shopping area.
Florists: Donofrio's Florists: 254-6761
My Florists: 258-7401

PITTSBURGH

Area Code: 412
Time Zone: Eastern
Weather: 936-1212
Police: 255-2830
Emergency: 911

Pittsburgh still conjures up images of steel mills, coal mining, and raw industrial might. That image is woefully outdated. Pittsburgh has artfully made the transition to a modern city. Steel, glass, and aluminum are all still major players in the local economy, but they've been joined by industries like pharmaceuticals, robotics, and data processing. Companies headquartered here include Heinz, USX, (formerly US Steel), Rockwell International, Westinghouse, and Alcoa.

Business Profile
Population: City, 410,000; Metropolitan area, 2 million
Population Growth (1980-1989): -6%
Unemployment Rate: 4.7%
Fortune 500 Corporate Headquarters: 16

General Information Sources
Greater Pittsburgh Convention and Visitors Bureau: 281-7711, out-of-state 800-821-1888
Greater Pittsburgh Chamber of Commerce: 392-4500
24-Hour Visitor Information Line: 391-6840
Duquesne University Small Business Development Center: 434-6233

Getting There
By Air: Pittsburgh International Airport: 778-2500

Private planes can land at Allegheny County Airport, 461-4300. Corporate Jets, Inc., 466-2500, specializes in 24-hour executive aircraft charter, management, and maintenance services.
Once you've landed: The airport is 16 miles west of downtown, usually, a 40-minute ride. Airlines Transportation, 471-8900, provides ground transportation to and from the airport. Motorcoach service to downtown costs $8; to Oakland and South Hills, $8.50; and to Monroeville, $12. A taxi ride downtown from the airport should cost about $25. People's Cab, 681-3131 or 441-5334; Yellow Cab of Pittsburgh, 665-8100.
Limousines (private): Try Allegheny Limousines, Inc., 731-8671; Landmark Limousine Service, 321-0802; The Limo Center, 923-1650.
Directions Downtown: Take Airport Parkway, (Route 60) to Route 279, across the Fort Pitt Bridge to downtown.
Overland Adventures: *Route Map:* The city's down-

town district is roughly bounded to the west and northwest by Route 279, to the south by Route 376, and to the east by route 579. Downtown, the streets are not laid out in any particularly regular fashion: numbered streets run from south to north, but they are interrupted by named streets. The best bet is to consult the map. The downtown area is small enough that most destinations can be reached by walking.
Bottleneck Busters: I-579 is often jammed up; as are I-279 and I-376. The Fort Pitt Bridge across the Monongahela, and the Fort Duquesne Bridge tend to be bottlenecks. Radio station WKQV-AM 1410 broadcasts regular traffic reports.
Trains: Amtrak, Liberty Ave. and Grant St., 800-872-7245
Bus Service: Greyhound/Trailways Lines Bus Terminal is at 11th St. and Liberty Ave., 391-2300.
Public Transportation: The Port Authority Transit (PAT) operates The Light Rail Transit System, a subway which connects downtown with Pittsburgh's southern suburbs. Passengers ride free between the downtown stations: Gateway Center, Wood Street, Steel Center, and Penn station. PAT also operates extensive bus service. Call 231-5707 for information about both services.
Road Service and Repairs: West Penn AAA: 362-3300
Towed? Call the Police Department's Tow Pound, 255-2500

International Travelers
International Services: Pittsburgh Council for International Visitors: 624-7800
Foreign Currency Exchange: Pittsburgh National Bank, 5th and Wood, 762-2000
Translation Services: Berlitz Translation Services, 355 5th Ave., 471-0900
The Language Center, 313 6th Ave., 261-1101
Takahashi Consulting, 2 Gateway Ctr., 391-0607 (Japanese and English)
Foreign Books and Periodicals: Smithfield Street News, 115 Smithfield St., 391-6980

FLYING TIMES
(in hours)
FROM
Pittsburgh
TO
Chicago: ½
Los Angeles: 6
New York: 1
Miami: 2½

Business Visitor's Needs
Banking: Large full service banks include Mellon Bank, 3 Mellon Bank Ctr., 234-5000; Pittsburgh National Bank, 5th and Wood, 762-2000; and Union National Bank of Pittsburgh, 4th and Wood, 644-8111.
Secretarial Services: Accountemps: 471-5946
Executaries Four: 456-1070
Executive Secretarial Service Inc.: 561-1717 and 561-2360
Copying and Printing: Kinko's: 687-8680 (open 24 hours; call for other locations)
Matthew's Printing: 391-3431
Sir Speedy: 391-7447
Fax and Telex Facilities: Kinko's: 687-8680 (open 24 hours)
Western Union: 800-325-6000
Messengers: First Courier: 771-1000
Fleet Feet: 471-0933

Medical Needs: Doctor referral: Allegheny County Medical Society: 321-5030
Dental referral: Dental Society of Western Pa.: 321-5810
Pharmacies: Rite Aid and Thrift Drug have numerous outlets throughout the city.
Hospitals: Allegheny General Hospital: 359-3131
Central Medical Center and Hospital: 562-3000
Mercy Hospital: 232-8111

Convention Center

David L. Lawrence Convention Center, 1001 Penn Ave., 565-6000. 131,000 sq. feet of space.

Entertainment, Sports, and Culture

Sports: Baseball: Pittsburgh Pirates, Three Rivers Stadium, 800-366-1212
Football: Pittsburgh Steelers, Three Rivers Stadium, 323-1200
Hockey: Pittsburgh Penguins, Civic Arena, 333-7328
The Arts: Benedum Center for the Performing Arts, 456-6666, houses Broadway, dance, and opera.
Pittsburgh Ballet Theatre: 281-0360
Pittsburgh Public Theater, 321-9800. Professional resident theater company; September-June.
Pittsburgh Symphony Orchestra: 392-4800. September-May.
Museums: Carnegie Institute Museum of Art: 622-3270
Frick Art Museum: 371-0600
Pittsburgh Center for the Arts: 361-0873

Dining: Four Stars and Our Stars

Carlton, 391-4099. Charcoal-grilled steaks are a specialty at this favorite spot of business executives. Prices are moderate. Lunch M-F, dinner M-Sat.
Common Plea, 281-5140. Not surprisingly, this restaurant, located near the Courthouse, is a lunchtime favorite among local lawyers, business executives, and city officials. Seafood is the house specialty. Reservations suggested for lunch.
Hyeholde (Coraopolis), 264-3116. Hyehold looks like an English Tudor mansion, complete with tapestries and wooden beams. Continental cuisine, extensive wine list. Expensive.
Top of the Triangle, 471-4100. Since this restaurant sits atop the 64-story USX Building, the view is the biggest attraction. Continental cuisine. Expensive. Open daily.
Tequila Junction, 262-3265. Located across the river from downtown in Station Square, the popular shopping arena. A comfortable and popular Mexican restaurant. Inexpensive. Reservations not necessary. Open 7 days.

Home Away from Home: Where to Stay

The Ramada Hotel, One Bigelow Square, 281-5800. This all-suite hotel offers Nautilus, indoor pool, and saunas. Prices: studios $90, 1-bedrooms $110, 2-bedrooms, $140.
Hyatt Pittsburgh at Chatham Center, 112 Washington Pl., 471-1234 and 800-228-9000. Convenient to the Civic Center,

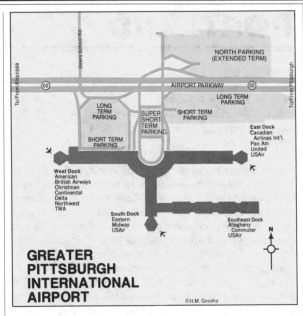

GREATER PITTSBURGH INTERNATIONAL AIRPORT

©H.M. Gousha

this 400-room hotel has the amenities of most modern hotels, including pool and health club. The top 2 floors have the best accommodations.
Pittsburgh Hilton & Towers, 600 Commonwealth Pl., Gateway Ctr., 391-4600. The Hilton is situated at the edge of Point State Park, overlooking the 3 rivers. It has 718 rooms; the top 3 floors are set aside as executive suites. Health club, sauna.
Vista International, 1000 Penn Ave., 281-3700. A pedestrian overpass connects this 614-room contemporary hotel with the Lawrence Convention Center. The hotel has 3 VIP floors.
Westin William Penn, 530 William Penn Pl., 281-7100. A local historic landmark. The hotel's top 2 floors have the most luxurious rooms. Well-located on Mellon Square.

Keeping Your Tone Away from Home

Joggers and Bikers: Joggers often use Point State Park, where the 2 major rivers meet, as well as Schenley Park and North Park. Bicycle rentals available at North Park, 935-1971.
Health Clubs: The City Club: 391-3300
YMCA: 227-3800

Shopping

Joseph Horne and Kaufmann's are 2 large downtown department stores. Larrimor's is a local upper-crust clothing store for men and women. John M. Roberts & Son. is a well-established local jeweler. A downtown office building, One Oxford Centre, has 3 lower floors with designer boutiques. Station Square, a restored Pittsburgh and Lake Erie Railroad complex has been converted into a museum and shopping center.
Florists: Hepatica: 241-3900
Lubin & Smalley: 471-2200

PORTLAND

Area Code: 503
Time Zone: Pacific
Weather: 236-7575, 778-6000
Police: Metro: east Portland, 248-5696; north Portland, 248-5720; west Portland, 796-309; State: 238-8434
Emergency: 911

Oregon's majestic, snow-capped Mt. Hood, visible from almost anywhere in downtown Portland, is more than a scenic backdrop for the city. It is symbolic of the city's devotion to the great outdoors, environmentalism, and an excellent quality of life. Thanks to careful city planning, Portland is one of those places constantly described as "livable." It has a reasonable cost of living, tremendous recreational and cultural opportunities, and a solid employment base.

The city boasts an abundance of recreational diversions. The beach and the mountains are each only 90 minutes away from Portland; and, as might be expected, tourism is big business. But so are industries like lumber, electronics, aluminum, and apparel. The city also has an active seaport, even though it is about 100 miles east of the Pacific. Companies headquartered here include Louisiana-Pacific, Pope & Talbot, Tektronix, Willamette Industries, NERCO, U.S. Bancorp, and NIKE. Other companies which are large employers locally include: Boeing Portland, Intel, James River Corp., Jantzen, Pendleton Woolen Mills, and the Reynolds Metal Company.

Business Profile
Population: 1.2 million
Population Growth (1980-1989): 8%
Unemployment Rate: 4.3%
Fortune 500 Corporate Headquarters: 10

General Information Sources
Portland Metropolitan Chamber of Commerce: 228-9411
Portland, Oregon Visitors Association: 222-2223; cultural events recorded message, 233-3333
Portland Development Commission: 796-5300

Getting There
By Air: Portland International Airport is 9 miles northeast of the city. Airport information: 234-8422 and 231-5000, ext. 422; to have someone paged, 249-4747. The airport has a new service, PDX Conference Center, which serves as a working space for business travelers. It has meeting rooms, copiers and fax machines, computer workstations, and secretarial help available, all at a cost. For prices and reservations, call 231-5000, ext. 507.

FLYING TIMES (in hours)
FROM
Portland
TO
Chicago: 4½
Los Angeles: 2½
New York: 7½
Miami: 7

Once you've landed: By taxi, the trip from the airport to downtown takes about 20 minutes and costs about $20 or $25. Taxis: Broadway Deluxe Cab, 227-1234; Portland Taxi, 256-5400; Radio Cab, 227-1212.

The RazTrans Portland Airporter, 246-4676, is a bus to major downtown hotels which leaves every 30 minutes One-way fare is $6, and the trip takes about a half-hour. The city's Tri-Met bus No. 12 leaves from the airport and stops at the Portland Mall in the city. The fare is $1.15.

Limousines (private): Corporate Plus Limousine Services, 249-2866; Oregon Limousine Service, 252-5882; Prestige Limousine, 282-5009

Directions Downtown: Take I-205 South to I-84 West. Take I-84 and I-5 to the Morrison Bridge and cross bridge to downtown.

Overland Adventures: *Route Map:* For travelers trying to find their way around the city, it helps to know that Portland's downtown business district is bounded on the west by I-405 and on the east by I-5. The Willamette River bisects the city in an east-west direction, while Burnside Street does the same from north to south. I-5 North will take you to Vancouver, WA and on to Seattle.

Driving Regulations: Right turn on red permitted unless posted. Seat belts are not required.

Bottleneck Busters: Rush hour traffic typically backs up on I-5 North and South, I-84 East, and on I-205, and the I-205 Bridge. U.S. 26 (Sunset Highway) and Route 217 (between U.S. 26 and I-5) are also hot spots.

Trains: Amtrak, Portland Union Station, 800 N.W. 6th Ave., 800-872-7245

Bus Service: Greyhound/Trailways Lines, 550 N.W. 6th Ave., 243-2323

Public Transportation: The Tri-Met bus system extensively covers the 3-county area; fares are exact change only. Within a downtown 300-block area, called Fareless Square, service is free. There is also a light rail system called MAX, which travels from downtown past the new Oregon Convention Center, and then on to the city's eastern suburbs. For information call 233-3511.

Road Service and Repairs: AAA, 600 S.W. Market St., 222-6734. 24-hour emergency line, 222-6777; Auto travel information line, 222-6700

Parking Regulations: Streets are metered. Some meters are restricted for car pool use only; parked cars must display a car pool pass. Downtown parking garages are plentiful; full-day rates range anywhere from $8 to $15.
Towed? Call 255-8141

International Travelers
Foreign Currency Exchange: First Interstate Bank of Oregon, 1300 S.W. 5th Ave., 225-2531. Currency exchange services located on the 2nd level of the First Interstate Bank Tower.
Tele-Trip Insurance and Foreign Exchange, Portland Interna-

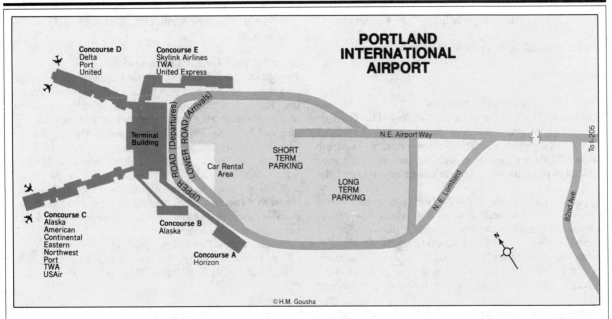

PORTLAND INTERNATIONAL AIRPORT

Concourse D
Delta
Port
United

Concourse E
Skylink Airlines
TWA
United Express

Terminal Building

UPPER ROAD (Departures)
LOWER ROAD (Arrivals)

Car Rental Area

SHORT TERM PARKING

LONG TERM PARKING

N.E. Airport Way

N.E. Lombard

82nd Ave.

To I-205

Concourse C
Alaska
American
Continental
Eastern
Northwest
Port
TWA
USAir

Concourse B
Alaska

Concourse A
Horizon

© H.M. Gousha

tional Airport, 281-3045
Translation Services: Asian Type and Printing Co., 1234 S.E. 7th, 234-3442
Portland Translation Service, 1422 E. Burnside, 232-7440; fax 232-8168
Sarjam Communications Ltd., 4004 S.E. Woodstock, Suite 102, 777-4950; fax 777-8286
Foreign Books and Periodicals: Rich's Cigar Store, 801 S.W. Alder, 228-1700 or 706 N.W. 23rd, 227-6907

Business Visitor's Needs

Banking: First Interstate Bank of Oregon, 1300 S.W. 5th Ave., 225-2531
Key Bank of Oregon, 1211 S.W. 5th Ave., 790-7500
Security Pacific Bank Oregon, 1001 S.W. 5th Ave., 222-7777
U.S. Bank, U.S. Bancorp Tower, 111 S.W. 5th Ave., 275-6111
Full Service Assistance: HQ-Headquarters Companies: 221-0617 (call for other locations)
Secretarial Services: Alpine Secretarial Service: 233-7756
BP&K Professional Office Services: 224-3366
Dixie's Executive Business Services: 222-2715
Copying and Printing: Kinko's: 223-2056 (open 24 hours; fax services; call for other locations)
Pip Printing: 281-8666
Quik Print: 228-6253 (fax services; call for other locations)
Fax Facilities: Try the firms listed under "Copying and Printing," above, as well as:
Minuteman Press: 241-3306; fax 224-5006
Readi-Print: 292-6625; fax 292-8772
Messengers: Custom Courier Service: 223-3648
Pronto Messenger Service: 239-7666; fax 239-7686

Medical Needs: Doctor referral: Multnomah County Medical Society: 222-0156
Dental referral: Multnomah Dental Society: 223-4731
Pharmacies: Mt. Scott Pharmacy: 771-9025
St. Vincent Hospital & Medical Center Pharmacy: 791-2630 (open M-F 7:30am-10:30pm, Sat. 8:30am-4:30pm)
Also: Safeway stores (there are several in Portland) have in-store pharmacies which are open 7 days a week.
Hospitals: Emanuel Hospital & Health Center: 280-3200
Good Samaritan Hospital & Medical Center: 229-7711
Oregon Health Sciences University Hospital: 279-8311

Convention Centers

Memorial Coliseum Complex, 1401 N. Wheeler Ave., 235-8771. Exhibition area: 100,800 sq. feet.
Multnomah County Exposition Center, 2060 N. Marine Dr., 285-7756. Exhibition area: 220,000 sq. feet.
Oregon Convention Center, 777 N.E. Martin Luther King Jr. Blvd., 235-7575. New convention center scheduled to open in the fall of 1990.

Entertainment, Sports, and Culture

Sports: Baseball: The Portland Beavers (AAA Team—affiliate Minnesota Twins), Civic Stadium, 223-2837
Basketball: Portland Trail Blazers, Memorial Coliseum, 231-8000
Hockey: Portland Winter Hawks, Memorial Coliseum, 238-6366
The Arts: Oregon Ballet Theatre: 227-6867
Portland Center for the Performing Arts, 248-4496. Center includes 2 theaters, and is home to the Portland Opera, the Oregon Shakespeare Festival, the Music Theater of Oregon, and the Oregon Symphony. For tickets and information on perfor-

mances in any of the theaters or in the Civic Auditorium, call 248-4496.

Portland Civic Theatre, 226-3048. Musical theater productions. Portland Repertory Theater, 224-4491. Professional Equity theater company.

Dining: Four Stars and Our Stars

Atwater's, 275-3600. Located on the 30th floor of the U.S. Bancorp Tower, Atwater's serves up dazzling views of Portland, as well as delicious Pacific Northwest cuisine. The fresh seafood is always a good bet, although the menu is varied enough to please anyone. Daily for dinner; Sun. brunch 10am to 3pm.

Cajun Cafe and Bistro, 227-0227. Northwest cuisine meets Creole cooking. The result is some spicy seafood. Reservations suggested for this popular spot. Lunch M-F; dinner M-Sat.

Ringside West, 223-1513, and **Ringside Northeast**, 255-0750. Steak and fried chicken in a casual atmosphere. Moderately priced. Ringside West serves dinner only; Ringside Northeast serves breakfast, lunch, and dinner. Both are open 7 days a week.

Harborside Restaurant and Shanghai Lounge, 220-1865. Almost all tables have a stunning view at this riverfront eatery. Seafood and steaks are featured on the menu. Open 11am-11pm; Sun. brunch 10:30am to 2:30pm.

Home Away from Home: Where to Stay

The Heathman Hotel, 1009 S.W. Broadway, 241-4100. Absolutely first class. The Heathman combines the best of the old and new. It is located in an old (1927) palace, complete with all the ornate decorative touches, but it has been recently renovated. Still fairly small, 152 rooms, and near the city's Center for the Performing Arts. Prices ranges from $110 and up for rooms, suites run $150 and up.

Portland Marriott Hotel and Resort, 1401 S.W. Front Ave., 226-7600. Popular for conventions, this 500-room hotel has a pool, health club, spacious rooms, all the amenities a business traveler would expect. Prices: rooms $110 and up, suites $350 and up.

Portland Hilton, 921 S.W. 6th Ave., 226-1611. Located in the heart of the business district, this large, modern hotel (455 rooms) also has an outdoor pool. The hotel has a currency exchange service for foreign visitors. Rooms range from $95 and up, suites $300 and up.

Riverplace Alexis, 1510 S.W. Harbor Way, 228-3233. This lovely, small luxury riverfront hotel (74 rooms and suites) is known for its attentive service. Free continental breakfast. Full health club facilities are available for guests. Rooms start at $130, suites at $170.

The Benson Hotel, 309 S.W. Broadway, 228-2000. This was built in 1913, and was for a long time, the city's premier grand old hotel. Well-situated in the heart of downtown, this 320-room establishment was renovated this year. Guests have privileges at a nearby health club. Rooms $95-$135, suites $250-$425.

Keeping Your Tone Away from Home

Joggers and Bikers: Portland is an outdoor enthusiast's dream. Jogging and bike paths dot the cityscape. Waterfront Park which hugs the Willamette River and is convenient to downtown hotels, has a 2-mile promenade ideal for jogging and bicycling. For the more ambitious there is also the 10-mile-long Terwilliger Path, leading from Portland State University up Terwilliger hill and along Terwilliger Blvd. to Tryon Creek State Park.

Bicycle rentals available from Agape Cycle and Sports, 230-0317.

Health Clubs: YMCA: 294-3311 (call for other locations)

Public Golf Courses: Portland has more than a dozen public golf courses. A sampling:

Colwood National Golf Course: 254-5515

City of Portland Courses: Eastmoreland Golf Course, 775-2900; and Rose City Golf Course, 253-4744

Shopping

Currently there is no sales tax in Oregon.

Nordstrom's and Meier & Frank are 2 full service department stores located downtown. Morgan's Alley and Old Town are filled with offbeat little shops, galleries, and boutiques. Lloyd Center has 100 stores and an indoor skating rink in winter. Pioneer Place is scheduled to open mid-1990 and will have 90 specialty shops including Saks Fifth Avenue.

Florists: Flowers by Dorcas: 227-6454

Richard Calhoun Design Studio: 223-1646

RALEIGH – DURHAM

Area Code: 919
Time Zone: Eastern
Weather: 860-1234
Police: Raleigh, 890-3335; Durham, 560-4427

Raleigh is the state capital of North Carolina, and along with Durham, is one of the fastest-growing areas in the south. Fifteen miles northwest of Raleigh is Research Triangle Park. RTP, as it's called, is the country's largest planned research and development park (6,650 acres), and home to dozens of large companies.
A major university sits at each of the 3 points of Research Triangle: Duke University in Durham, the University of North Carolina in Chapel Hill, and North Carolina State in Raleigh. Major local employers include IBM, Burroughs Wellcome, Northern Telecom, and Liggett & Myers Tobacco Co.
Note: Addresses in this section are in Raleigh unless noted otherwise.

Business Profile
Population (1988): 686,367
Population Growth (1980-1988): 22.3%
Unemployment Rate: 2.3% (Raleigh); 2.6% (Durham)
Fortune 500 Corporate Headquarters: 0

General Information Sources
Capital Area Visitor Center in Raleigh: 733-3456
Raleigh Convention and Visitors Bureau: 834-5900 and 800-868-6666
Durham Convention and Visitors Bureau: 687-0288 and 800-446-8604

Getting There
By Air: Raleigh–Durham International Airport is located 15 miles northwest of downtown Raleigh, and approximately 6 miles southeast from Durham. Information, 840-2123.
Once you've landed: Taxi service is available from the airport to the downtown district of each city and to Research Triangle Park (RTP). A taxi to Raleigh will cost $20-$25; to Durham, about $15-$20, and a cab to RTP will cost $10-$15. Taxis: Raleigh: American Cab, 821-0095; National Cab, 740-7122; Yellow Cab, 832-5814. Durham: Pine St. Taxis, 688-1394; Yellow Cab Co., 682-6111. Raleigh Transportation offers service from the airport to downtown Raleigh and Durham; cost is $14, and 24-hour reservations are required. 821-2111.

Many local hotels have complimentary airport shuttle service.
Limousines (private): Raleigh: CEO Limousine Service, 870-9294; ExecuCoach Limousines, 876-1001. Durham: Airport Express, 596-2361; Carolina Livery Service, 544-5828.
Directions Downtown: To Raleigh: Take I-40 east to Exit 285. Take Wade Ave. East to Downtown Blvd. South. To Durham: Take I-40 West to the Durham Freeway.
Overland Adventures: *Route Map:* The Raleigh Beltline circles the perimeter of the city and provides access to all major highways. I-40, known locally as the "High Tech Highway," links Raleigh, Durham, and RTP. Chapel Hill can be reached via U.S. 501 southwest from Durham, or I-40 to U.S. 501 from Raleigh and RTP. North Carolina Highway 54 also links Raleigh and Chapel Hill.
U.S. 70 also connects Raleigh and Durham; it links up to to I-85 in Durham (which cuts through the city in an east-west direction), and I-95 southeast of Raleigh.
Bottleneck Busters: Traffic jams are a problem. Raleigh's northern section tends to be particularly congested, especially Six Forks Road north. I-40 and I-70 can also be slow-moving. The Raleigh Beltline (which encompasses sections of U.S. 1 and U.S. 64) is also a problem, as are U.S. 1 and U.S. 64 by themselves. Durham's traffic is noticeably lighter; there are few consistent trouble spots.
Radio station WPTF-AM 680 has frequent traffic updates.
Trains: Amtrak, 320 W. Cabarrus St., 833-7594

FLYING TIMES
(in hours)
FROM
Raleigh–Durham
TO
Chicago: 2½
New York: 1½
Miami: 1¾

Bus Service: Greyhound/Trailways Lines and Carolina Trailways, 321 W. Jones St., Raleigh, 828-2567; 820 S. Morgan St., Durham, 687-4800
Road Service and Repairs: Raleigh: AAA 24-hour emergency service and general information, 832-0543. Durham: 24-hour emergency service, 683-1968; AAA information, 489-3306
Towed? Call the general information number for the police: Raleigh, 890-3335; Durham, 560-4427

International Travelers
International Visitors Council: 549-9191
Foreign Currency Exchange: Central Carolina Bank, 111 Corcoran St., Durham, 683-7777
First Citizens Bank, Raleigh–Durham Airport, Terminal C (American Airlines Terminal), 840-5150. Hours: M-F 10am-6pm, 7pm-9pm; weekdays 7pm-9pm
Translation Services: Berlitz Translation Services, 6512 Six Forks Rd, 848-1888
Dialogos International Corp., 8921 Glenwood Ave., 782-2630
DTS Language Services, 100 Europa Dr., Chapel Hill, 942-0666; fax 942-0686
Foreign Books and Periodicals: University News & Sundry, University Mall, Chapel Hill, 967-1230

Business Visitor's Needs:
Banking: First Union National Bank, 234 Fayetteville Street

Mall, 829-6161
North Carolina National Bank: One Hanover Sq., 829-6500; 123 W. Main St., Durham, 956-2000
Wachovia Bank: 227 Fayetteville St., 755-7600; 201 W. Main St., Durham, 683-5211
Full Service Assistance: EBC Office Center (Durham): 544-3513
Executive Dimensions: 781-9000
Secretarial Services: Data Group Management: 848-3237
Kelly Services: 846-1130
Office Solutions: 834-7152
Roger's Word Service: 834-0000; fax 834-4537
Copying and Printing: Alphagraphics Printshops of the Future: 783-5179
Copytron: 832-1196; Durham, 286-1809; Chapel Hill, 933-2679
Kinko's: 832-4533; Durham, 682-4346 (open 24 hours)
Fax and Telex Facilities: Copytron, Kinko's, and EBC Office Centers, listed above, have fax services, as well as:
Mail Boxes Etc. USA (Durham): 382-3030
Sir Speedy Printing Center (Durham): 477-7362 (fax only)
Messengers: A-Plus Delivery Service (Durham): 477-7290
Eastern Courier Corp.: 772-9428
Mr. P's Quik Delivery Service (Durham): 477-6196
Medical Needs: Doctor referral: Wake County Medical Society: 821-2227
Durham-Orange Medical Society (Durham and Chapel Hill): 383-2602
Dental referral: North Carolina Dental Society: 832-1222
Pharmacies: Eckerd Drugs: 847-8663 (call for other locations); Durham, 383-5591 (open 24 hours; call for other locations)
Hospitals: Rex Hospital: 783-3100
Wake Medical Center: 250-8000
Duke University Medical Center (Durham): 684-8111
North Carolina Memorial Hospital (Chapel Hill): 966-4131

Convention Centers

Raleigh Civic and Convention Center, 500 Fayetteville Street Mall, 831-6011; box office 831-6060. Exhibition space: 80,000 sq. feet.
Durham Civic Center and Omni Durham Hotel, 201 Foster St., 683-6664. 71,000 sq. feet of exhibition space.
Also, several of the local hotels have extensive meeting and convention facilities.

Entertainment, Sports, and Culture

Sports: Basketball: Some of the nation's finest college basketball takes place in the Raleigh–Durham area. Atlantic Coast Conference teams include North Carolina State, 737-2106; Duke University, 681-2583; University of North Carolina at Chapel Hill, 962-2296.
The Arts: Durham Symphony: 560-2736
Memorial Hall: 962-1449, Carolina Union box office
North Carolina Symphony Raleigh: 831-6060
Raleigh Civic Symphony: 737-7952

Dining: Four Stars and Our Stars

Angus Barn, Ltd., 787-3505. Specializes in steak and prime rib. Open for dinner 7 days. Reservations recommended.
Bakatsias Cuisine (Durham), 383-8502. Classic French cuisine. Lunch and dinner weekdays, dinner Sat., closed Sun.
Charter Room, Velvet Cloak Inn, 828-0333. Continental cuisine; traditional elegance in the area's premier hotel. Lunch and dinner daily, Sun. brunch.
Top of the Tower, 832-0501. Located at the top of the Holiday in downtown Raleigh.
Bullock's Bar-B-Cue (Durham), 383-3211. Barbecue is a North Carolina specialty; this informal spot is a local favorite.

Home Away from Home: Where to Stay

The Velvet Cloak Inn, 1505 Hillsborough St., 828-0333. The Velvet Cloak Inn is a class act. Fresh flowers are in abundance; high tea is served each afternoon. Rooms $65, suites $125-$300.
Omni Durham Hotel, 201 Foster St., Durham, 683-6664. Convenient to the new Civic Center. Rooms $76-$99, suites $150-$225.
Sheraton Imperial Hotel & Towers, 4700 Emperor Blvd., Morrisville, 941-5050. This is a popular convention hotel. Full fitness facilities.. Rooms $88-$98, suites $150-$170. Towers: rooms $105-$135, suites $160-$400.
Raleigh Marriott Crabtree Valley, 4500 Marriott Dr., U.S. 70W near Crabtree Valley Mall, 781-7000. Rooms $109-$119. Luxury level $115-$125.
North Raleigh Hilton & Convention Center, 3415 Old Wake Forest Rd., 872-2323. Large hotel, popular for meetings. Rates: $74-$109, suites $110-$375. Executive Towers: rooms $99-$109, suites $275-$375. Airport transportation is free.
Guest Quarters (formerly the Pickett Suite), 2515 Meridian Pkwy., Research Triangle Park, 361-4660. All-suite hotel. Rooms start at $109. Ask about corporate rates.

Keeping Your Tone Away from Home

Joggers and Bikers: In Raleigh, popular jogging spots include Shelley Lake and the track at North Carolina State University. Raleigh has set aside 20 miles of paths for bicycling; maps and information are available from the Raleigh Parks and Recreation Department at 831-6640 or 831-6575. In Durham, The Sheraton Imperial Hotel has jogging trails.

Shopping

The Crabtree Valley Mall in Raleigh is the area's largest. It has over 200 stores, including The Limited, Crabtree & Evelyn, Waldenbooks, and Benetton. Raleigh's North Hills Mall's tenants include J.C.Penney, Jos A. Bank Clothiers, and The Gap. In Durham, Northgate Mall's shops include The Limited, Paul Harris, and Esprit Sport. Brightleaf Square is a downtown shopping complex set in a renovated tobacco warehouse. In Chapel Hill try the University Mall. Sales tax is 5%.
Florists: Carlton: 821-3862
Sanders Florist (Durham): 286-1288

SAN ANTONIO

Area Code: 512
Time Zone: Central
Weather: 223-1400
Police: 299-7484
Emergency: 911

When thinking of an appealing business location, one would do well to remember San Antonio. Retaining its Spanish heritage—embodied by its river which meanders 20 feet beneath the business district and its famous missions—San Antonio is a modern city that has shed a long shadow from its gunslinging days. Its diverse economy includes manufacturing of oil field equipment and airplane parts as well as tourism and 5 military bases. And San Antonio is one of the Southwest's leaders in medical research. Living costs are quite low, but a plentiful workforce may need extensive training and language education. It's hard to "Remember the Alamo" in the new, pro-business atmosphere of San Antonio.

Business Profile
Population: 785,023
Population Growth (1980-1987): 2.8%
Unemployment Rate: 6.3%
Fortune 500 Corporate Headquarters: 2

General Information Sources
San Antonio Convention and Visitors Bureau:
270-8700
Visitors' Information Center: 299-8155
Greater San Antonio Chamber of Commerce:
229-2100

Getting There
By Air: San Antonio International Airport (SAIA) general information: 821-3411
Once you've landed: VIA Metropolitan Transit has an Express Airport Bus No. 12 to the downtown area. The bus leaves the airport between 6:30am and 6:25pm M-F. The fare is 75 cents. Service from downtown to the airport begins at 6am; hop on the bus downtown at Commerce and Alamo. Information and schedules, 227-2020.
A 15-minute taxi ride from SAIA to downtown will cost about $12. Since taxis are difficult to signal from the street, look for them at major hotels or at taxi stands. Taxi Express, 222-2222; Yellow Cab, 226-4242.
Limousines (private): Services request 24-hour notice. Fiesta Limousine Service, Inc., 431-LIMO (431-5466); River City Limo, 824-2275
Directions Downtown: From the airport take Airport Blvd.

over the overpass of 410 Loop and pick up I-37. Stay on this highway for 8 miles when exit signs for downtown will appear.

Overland Adventures: *Route Map:* San Antonio is surrounded by 410 Loop. In addition to this super highway are 3 interstates: I-10 runs east and northwest; I-37 runs south; I-35 runs northeast and southwest. The central downtown area was built around the San Antonio River—the streets are like spokes on a wheel radiating out from the downtown hub.
Driving Regulations: Seat belts required, $25-$50 fine. Right turn on red unless otherwise indicated. Left turn on red from one-way to one-way.
Bottleneck Busters: Downtown has been under construction for 3 years, check such papers as *San Antonio Light* and *Express-News* for daily traffic updates.
Trains: Amtrak operates an Intercity Rail Passenger Service from its 1174 E. Commerce St. location, 223-3226. For information and schedules call 800-872-7245.
Bus and Streetcar Service: VIA Metropolitan Transit Service, 227-2020, provides both bus service and streetcar service along 5 routes.

Greyhound/Trailways Lines suburban bus stations are in 3 locations: 10014 McCullough, 340-5437; 151 Crossroads Blvd., 732-7441; 700 Division, 923-3787. Greyhound/Trailways serves such western locations as Laredo, Houston, Dallas, and Austin. For fares and schedules call 270-5800.
Road Service and Repairs: For 24-hour road repair or towing call: AAA, 736-4691; Alamo Wrecker Service, 227-0652; Perez Gulf Service, 223-7353.
Parking Regulations: Since limited street parking is available, use the many garages and parking lots.
Towed? Call the San Antonio Car Pound, 299-7455

FLYING TIMES (in hours)	
FROM	
San Antonio	
TO	
Chicago:	2¾
Los Angeles:	3½
New York:	4
Miami:	3

International Travelers
Foreign Currency Exchange: International Bank of Commerce, 1500 N.E. Loop 410, 828-2500
NCNB Texas San Antonio Banking Center, 300 Convent, 270-5555
Translation Services: Ad-Ex Worldwide: 800-223-7753
Berlitz Translation Services: 681-8944
Consulates: Honduras Consulate General: 342-1011
Mexican Consulate General: 227-9145
Foreign Books and Periodicals: Alamo News Bookstore, 110 Broadway, 223-3133

Business Visitor's Needs
Banking: Frost National Bank, 100 W. Houston St., 220-4011
NBC Bank-San Antonio, 430 Soledad St., 225-2511
Secretarial Services: Ande & Associates: 366-3891
Kelly Services: 680-1000
Copying and Printing: Kinko's: 732-1177 (open 24 hours)

Kwik-Kopy Printing: 828-5845
Messengers: Mission Couriers: 377-2387
Telex Facilities: BCS-Western Union: 525-8461
Communication Services, Inc.: 657-9755
Medical Needs: Doctor referral: Physician Referral-Humana Hospital San Antonio: 692-8242
Dental referral: San Antonio District Dental Society: 732-1264
Pharmacy: Drug Emporium: 680-4169
Hospitals: Baptist Medical Center: 222-8431
Humana Hospital San Antonio: 692-8110
Santa Rosa: 228-2011

Convention Centers
The San Antonio Convention Center, HemisFair Plaza, Market St., 299-8500, is a very large all-purpose facility. Within its structure are 2 exhibition halls, 2 banquet halls, 46 meeting rooms, and a total of 793,506 sq. feet. The theater for the performing arts and the arena together seat almost 19,000 people. The San Antonio Municipal Auditorium, 100 Auditorium Circle, 270-8800, has 24,000 sq. feet of meeting and exhibition space on its lower level and can seat almost 5,000 people in the main hall.

Entertainment, Sports, and Culture
Ticket Services: Ticketmaster: 800-992-8000
Sports: Baseball: Los Angeles Dodgers AA Farm Team, V.J. Keefe Field, 434-9311
Basketball: Spurs, Convention Center Arena, 224-9578
The Arts: Alamo City Theatre: 734-4646
Arneson River Theatre: 299-8610
San Antonio Little Theater: 733-7258
The San Antonio Performing Arts Association, 224-8187, promotes interesting and varied repertory around town. The season runs from mid-September to mid-May.
The San Antonio Symphony, 554-1010, attracts quality performers and conductors.

Dining: Four Stars and Our Stars
Three Stars: La Provence, 225-0722. Reservations are necessary and the menu is heavily French. Located in a renovated 1920s mansion, the pianist complements the elegance. Moderately priced.
Our Stars: Settlement Inn, 698-2580. This former stagecoach stop has the flavor of the old West with its outdoor dining, barbecue pits, and specialties of barbecued brisket, sausage, and ribs. Reasonably priced.

Home Away from Home: Where to Stay
La Mansion Del Rio, 112 College St., 225-2581. Offering either courtyard or river views, the hotel is located by the San Antonio River. Singles range from $110-$185. The hotel books up quickly for the April Fiesta.
Four Seasons San Antonio, 555 S. Alamo, 229-1000, 800-421-

1172. Tiled courtyards, private patios, and balconies plus an abundance of amenities. Singles start at $140.
St. Anthony Park Lane, 300 E. Travis, 227-4392. This charmingly renovated 1909 hotel has antiques, afternoon tea, a roof garden, and excellent service. Singles begin at $85.

Keeping Your Tone Away from Home
Joggers and Bikers: Friedrich Park sports spectacular wilderness trails. Be sure to jog with a friend or partner. Likewise, San Antonio Missions Hike and Bike Trail can be isolated so make sure you aren't alone. You won't want to miss the 3 or 4 missions along the trail. Bicycle rentals: Four Seasons San Antonio rents bikes to its guests.
Health Clubs: International Fitness Center: 349-3911
Presidents Health Club: 647-9600
YMCA: 227-5221
YWCA: 692-9922
Public Golf Courses: Carpenters Golf Range and Par Three: 696-3143
Devine Golf Association: 663-9943

Shopping
For designer goods from such stores as Saks Fifth Avenue and Marshall Field's, go to North Star Mall. For leisurely walking, try Rivercenter—the San Antonio River, river cafes, crafts people, and 135 shops are all housed in a glass structure. For antiques and collectibles, try the Antique Sampler Mall. Marketsquare, El Mercado, west of downtown, offers Mexican and Central American attractions. Joske's and Frost's are 2 traditional downtown department stores.
Florists: Alamo Plants and Petals: 828-2628
Flowers to Go: 524-1003
The Rose Shop: 732-1161

SAN DIEGO

Area Code: 619
Time Zone: Pacific
Weather: 289-1212
Police: 236-5911
Emergency: 911

San Diego can't help being popular; who wouldn't enjoy the sunny climate and beautiful ocean sweeps. Fortune 500 ranks this city as the fastest-growing of the 31 cities polled. High-tech companies are locating here, helping San Diego's economy diversify (from a Navy town into a biomedical research and aerospace manufacturing center). Rohr Industries and General Dynamics are big employers, but the military bases and tourism are economic lifelines for the area. Both the San Diego Zoo—one of the world's finest—and the San Diego Wild Animal Park, set miles away in the natural mountain-desert climes, are spectacular San Diego attractions.

Business Profile
Population: 2,403,000
Population Growth (1980-1989): 29.1%
Unemployment Rate: 4.3%
Fortune 500 Corporate Headquarters: 4

General Information Sources
San Diego Convention and Visitors Bureau: 232-3101
San Diego Chamber of Commerce: 232-0124

Getting There
By Air: San Diego International Airport (SAN) general information: 231-5220; traveler's aid desk, 231-7361. SAN is sometimes referred to as Lindbergh Field.
Once you've landed: SAN is simple to understand and to get around; East and West Terminals abut each other and are within a few minutes walk to the baggage claim.
Taxi rides are a quick way to reach downtown San Diego. It is advisable to agree upon a fare beforehand since taxis are deregulated. The usual cost is about $6, and the ride takes about 10 minutes. Co-op Silver Cabs, 280-5555; Orange Cab (Independent Cab Owners Association), 291-3333; Yellow Cab of San Diego, Inc., 234-6161
Van rides are offered by 2 services, Peerless Vans, 800-367-4093, and Greg Ware Limos, 280-1789. These shared-ride vans cost about $4 one way, and operate 24 hours daily.
Limousines (private): Service is available with 24-hour reservations. Distinctive Limousine, 692-3263; Liberty Limousines of San Diego, Inc., 579-9910; Travel and Limousine Enterprises, 279-3344

FLYING TIMES
(in hours)
FROM
San Diego
TO
Chicago: 5
Los Angeles: ½
New York: 5
Miami: 5¼

Directions Downtown: San Diego is 3 miles southeast of SAN. When leaving the airport, follow the signs for Harbor Rd. and downtown San Diego. Harbor Rd. is a direct route to downtown.
Overland Adventures: *Route Map:* One half-hour south of San Diego is Mexico. Next to the Pacific Ocean, San Diego is bordered by Anza-Borrego Desert State Park to the east and is 90 miles away from Disneyland and Los Angeles to the north. Via I-5, which stretches from Mexico to Canada, San Diego is just a few hours from Los Angeles. I-8 connects the city with Yuma, AZ. I-15 serves Riverside County, NV, and the inter-mountain West. The Pacific Coast Highway is a particularly scenic way to see the California coast.
Driving Regulations: Right turn on red is permitted unless otherwise posted. Left turn from a one way street to a one way street is permitted. Seatbelts are mandatory; failure to buckle-up results in a $20 fine.
Bottleneck Busters: Tune into KFMB 100.7 FM on your radio for the latest in traffic updates, but generally traffic is as laid back as the city.
Trains: Amtrak, 1050 Ketna Blvd., 239-9021 or 800-872-7245. Provides daily passenger service to and from Los Angeles.
Bus Service: Greyhound/Trailways Lines Travel Services, 120 Broadway, 800-528-0447
Public Transportation: San Diego Transit Corporation, 233-3004 or 238-0100. The public bus system has many routes in San Diego. The local bus fare is $1 and express bus fare is $1.25. The San Diego Transit Store, 449 Broadway at Fifth Ave., has tickets and passes for sale and route information.
San Diego Trolley, Inc., 231-8549. This rail system has a South Line which is a 40-minute ride from downtown to Mexico, and an East Line which provides service to East County. Water Taxi Service began a year ago, and it serves the Convention Center, San Diego Bay hotels, restaurants, and attractions. Contact Harbor Hopper, 229-8294, for further information.
Road Service and Repairs: AAA Auto Club, 668-0250
Towed? Call Police Impound, 531-2844

International Travelers
International Services: International Visitor Information Center, 11 Horton Plaza at 1st Ave. and F St., 236-1212
Foreign Currency Exchange: Deak International, 177 Horton Plaza, 235-0900
San Diego International Airport: Tele-Trip Insurance, 295-1501 and California East Bank in the East Terminal, 230-4340
Translation Services: Berlitz Translation Services, 7801 Mission Center Court, 297-8392
International Visitor Information Center, 11 Horton Plaza at 1st Ave. and F St., 236-1212
Consulate: Mexican Consulate: 231-8414
Foreign Books and Periodicals: Butler & Mays Booksellers, 8657

Villa La Jolla Dr., La Jolla, 450-1698
Para Newsstand, 3911 30th St.,
296-2859

Business Visitor's Needs
Banking: Bank America, 450 B St.,
230-5463
San Diego Trust and Savings, 530
Broadway, 557-2200
Union Bank, 445 S. Figueroa, 230-
4567
Secretarial Services: A Personal
Touch: 238-1623
Kelly Services: 268-2290
Copying and Printing: Pip Print-
ing: 239-2079
Sir Speedy: 231-2799
Messengers: Courier Express: 292-4668
Telegram Facilities: Western Union: 236-0777
Medical Needs: Doctor referral: Hillside Hospital Doctor Re-
ferral Service: 297-2251
Dental referral: Dental Society Referral Service: 223-5391
Pharmacies: Fed Rx Pharmacy: 279-3600
Uptown Pharmacy: 291-7377
Hospitals: UCSD Medical Center: 543-6222
Hillside Hospital: 297-2251
Mercy Hospital: 294-8111

Convention Centers
Convention Center, 111 West Harbor Dr., 525-5000. This facility has 760,000 sq. feet of space. The roof structure is particularly striking because of the sail motif.
Convention and Performing Arts Center, 202 C St., 236-6500
or 236-6510. A multi-purpose convention and arts complex.

Entertainment, Sports, and Culture
Ticket Services: Teleseat, 283-SEAT (238-7328)or 452-1950;
Ticketmaster, 298-5070 for recorded information, 278-8479 to
charge tickets
Sports: Baseball: Padres, Jack Murphy Stadium, 283-4494
Football: Chargers, Jack Murphy Stadium, 280-2111; 563-8281
for tickets
The Arts: Ticket Services: Times Arts Tix Center, 238-3810.
Half-price tickets; cash only.
The Civic Theatre, Convention and Performing Arts Center,
236-6510. Provides plays, ballets, and a variety of concerts.
Edison Center for the Performing Arts, 239-2255, is home to
the Old Globe Theatre, Cassius Carter Center Stage, and Festival Stage. A variety of programs from Shakespeare to musical treats can be found here.

Dining: Four Stars and Our Stars
Four Stars: Islandia Bar and Grill, 224-1234. The beauti-

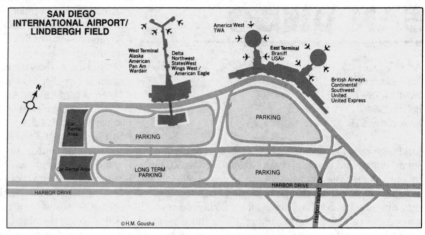

ful Mission Bay vistas make the outdoor dining in the summer months a must. The specialty of the house is seafood.
Le Fontainebleau, 238-1818. Splendid 17th-century furnishings, oil paintings, and antiques surround diners who can expect a French menu.
Our Stars: Lubach's, 232-5129. From Lubach's, diners can
catch the panoramic view of the Bay and in the winter
months, the fireplaces are welcome. The menu is continental,
the specialties are Dover sole and sea bass sauté.

Home Away from Home: Where to Stay
San Diego Marriott, 333 W. Harbor Dr., 234-1500. Single
rooms cost $130-$180.
Westgate, 1055 2nd Ave., 238-1818. Single rooms are $114-
$134. A central downtown location; expect concierge, health
club, free transportation, and high tea.
Rancho Bernardo Inn, 17550 Bernardo Oaks Dr., 487-1611.
Single rooms cost $150-$175.

Keeping Your Tone Away from Home
Joggers and Bikers: The best place for jogging and
biking is extensive Balboa Park, with marked jogging and
biking trails.

Shopping
The most modern and up-to-date shopping can be found at
Horton Plaza in downtown San Diego. For boutiques and art
galleries, try Girard Ave. and Prospect St. in La Jolla. For local
Mexican and South American wares, Bazaar del Mundo and
Galleria are 2 good places in Old Town. Antique worshippers
should try T and R Antiques Warehouse, Inc.
Sales tax in San Diego is 7 1/4%.
Florists: A Crowning Touch: 696-9601
Broadway Florist: 239-1228

SAN FRANCISCO

Area Code: 415, 408 (Telephone numbers in this section are within the 415 calling area unless otherwise noted.)
Time Zone: Pacific
Weather: 936-1212
Police: 553-0123

San Francisco claims to be everybody's favorite city and to be a window on the world. Offering 40 hills with spectacular water views, international dining and shopping, and a world-renowned wine country, it's no wonder that San Francisco's tourism industry is thriving. Located on the western edge of the continent, San Francisco's bay and port are important links to the Orient. Companies like Chevron, Bank of America, and Apple Computer have helped to make the area's economy prosper, and at the same time have attracted bright and skilled workers who can afford the steep cost of living. The same excitement that energized San Francisco during the gold rush is alive today in this cosmopolitan city.

Business Profile
Population: 6,118,000
Population Growth (1980-1989): 38.2%
Unemployment Rate: 3.7%
Fortune 500 Corporate Headquarters: 27

General Information Sources
San Francisco Convention and Visitors Bureau: 974-6900
San Francisco Chamber of Commerce: 392-4511

Getting There
By Air: San Francisco International Airport (SFO) general information: 761-0800
Oakland International Airport general information: 577-4015
San Jose International Airport general information: 408-277-4759
Once you've landed: SFO has 3 terminals: North, South, and International. Use the covered walkways or try the intra-terminal shuttle service which circles the upper level and operates daily, early morning-midnight. The North and South Terminals handle domestic flights. On the upper level find the intra-airport shuttle service and the car rental parking lot. The lower level has baggage claims, hotel information, bus schedules, car rental agencies, taxi stands, buses and vans.
Taxi rides to downtown take 20 minutes. The flat rate for anywhere in town is about $24, but up to 5 people can share a ride. Luxor Cab, 282-4141; Yellow Cab, 444-1234.
The SFO Airporter provides daily van service to major downtown hotels and Union Square. Vans leave every 20 minutes and cost $4 one way, $7 round trip.

Quite a few vans offer door-to-door service. Reservations are required, and drop-off and pick-up are on the center island of the upper level. Shared rides within the city limits cost $7. Downtown Airport Express, 775-5121; Good Neighbors Airport Shuttle, 777-4899, Lorrie's, 334-9000; Supershuttle, 558-8500; Yellow Airport Shuttle, 282-7433.
Limousines (private): Service is available with 24-hour reservations. A-1 Limousine Service, 550-0331; Gateway Limousine Service, 345-7077; Sam's Limousine Service, 567-LIMO; Silver Cloud Limousine Service, 821-3851
Directions Downtown: San Francisco is 14 miles north of the airport. Follow the airport signs for San Francisco and take U.S. 101 North. Exit on 3rd or 5th Sts., both lead to downtown Market St.
Overland Adventures: *Route Map:* San Francisco is on the tip of a peninsula surrounded by the Pacific Ocean and San Francisco Bay. Although the city's streets are particularly hilly, they are in a grid pattern and are fairly simple to follow. The city has distinct sections like the Financial District, Chinatown, Nob Hill, North Beach, Mission District, and the once infamous 60s hangout, Haight-Ashbury. Several interstates and highways make travel through the Bay Area palatable. I-5, just east of the city, serves a northern route to Oregon and a southern route to Los Angeles. I-580 joins I-5 at San Jose. By traveling northwest on I-580, it's possible to go to Oakland, which is opposite San Francisco across the San Francisco Bay in Alameda County. At Oakland, the choices are I-80 across the Oakland Bay Bridge to San Francisco, or I-80 northeast to Lake Tahoe. I-680 is the north and south bypass of Oakland connecting I-80 north of Oakland with I-580 south of Oakland. I-280 runs north and south between San Jose and San Francisco. Route 1 serves points north all along the Pacific coast.

Bottleneck Busters: Coming up the peninsula via the freeways or from the bridges, drivers may expect problems from the city's crosstown traffic. Traffic jams occur daily during rush hour at the approaches to the Bay Bridge. Steep hills may complicate things for visitors. Try the California Road Conditions Report at 557-3755.
Trains: Amtrak, Transby Terminal, 1st and Mission Sts., 800-USA-RAIL (800-872-7245).
CalTrain Peninsula Commute Service, 4th and Townsend Sts., 557-8661 or 800-558-8661 (from Northern California), has daily trains between San Francisco and San Jose.
Bus Service: Greyhound/Trailways Lines, Transby Terminal, 1st and Mission Sts., 558-6789
AC Transit, Transby Terminal, 839-2882. AC is an East Bay communities bus service which has routes between Oakland and San Francisco via the Oakland-Bay Bridge.
Golden Gate Transit, Transby Terminal, 332-6600. Bus service is provided between Marin and Sonoma Counties via the Golden Gate Bridge.

FLYING TIMES
(in hours)
FROM
San Francisco
TO
Chicago: 4½
Los Angeles: 1
New York: 5
Miami: 5½

SamTrans, Transby Terminal, 367-1500. This bus service provides rides between San Francisco and San Francisco International Airport. Service further south to places like Palo Alto is also available.

Public Transportation: Bay Area Rapid Transit (BART), 788-BART (788-2278). BART has 71 miles of rail, and its fleet links 8 San Francisco stations with Daly City to the south. In the Oakland area, BART links 25 stations to East Bay. Trains operate daily 6am until midnight M-Sat., Sundays from 9am until midnight. Obtain tickets from the station machines; a $2.50 ticket entitles a passenger to "ride forever" while remaining on the train. Exact change machines are in the stations; color-coded wall maps explain routes and destinations.

San Francisco Municipal Railway (MUNI), 673-MUNI (673-6864). This multi-transportation system includes light rail vehicles, electric buses, motor coaches, trolley, and cable cars. Muni Metro or light rail vehicles operate underground downtown and on the streets in the outer neighborhoods. Owl Service motor coaches are the transporters during the hours of midnight to 6am and serve major transit routes. Fare is 85 cents in exact change.

Cable Cars, a part of the MUNI service, has 3 routes which operate between the financial district and Nob Hill hotels: Powell-Hyde, Powell-Mason, and California Street lines. The Powell lines operate north and south routes, and the California line operates east and west routes.

Ferries: Ferry service across the Bay is provided by Golden Gate Ferries, Ferry Building on Market St., 332-6600; and Red and White Fleet, Pier 41, Fisherman's Wharf, 546-2896.

Road Service and Repairs: AAA, 863-3432

Towed? Call the city police non-emergency number, 553-0123

International Travelers

International Services: International Visitors Center, 312 Sutter St., Suite 402, 986-1388

Foreign Currency Exchange: American Foreign Exchange, 315 Sutter St., 391-9913

Bank of America, SFO International Terminal, 742-8079; Powell and Market Sts., 622-4498

Citicorp, SFO International Terminal, 627-6000

Deak International, SFO International Terminal, 583-4029; 100 Grant Ave., 362-3452

Translation Services: AT&T Communications Center, SFO International , lower level

Berlitz Language and Translation Services, 660 Market St., 986-6474; 430 Cambridge Ave., Palo Alto, 323-0076

Langauge Resource Institute, 1336 Polk St., 441-8145

Foreign Books and Periodicals: De Lauer's, 1300 Broadway, Oakland, 451-6157

Printer's Ink, 310 California Ave., Palo Alto, 327-6500

Business Visitor's Needs

Banking: Bank of America, 345 Montgomery, 622-9472

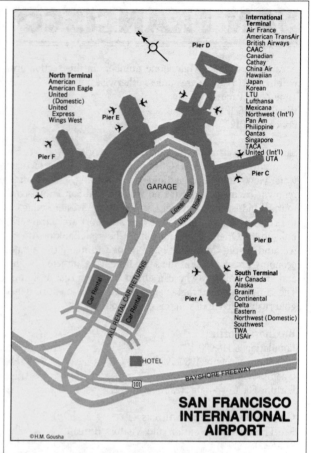

SAN FRANCISCO INTERNATIONAL AIRPORT

International Terminal: Air France, American TransAir, British Airways, CAAC, Canadian, Cathay, China Air, Hawaiian, Japan, Korean, LTU, Lufthansa, Mexicana, Northwest (Int'l), Pan Am, Philippine, Qantas, Singapore, TACA, United (Int'l), UTA

North Terminal: American, American Eagle, United (Domestic), United Express, Wings West

South Terminal: Air Canada, Alaska, Braniff, Continental, Delta, Eastern, Northwest (Domestic), Southwest, TWA, USAir

©H.M. Gousha

Citibank International, 1 Sansome St., 627-6008

Secretarial Services: Kelly Services: 982-2200; 852-9922 in Palo Alto

Office Overload: 434-3770

Copying and Printing: Copy Factory: 781-2990

Kinko's (Palo Alto): 328-3381

Pip Printing: 421-7703

Messengers: Aero Special Delivery Service: 982-1303

Quicksilver Messenger Service: 495-4360

US Courier: 676-1213; 408-295-2992 in San Jose, Silicon Valley

Telex Facilities: Western Union: 956-1171

Medical Needs: Doctor referral:

Physician Referral: 991-6677

Dental referral: San Francisco Dental Society: 421-1435

Pharmacies: Merrill's Drug Center: 781-1669

Walgreen's: 391-4433

Hospitals: The Medical Center at the University of California, San Francisco: 476-1000

St. Francis Memorial Hospital: 775-4321

San Francisco General Hospital: 821-8200

Seton Medical Center: 992-4000

Convention Centers

Civic Auditorium and Brooks Hall, Grove and Polk Sts., 974-4058 or 974-4060, consists of the auditorium, 2 other halls, a main arena, and the adjoining Brooks Hall. This facility can handle about 8,000 people, 600 booths, and 800 cars.

Moscone Center, 747 Howard St., 974-4000, has an 11-acre site, a main exhibit hall which can be divided into 3 sections, meeting rooms, and a ballroom. The Center has 261,000 sq. feet, seats for 17,000 people, 43 meeting rooms, and parking for 4,000 cars. In addition, the use of closed circuit TV and simultaneous translation are available.

The Cow Palace, Geneva Ave. and Rio Verde St., 469-6065 or 469-6000, has 4 exhibit arenas, meeting rooms, 3 restaurants, food stands, cocktail bars, and a catering service. Located on the southern edge of the city, the Palace has about 270,000 sq. feet, seats for 14,500 people, 6 meeting rooms for up to 600 people, and parking for 5,000 cars.

Entertainment, Sports, and Culture

Ticket Services: Bass, 762-2277; Ticketron, 392-7469 or 243-9001; STUBS, 433-7827 (half-price same-day tickets)

Sports: Baseball: Giants, Candlestick Park, 467-8000
Oakland Athletics, Oakland Coliseum, 638-0500
Football: 49ers, Candlestick Park, 468-2249

The Arts: Louise B. Davies Symphony Hall, Civic Center, 431-5400, is home to the San Francisco Symphony.

The Opera House, Civic Center, is home to both San Francisco Opera, 864-3330, and San Francisco Ballet, 621-3838.

Dining: Four Stars and Our Stars

Ernie's, 397-5969. A la carte prices are expensive, but Ernie's specializes in a top-of-the-line wine list and diners rub elbows with celebrities.

Donatello, 441-7182. Donatello is formal, ornate, and has the best northern Italian cuisine. Expensive.

Washington Square Bar and Grill Restaurant (North Beach), 982-8124. Offers late-night dining, live jazz, and a menu that changes daily. Prices are moderate.

Pacific Heights Bar and Grill (Pacific Heights), 567-3337. An oyster bar featuring 17 varieties of oysters and fresh seafood is the main attraction. Revel in the restored Victorian setting while sipping a glass of California wine. Moderately priced.

Chez Panisse Grill (Berkeley), 548-5525. Be ready for a 5-course menu set daily. Cafe dining is also available. Moderately expensive.

Doros, 397-6822. Doros has won awards for their wine list, and the very best continental menu offers tantalizing selections like veal picatta with capers.

Kan's, 982-2388. This Cantonese menu is unbeatable. The prices are right; reservations a must.

Lion and Compass (Sunnyvale, Silicon Valley), 408-745-1260. Very popular with business people, the restaurant has a good wine selection and a ticker tape service.

Home Away from Home: Where to Stay

Four Seasons Clift, 495 Geary St., 775-4700. Single rooms are $150-$235. This hotel is quiet yet quite fashionable, well-equipped for business people yet offers personalized service.

The Stanford Court, 905 California St., Nob Hill, 989-3500. A lavish hotel: Antiques, marble bathrooms, and oversized beds make this a traveler's heaven. Singles $145-$210.

Westin St. Francis, 335 Powell St., 397-7000. Single rooms are $125-$215. This hotel has a marvelous location across the street from Union Square and a short walk to the financial district.

Hotel Huntington, 1075 California St., Nob Hill, 474-5400. Single rooms are $140-$210. The spectacular views of the Bay and of the city make these rooms unmatchable. Concierge, health club, and uniquely decorated rooms are standard fare.

Campton Place, 340 Stockton St., 781-5555. Singles are $170-$230. In the heart of the financial district, this small hotel has an excellent location and tremendous service; service with a smile is in the European tradition. Tennis club, Nob Hill Club, and resplendent furnishings are the guest's privileges.

Hyatt Palo Alto, 4290 El Camino Real, Palo Alto (Silicon Valley), 493-0800. Single rooms are $140. Amenities include tennis, pool, and exercise room. Both Tempo's bar and the Echo Italian restaurant are here.

Keeping Your Tone Away from Home

Joggers and Bikers: Try markéd bike routes at Golden Gate Park or the south end of the city across the Golden Gate Bridge into Marin County. Bike rentals are available in Golden Gate Park or along Stanyan St. and Geary Blvd. Golden Gate Park is the best place for joggers. Park headquarters, 441-5705.

Health Clubs: Decathlon Club (Santa Clara, Silicon Valley): 408-738-8743
Nob Hill Club: 397-2770
Physis: 989-7310

Shopping

World-class shopping abounds in the city. The streets to remember are Post and Sutter. Union Square has big-time department stores like Saks Fifth Avenue. Brooks Brothers and Wilkes Bashford are 2 fine men's clothing stores. For an adventure in jade and other fine items, Gumps is the place. Pier 39 on Embarcadero has specialty shops. A few blocks away from Fisherman's Wharf are some great shopping centers: The Cannery, The Anchorage and Ghirardelli Square. Finally, for antique-browsers, try Collective Antiques and Telegraph Hill Antiques. Sales tax is 7 1/4%.

Florists: Ah Sam (San Mateo, Silicon Valley): 341-5611
Floratek: 563-1166
Rossi and Rovetti Flowers and Gifts: 566-2260
Somewhere In Time: 882-9696

SEATTLE

Area Code: 206
Time Zone: Pacific
Weather: 382-7246
Police: 526-6087
Emergency: 911

Located on Puget Sound in the northwest corner of Washingotn State, Seattle is an important gateway to the Far East, the North, and the Pacific Rim countries. Because of Seattle's terrific harbor, American President and Hanjin Container Lines are important industries. Lockheed and Todd Shipyards are kept busy building and repairing boats. Boeing, PACCAR, Weyerhauser, and Microsoft are also large corporations bolstering Washington's economy, the fastest-growing in the U.S. With its 150-year-old logging camp history, Seattle is an attractive and verdant city which prides itself on maintaining such attractions as the Klondike Gold Rush National Historic Park and the waterfront's Pike Place Market.

Business Profile
Population: 491,000
Population Growth (1980-1989): 13.8%
Unemployment Rate: 3.9%
Fortune 500 Corporate Headquarters: 3

General Information Sources
Seattle-King County Convention and Visitor's Bureau: 461-5840
Greater Seattle Chamber of Commerce: 461-7200
Seattle-King County Economic Development Council: 386-5040

Getting There
By Air: Seattle-Tacoma International Airport (Sea-Tac) public information: 433-4645
Sea-Tac Skyline, a computer-operated system, provides the following information on a 24-hour basis: parking, ground transportation alternatives, schedules and rates, airport weather, and air traffic conditions, 431-4444 or 800-544-1965. The facility also has an all-night post office.
Once you've landed: Regular subway service running every 2 minutes links the 2 satellite concourses with the main terminal. The Grayline Airport Express Charter Bus, 626-6088, leaves every 15-30 minutes from 5:30am-12am and costs about $6. The Express makes connections with downtown Seattle.
A 20-30 minute taxi ride even during rush hour is probably the most efficient transportation from the airport to the business district and will cost approximately $20. Taxi's: Farwest, 622-1717; Yellow Cab, 622-6500. Major credit cards accepted.

FLYING TIMES (in hours)
FROM
Seattle
TO
Chicago: **3**
Los Angeles: **2½**
New York: **6**
Miami: **6**

Limousines (private): 24-hour advance reservations. Elite Limousine Service operating 24 hours daily, 575-2332.
Directions Downtown: Follow airport signs for I-5 North and 518 East. Take 518 East to I-5 North. Seattle is 13 miles north of Sea-Tac, and you will take either the Madison St. or Seneca St. exits to get to the downtown business district.
Overland Adventures: *Route Map:* I-5 runs north and south bisecting both Seattle and its airport. Continuing north of Seattle it connects with Everett and Canada, and continuing south it connects with Tacoma, Portland, and California. I-405, parallel to I-5, acts as a beltway around Seattle and runs through Bellevue, which is Seattle's rapidly growing Silicon Valley. I-405 connects with I-5 north and south of Lake Washington. Highway 520 and I-90 run east and west across Lake Washington and connect I-5 and I-405 by the use of floating bridges; Evergreen Floating Bridge (Highway 520) is to the north, and Mercer Island Bridge (I-90) is to the south.
Bottleneck Busters: In the downtown area, beware of Pike Street. Since the Metro bus tunnel is undergoing repairs, this street is closed. On I-405, both north and south of Seattle, traffic is slow due to construction.
Trains: Amtrak, 3rd and South Jackson, 800-USA-RAIL (800-872-7245)

Bus Service: Greyhound/Trailways Lines Terminal, 8th Ave. and Stewart St., 624-3456. Cascade Trailways, 728-5955; departures from Greyhound Terminal.
Public Transportation: Metro operates a wide range of bus services for Seattle and Cook County between the hours of 5:21am and 12:20am, 447-4800. A monorail connects Seattle's shopping area at 4th St. and Pine with the Seattle Center.
Road Service and Repairs: AAA Washington Emergency Road Service, 448-5409 or 800-637-2010 from within Washington state (open 24 hours); Airport Towing, 243-6252.
Towed? Call 684-5444

International Travelers
International Services: International flights arriving at Sea-Tac's South Satellite will find translation services, interpreters, and foreign currency exchange.
Translation Services: Berlitz Translation Services, 1525 4th Ave., Suite 710, 682-0312
Red Cross Language Bank, 1900 25th Ave. S., 323-2345
Consulates: British Consulate-Seattle: 622-9255
Canadian Consulate General: 443-1777
Coordination Council for North American Affairs-Republic of China in Taiwan: 441-4586
Philippine Consulate General: 441-1640
Foreign Books and Periodicals: Magazine City, 3rd Ave. and Stewart, 441-4235; and Pike Place Market Newsstand, Pike St., 624-0140

Business Visitor's Needs

Banking: Seafirst Bank, 1001 4th Ave., 358-3000
Security Pacific Bank, 1301 5th Ave., 621-4111
Secretarial Services: Globe Secretarial: 624-3822
Copying and Printing: Kinko's: 292-9255
Messengers: American Messenger: 441-4555
Farwest Taxi: 622-1717
Medical Needs: Doctor referral: Valley Medical Center: 251-5129 (open 24 hours)
Dental referral: Seattle-King County Dental Society: 443-7607 (open 24 hours)
Pharmacies: Fred Meyer: 323-5256
Kelly Rose: 622-3565 (will deliver)
Hospitals: Saint Cabrini: 682-0500
Swedish Hospital Medical Center: 386-6000
Virginia Mason: 624-1144

Convention Centers

Washington State Convention and Trade Center, 700 Convention Pl., 447-5000, has 40,000 sq. feet of convertible exhibition space on the upper level and accommodates 10,000 people.
The Kingdome, 201 South King St., 296-3128; ticket information, 296-3111. Seats 65,000 people and has 153,000 sq. feet of floor space available.
Seattle Center, 305 Harrison St., 684-7200, can accommodate almost any convention, meeting, or banquet.
Seattle Trade Center, 2601 Elliot Ave., 728-8000, is a 55,000-sq.-foot area that encloses an atrium.

Entertainment, Sports, and Culture

Ticket Services: Ticketmaster Northwest: 628-0888
Sports: Baseball: Mariners, Kingdome, 296-3128
Basketball: Supersonics, Coliseum, 281-5850
Football: Seahawks, Kingdome, 827-9766
The Arts: The Seattle Center houses the Coliseum and is home to the Seattle Opera Company (443-4711), the Seattle Symphony (443-4747), and the Pacific Northwest Ballet (628-0888).

Dining: Four Stars and Our Stars

Hunt Club, 622-6400. Outdoor dining (seasonal) and English Inn decor; specialty is Northwest seafood.
Fuller's, 621-9000. Northwestern artists' original art throughout formal dining room and hotel. Moderately expensive Northwestern seafood and fowl.
Ivar's Indian Salmon House, 632-0767. Informal eating; specialty is alder-smoked salmon eaten Indian-style. Authentic tribal longhouse decor; very reasonably priced.
Mikado, 622-5206. Japanese cuisine; moderately priced; dark and funky ambiance.

Home Away from Home: Where to Stay

Alexis Hotel, First and Madison, 624-4844. Late 1800s building specializing in European-style luxury, elegance, and per-

SEATTLE TACOMA INTERNATIONAL AIRPORT
©H.M. Gousha

sonal service. Seattle Athletic Club and Rooftop Tennis. Singles start at $115.
Four Seasons Olympic Hotel, 411 University St., 621-1700. This historic landmark, opened in the 1920s, attracts Seattle society and top business executives. Features a solarium, health facilities, and fine dining. Singles from $140.
Westin, 1900 5th Ave., 728-1000. Tower rooms have a panoramic view of downtown Seattle while the opulent Palm Court and the restaurant Trader Vic's are business-savvy spots. Single rooms begin at $100.

Keeping Your Tone Away from Home

Bikers: Bicycle rental at the Bicycle Center, 523-8300, is a popular activity because Seattle's weather is so mild year round. King County Bicycle Hotline, 296-RIDE (296-7433).
Health Clubs: Metropolitan Health Club: 682-3966
Nautilus Northwest Athletic Club: 443-9944
YMCA: 382-5000

Shopping

The large department stores such as I. Magnin, Nordstrom, and Fredrick and Nelson offer some designer names like Gucci and Ralph Lauren. Rainer Square holds expensive shops like Littler's and Talbots.
At Pioneer Square specialty shops for antiques, handmade items, fresh fruits, vegetables, and seafood abound.
Tourist shops line the waterfront.
Florists and Gift Baskets: Charles E. Sullivan Florist: 624-1300
Cheers and Chocolates: 454-7780
Totem Smokehouse Gourmet Seafood: 443-1710

ST. LOUIS

Area Code: 314
Time Zone: Central
Weather: 321-2222
Police: 231-1212
Emergency: 911

St. Louis has had a history of rivers, roads, and rendezvous. The Missouri, Illinois, and Mississippi Rivers flow in and around St. Louis, making it the central interchange for any westward movement. St. Louis—with its welcoming Arch—remains the crossroads for 4 interstate highways, boasts an international airport, and services landlocked riverport traffic. Taking a trip on a riverboat is still possible; Dixieland jazz is the usual shipboard tune. And large corporations like McDonnell-Douglas, Ralston Purina and Anheuser-Busch help to make St. Louis stand out on the map.

Business Profile
Population: 2,492,000
Population Growth (1980-1989): 4.8%
Unemployment Rate: 5.5%
Fortune 500 Corporate Headquarters: 15

General Information Sources
St. Louis Convention and Visitors Commission: 421-1023
Visitors Center: 241-1764
Fun Phone: 421-2100

Getting There
By Air: Lambert-St. Louis International Airport (STO): 426-8028
Once you've landed: STO has one main terminal and 4 adjacent concourses. The baggage claim area abuts parking and public transportation.
Taxi rides take about 30 minutes and cost $17. Additional passengers are 50 cents. Try: Allen, 241-7722; Laclede, 652-3456; Yellow, 361-2345.
Bi-State Transit System, 231-2345, has a No. 104X express bus which operates M-F. The ride takes about 55 minutes and costs $1. Four buses are inbound for the airport, and 4 buses are outbound for downtown. Service from 6:30am to 8pm.
Limousines (private): Service is available with 24-hour reservations. Carey Limousine of St. Louis, 946-4114; Panache Limousine Service, 391-6981; Top Hat Limousine Service, 800-842-3998
Directions Downtown: St. Louis is 13 miles southeast of the airport. When leaving the airport from the car rental agency, turn left at the first light. Stay in the right lane and take I-70

East. Exit for downtown at Memorial Drive Stadium Exit.
Overland Adventures: *Route map:* St Louis has a beltway, I-270, which encircles the city on 3 sides and crosses over the Mississippi. I-70 travels through the city in a northwest to easterly direction. Highway 40 travels east and west through St. Louis, and I-170 is the north-south connector between Highway 40 and I-270. I-44 goes from St. Louis to the southwest, and I-55 comes from the south through the city and continues northeast into Illinois.
Bottleneck Busters: Avoid Highway 40 around rush hours. Downtown traffic is mild.
Trains: Amtrak, 550 S. 16th St., 800-872-7245. Amtrak connects St. Louis to major cites in the U.S. and in Canada.
Bus Service: Greyhound/Trailways Lines, 801 N. Broadway, 231-7800
Public Transportation: Bi-State Transit System, 231-2345, provides bus service to metropolitan St. Louis. Approximately 160 routes are available with the most heavily used routes on Kingshighway, Grant, Hanley, and Lindbergh. Local fares are 85 cents with 15-cent transfers; express fares are $1.15 and 15 cents for transfers.
Road Service and Repairs: AAA Auto Club, 576-7300; A&A Towing, 296-5222; Highway Patrol information, 434-3344
Parking Regulations: St. Louis has plenty of metered parking, or if you prefer parking garages, the daily fee is about $8.
Towed? Call 534-1204

FLYING TIMES
(in hours)
FROM
St. Louis
TO
Chicago: **1**
Los Angeles: **3½**
New York: **4**
Miami: **3**

International Travelers
International Services: World Affairs Council of St. Louis, 232 N. Kingshighway, 361-7333
Foreign Currency Exchange: Mercantile Bank, 8th and Locust, 425-2895
Mercantile Bank of St. Louis, STO, 429-1225
Translation Services: Accento Language Co., 6300 Harry Hines, 645-2214
Berlitz Translation Services, 200 S. Hanley, 721-1070
Foreign Books and Periodicals: Daily Planet News, 243 N. Euclid Ave., 367-1333

Business Visitor's Needs
Banking: Boatmen's National Bank, 1 Boatmen's Plaza, 466-6000
Commerce Bank of St. Louis County, 8000 Forsyth, 854-7463
Mark Twain Bank St. Louis, 620 Market, 621-4400
United Missouri Bank of St. Louis, 312 N. 8th St., 621-1000
Secretarial Services: A & R Secretarial Services: 458-2408
Kelly Services: 576-7787
Copying and Printing: Kinko's: 524-7549
Quick Print: 726-1110
Fax and Telex Facilities: Western Union: 800-325-6000
Messengers: Kwik Courier Systems: 569-1011
Lanter Company: 664-0643

Medical Needs: Doctor referral: Health Calls St. John's Mercy Medical Center: 569-6901

Dental referral: American Doctors and Dentist Referral Service: 429-1924

Pharmacies: 24-Hour Pharmacy: 721-2033

Walgreen's: 227-5828

Hospitals: St. Louis University Medical Center: 577-8000

Bethesda General: 772-9200

Barnes Hospital: 362-5000

Convention Centers

A. J. Cervantes Convention and Exhibition Center, 801 Convention Plaza, 342-5036; events line 342-5000. Convention Plaza covers 16 city blocks and 4 of those blocks make up the A. J. Cervantes Convention and Exhibition Center. 240,000 sq. feet of space is available for exhibits, and the center has 52 meeting rooms. The center is an easy walk from any downtown hotel. A large expansion of this convention center is slated to be finished by 1992. The new Convention Center Plaza Drive will connect 7th and 9th Sts. via an underground tunnel.

Kiel Auditorium, 1400 Market St., 241-1010. Kiel Auditorium is a multi-level facility with several separate areas. Exposition Hall has 90,000 sq. feet of exhibition space; Convention Hall can seat 10,500 and is the best spot for booths; the Opera House seats thousands; 4 large assembly halls and 11 meeting rooms round out the choices.

Entertainment, Sports, and Culture

Ticket Services: Gateway Tickets: 652-5000

Sports: Baseball: Cardinals, Busch Stadium, 421-3060

Hockey: Blues, Arena, 781-5300; box office 644-0900

Soccer: Storm, Arena, 781-6475; box office 644-0900

Horse Racing: Fairmount Park (Collinsville, IL), 436-1517

The Arts: The Muny, Forest Park, 361-1900, is an outdoor amphitheatre which presents musical theater during the summer months.

Opera Theatre of St. Louis, Loretto Hilton Center, 961-0644, presents both new and classic operas.

The Repertory Theatre of St. Louis, 968-4925. The Rep presents a variety of plays: classics, modern plays, musicals, comedies, and dramas.

St. Louis Symphony Orchestra, Powell Symphony Hall, 534-1700, is the second-oldest orchestra in America, has earned a Grammy Award, and presents a variety of musical programs throughout the year.

Dining: Four Stars and Our Stars

Anthony's, 231-2434, has a delectable French menu specializing in milk-fed veal and fresh seafood. Although expensive, the very good service diners receive makes this modern restaurant a must.

Faust, 241-7400. Reservations are required for this chef-owned restaurant which is decorated in the Tudor fashion with stained glass and tapestries. The continental menu has rack of lamb and jumbo shrimp, and the prices are moderate.

Agostino's Colosseum (Creve Coeur), 434-2959. This restaurant has a French and Italian menu with specialties like salmone al acciuga and costoletta di vitello. The dinners are moderately expensive, and the atmosphere is gracious with mirrored walls and background music. Reservations are required.

Home Away from Home: Where to Stay

Adam's Mark, 4th and Chestnut, 241-7400. Single rooms cost $90-$130, luxury level single rooms cost $125. When entering this hotel, be prepared to be greeted by 2 bronze horses in the lobby, and be sure to ask for a room with a riverfront view and a glimpse of the Gateway Arch. Good health facilities and nightly entertainment make this a popular place to stay.

Doubletree Hotel and Conference Center, 16625 Swingley Ridge Rd., 532-5000. Single rooms cost $100-$124, luxury level single rooms are $120. This hotel is away from the hustle and bustle of downtown, and yet it has great meeting and recreational facilities. Two pools, lighted tennis, golf, health club, and airport and local transportation are a few perks.

Hyatt Regency St. Louis Union Station, 1 Union Station, 231-1234 or 800-233-1234. Single rooms cost $90-$130, luxury level singles $135. The Hyatt is the focal point for the restored Union Station, once the heavily trafficked railroad station for trains traveling through the Midwest. The hotel's public areas have displays of rare marble, frescoed ceilings, and stained glass. The Hyatt has just about any service a business traveler might desire.

Keeping Your Tone Away from Home

Jogging and Biking: Forest Park is a terrific park for lots of activities but especially for jogging and biking. The park's paths are particularly scenic because they wander along a river. Wilmore Park and Queeny Park have biking paths. For more information call St. Louis City Parks and Recreation Department, 535-1503.

Health Clubs: YMCA: 436-4100

Public Golf Courses: Chesterfield: 469-1432

Forest Park: 367-1337

Shopping

Stores like Saks Fifth Avenue and Neiman Marcus reside in Plaza Frontenac. For shopping with an international flavor, try the boutiques offering gifts from around the world in West Port Plaza. St. Charles Rock Rd. and Lindburgh Blvd. sport some major department stores. Don't overlook St. Louis Centre and St. Louis Union Station which are in the heart of the downtown area. The sales tax is 5.9%.

Florists: Richter's Florists: 469-3800

Walter Knoll Florist: 352-7575

TAMPA

Area Code: 813
Time Zone: Eastern
Weather: 645-2506
Police: 223-1112
Emergency: 911

Tampa is the Suncoast's jewel in the crown, elected by executives as one of the 5 best cities for business. Often eclipsed by other Floridian hot spots like Miami or Orlando, Tampa's heat is generated from its astronomical growth and from its position as Florida's largest metropolitan area. Tampa, which means "sticks of fire," no longer relies upon cigar production as it did for 5 decades. Today the city has a balanced and diversified economy. Because Tampa is the state's largest port, it isn't surprising that it's also the world's largest shrimp center. Tourism, manufacturing, shipping, agricultural production, transportation, banking, and a growing medical and technology center are this city's major economic components. Teddy Roosevelt and his Rough Riders, who once trained in Tampa with Cuba's freedom fighters, would not have been surprised at Tampa's hard-won eminence.

Business Profile
Population: 271,523
Population Growth (1980-1990): 6%
Unemployment Rate: 5%
Fortune 500 Company Headquarters: 2

General Information Services
Tampa/Hillsborough Convention & Visitors Association: 223-1111
Greater Tampa Chamber of Commerce: 228-7777

Getting There
By Air: Tampa International Airport general information: 870-8700
Once you've landed: A taxi ride between the airport and downtown will take about 15 minutes and costs about $15. ABC Taxi, 872-TAXI (872-8294); United Cab, 253-2424; Yellow Cab, 253-0125.
Hillsborough Area Regional Transit (HART Line), 623-5835, has a downtown bus No. 30 which leaves from the red departure level about every 30 minutes, M-F, from 6:08am until 7:58pm. The fare is 60 cents and the trip takes about 30 minutes. Weekends, buses leave hourly: Sat. from 6:45am-7:35pm, and Sun. from 9:58am-5:40pm.
Limousines (private): Central Florida Limousine, 276-3730, provides 6am-to-midnight service to downtown Tampa. Follow baggage signs to the Ground Transportation lots. Reser-

vations are recommended; the cost is $10. Also: A VIP Limousine Service, 229-6555.
Directions Downtown: When leaving the airport take the exit to I-275 North. The airport is 5 miles from the city center. Take the Ashley Exit for the downtown area.
Overland Adventures: *Route Map:* A network of interstates and highways either skirt around or go through the Tampa Bay area. I-75 is the major north-south corridor which has just been completed. It runs north around and past Tampa toward Ocala and south to Sarasota and Fort Meyers. I-275 travels through St. Petersburg, heads east across Tampa Bay via the Howard Franklin Bridge, continues north into the heart of Tampa and connects again with I-75. Before the age of super highways, Route 41 (or the Tamiami Trail) was and continues to be a main north to south highway which passes through downtown Tampa. I-4 leads from the center of Tampa to points east as far as Daytona.
Bottleneck Busters: Rush hour in the morning, 7:30am-9am; and in the afternoon, 4:30pm-6pm. A toll is charged on the crosstown expressway between south Tampa and Brandon.
Trains: Amtrak connections for Miami in southern Florida or for as far north as Washington, D.C. can be made at 601 Nebraska Ave., 221-7600. The station is open from 8:30am-8pm.
Bus Service: Greyhound/Trailways Lines Terminal, 610 Polk St., 229-2112 or 800-531-5332 (Spanish speaking). Greyhound serves cities nationwide.
Public Transportation: Hillsborough Area Regional Transit (HART Line), 623-5835, has 50 bus routes in the Tampa Bay area. The fare is 75 cents and transfers are free.
Road Service and Repairs: AAA, 872-5911 (open 24 hours)
Parking Regulations: Downtown parking is limited. Try Allright Parking, 229-0325, a garage chain.
Towed? Call the Impound Lot, 225-5956

International Travelers
Foreign Currency Exchange: Tele-Trip Company, Inc., Tampa International Airport, main building opposite Airside E and F on the 3rd floor, 276-3665
Translation Services: Ad-Ex Worldwide: 800-223-7753
International Languages Services, 1944 Dodge Circle, Clearwater, 536-6309
Consulates: Mexican Consulate: 254-5960
Consulate of the Republic of Honduras: 229-2290
Colombian Consulate: 289-7949
Foreign Books and Periodicals: B. Dalton Books, 2009 Tampa Bay Center, 3302 Buffalo Ave., 879-5481
The Newsstand, Tampa Bay Center, 3302 Buffalo Ave., 877-5136

Business Visitor's Needs
Banking: Barnett Bank of Tampa, Barnett Plaza Office,101 E.

FLYING TIMES
(in hours)
FROM
Tampa
TO
Chicago: 2¾
Los Angeles: 5
New York: 2¾
Miami: 1

Kennedy Blvd., 225-2200
The Citizens and Southern National Bank of Florida, 402 E. Madison, 933-0331
First Florida Bank, 111 E. Madison, 224-1111
NCNB National Bank, 9389 N. Florida Ave., 935-4467
Secretarial Services: A Accurate Secretarial Services, Inc.: 264-2092
Executive Secretarial Services: 287-2587
Kelly Services: 264-0266
Copying, Printing, and Faxing: Kinko's: 988-3950 (24 hours)
Kwik-Kopy Printing: 289-1660
Sir Speedy: 273-0240
Messengers: Central Courier Systems: 247-7070
Corporate Courier, Inc.: 837-9198
Telex Facilities: Western Union: 800-527-5184
Medical Needs: Doctor referral: Ask-A-Nurse/St. Joseph's 24-hour Information and Physician Referral: 870-4444
Dental referral: Dental Association, Florida: 877-7597
Pharmacies: Rite Aid: 988-9876
Walgreen's: 985-8517
Hospitals: St. Joseph's: 870-4000
The Tampa General Hospital: 251-7100 (emergency room)
Doctors Hospital of Tampa: 879-1550

Convention Centers

Curtis Hixon Convention Center, 600 Ashley Dr., information: 223-8511; box office 223-8311. The main hall features 61,250 sq. feet of exhibition space; varied rooms provide an additional 25,000 sq. feet. Up to 8,000 people can be seated. Eight meeting rooms can also hold from 40 to 1,045 people.
Florida State Fairgrounds, 4800 U.S. 301, 621-7821. The exhibition hall has 86,000 sq. feet of space, room for 322 exhibits, and can seat 8,000 people. The facility is 6 miles from downtown Tampa.

Entertainment, Sports, and Culture

Ticket Services: Ticketmaster: 871-2993
Sports: Baseball: Cincinnati Reds (Spring Training), Plant City Stadium, 757-6712
Football: Tampa Bay Buccaneers, Tampa Stadium, 879-2827
Jai-Alai: Tampa Fronton, 831-1411
The Arts: Arts Council of Tampa, 229-ARTS (229-2787) provides recorded information about events.
Tampa Bay Performing Arts Center, 221-1045 or 800-955-1045. The Center is within walking distance of downtown hotels. However, walking to this location at night is not advised. Such entertainment as the Florida Orchestra, Tampa Ballet, and the Tampa Players perform here.
Tampa Theater, 223-8981, hosts theater performances, concerts, films, and lectures in a splendid Moorish Castle decor with an imaginative sky ceiling.

Dining: Four Stars and Our Stars

Four Stars: Bern's Steak House, 251-2421. Reservations required for this elegant dining and delicious food. Specialties include organically grown veggies, imported coffee, and excellent beef. Bathed in background music and surrounded by fine arts, this chef-owned restaurant's entrees range in price from $16 to $36.
Garrison's Harbour View, 229-5001. Lovely waterview and seafood specialties distinguish this eatery. Prices are moderate.

Home Away from Home: Where to Stay

Harbour Island, 725 S. Harbour Island Blvd., 229-5000. Tampa vistas and pretty Bay views abound. All the amenities like concierge, tennis, pool, health club benefits, plus bathroom phones in the suites. Singles $99 and up.
Sheraton Grand, 4860 W. Kennedy Blvd., 286-4400. Offers the usual advantages such as concierge, tennis and golf privileges, and a shopping arcade. Singles $99, doubles $114. Concierge or executive level is available: singles $150, doubles $155.
Hyatt Regency, 2 Tampa City Center, 225-1234. Singles cost $135. Pool, health club, concierge and valet parking are perks.

Keeping Your Tone Away from Home

Joggers and Swimmers: The city of Tampa's Parks and Playgrounds offers a variety of jogging opportunities: Horizon Park, Lowery Park, Bayshore Boulevard Drive. These locations also have public beaches so that weary runners can cool off pronto.
Health Clubs: American Fitness and Racquet Clubs: 831-9050
Nautilus Fitness Center Town & Country: 885-5190
YMCA of Tampa: 224-9622

Shopping

The Florida sales tax is 7%, but don't let this inhibit your enjoyment of this shopping mecca. In the Latin quarter of Tampa is Ybor City, a Cuban, Spanish, and Italian enclave 30,000 strong that dates back to the turn of the century when Vincente Martinez Ybor built his cigar factory—then the largest of its kind in the world. Now these splendidly renovated buildings contain among other attractions a variety of shops and boutiques. For more boutiques, as well as designers like Ralph Lauren and old stand-bys like Brooks Brothers, try Old Hyde Park Village. At The Shops on Harbour Island expect to find elite shopping like Land and Sea, Paul Harris, Alexanders, and Scruples. Both the Tampa Bay Center and Westshore Plaza are large malls.
Florists: Bel-Mar Florist and Greenhouses: 837-1498
Jennie's Flower Shop, Inc.: 872-8441
Si Simonds' Flower Fair: 253-0306

WASHINGTON, D.C.

Area Code: Washington, D.C.: 202; Virginia: 703; Maryland: 301 (Telephone numbers in this section are within the 202 calling area unless noted otherwise.)
Time Zone: Eastern
Weather: 936-1212
Police: 727-1010 or 727-4326
Emergency: 911

Now more than ever the place to be is Washington, D.C. Its major industries are tourism and government—not surprising given the fact that Washington houses the nation's treasures and that Capitol Hill is a power broker's dream. Ralph Nader's non-profit consumer watchdog organization coexists with defense contractors like Martin Marietta. The beauty and splendor of the Lincoln Memorial and the Washington Monument attract tourists while communications companies like MCI and Gannett are next door expanding their empires. This city probably has more variety than any other in the U.S., and the excitement that surrounds our nation's capital is infectious.

Business Profile
Population: 3,774,000
Population Growth (1980-1989): 16.1%
Unemployment Rate: 3%
Fortune 500 Corporate Headquarters: 8

General Information Sources
Washington, D.C. Convention and Visitors Association: 789-7000
Washington, D.C. Chamber of Commerce: 347-7201

Getting There
By Air: Washington National Airport general information: 703-685-8000
Dulles International Airport general information: 703-471-7838
Once you've landed: Washington National Airport handles domestic flights only and is across the Potomac River in Virginia about 4 miles from the capital. Although extremely busy, especially in the afternoons, the layout of this airport is simple. Baggage and ground transportation services are on the street level, and a quick walk will bring you to any of the 5 terminals. The airport has been under construction since 1988 and is scheduled to be finished in 1992 or 1993.
Dulles International Airport is about an hour from downtown Washington in northern Virginia. It handles both domestic

FLYING TIMES
(in hours)
FROM
Washington, D.C.
TO
Chicago: **2**
Los Angeles: **4**
New York: **1**
Miami: **2**

and international flights. Services are on the main floor in both the East and West wings. International flight passenger services are on the ground floor. Service on the Concorde is also provided at Dulles.
The Airports Terminal, 15th and K Streets, is an in-town terminal which makes checking into Washington-area airports a bit easier. Taxis offer the fastest transportation into Washington, D. C. From National, a rush hour ride takes about 30 minutes.; non-rush hour, 15 minutes; the cost is about $10. Some taxi services are: Capital Cab, 546-2400; Time Cab, 265-1367; Yellow Cab Co. of D.C., 544-1212.
A taxi cab ride from Dulles to downtown Washington costs about $30 and will take about an hour. Agree upon a price before leaving the airport. For 24-hour cab service call Airport Taxi, 703-471-5555.
Washington, D.C.'s Metrorail subway station is next to National's North terminal. Free shuttle rides are offered outside the baggage claim area. Either the Yellow or Blue Lines go from the airport station to downtown Washington. The subways run until midnight daily. For information call 637-7000.
Ground Transportation bus service, the Washington Flyer, 703-685-1400, makes stops at Washington National Airport, downtown Washington, Dulles International Airport, and the suburban Washington area. One way to downtown hotels is $5 and round trip is $8. One way to Dulles is $10 and round trip is $18.
For door-to-door service between Washington National Airport and Dulles International Airport, call Metropolitan Washington Airport Authority, 979-2803; Red Top Executive Sedan Co., 703-522-3300; Washington Car and Driver, 703-876-6700.
Limousines (private): Service is available with 24-hour advance reservations. To National: Congressional Limousine, 966-6000; Econo Sedan Service, 544-1846. To Dulles: Admiral Limousine, 554-1000; Moran, 337-2880 or 800-826-1119.
Directions Downtown: From Washington National Airport: Washington, D.C. is 4 miles north of Washington National Airport. When leaving the airport, take the George Washington Memorial Parkway into downtown Washington. From Dulles International Airport: Washington, D.C. is 26 miles east of Dulles. Leaving the airport take the Dulles Access Road. This road connects with I-66 which leads directly to downtown Washington.
Overland Adventures: *Route Map:* All major roads interchange with the Capital Beltway which surrounds the city. To the west the Beltway is numbered I-495. However, to the east the Beltway is part of I-95 which is the major link between Baltimore, MD in the north and Richmond, VA in the south. The Baltimore Washington Parkway, I-295, and U.S. 1 enter the city from the north; U.S. 1 and I-395 come to the city from the south in Alexandria and Arlington, VA. I-270 connects the Washington area with I-70 north at Fredrick, MD.

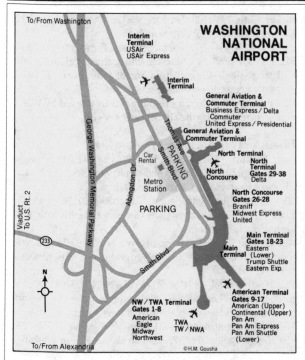

WASHINGTON NATIONAL AIRPORT

To/From Washington

Interim Terminal
USAir
USAir Express

Interim Terminal

General Aviation & Commuter Terminal
Business Express / Delta Commuter
United Express / Presidential

General Aviation & Commuter Terminal

Car Rental

North Terminal

North Concourse

North Terminal Gates 29-38
Delta

North Concourse Gates 26-28
Braniff
Midwest Express
United

Metro Station

PARKING

Main Terminal

Main Terminal Gates 18-23
Eastern
(Lower)
Trump Shuttle
Eastern Exp.

NW / TWA Terminal Gates 1-8
American Eagle
Midway
Northwest

TWA
TW / NWA

American Terminal Gates 9-17
American (Upper)
Continental (Upper)
Pan Am
Pan Am Express
Pan Am Shuttle
(Lower)

George Washington Memorial Parkway
Thomas Ave
Smith Blvd.
PARKING
Abingdon Dr.
Viaduct To U.S. Rt. 2
233
Smith Blvd.

To/From Alexandria

©H.M. Gousha

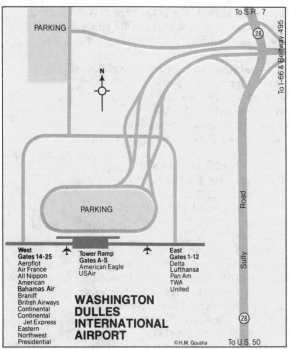

WASHINGTON DULLES INTERNATIONAL AIRPORT

To S.R. 7

PARKING

28

To I-66 & Beltway-495

PARKING

Road

Sully

West Gates 14-25
Aeroflot
Air France
All Nippon
American
Bahamas Air
Braniff
British Airways
Continental
Continental Jet Express
Eastern
Northwest
Presidential

Tower Ramp Gates A-S
American Eagle
USAir

East Gates 1-12
Delta
Lufthansa
Pan Am
TWA
United

28

To U.S. 50

©H.M. Gousha

Traveling east and west through D.C. is U.S. 50, and I-66 takes a short jog east and west between I-495 and downtown Washington.

The city has 4 quadrants, Northwest, Northeast, Southwest, and Southeast. Streets act as spokes connected to a wheel with the U.S. Capitol as the wheel's hubcap. North and south streets are numbered, east and west streets are lettered and diagonal streets are named after states. Remember to check the quadrant before going to any downtown address.

Bottleneck Busters: During the rush hours of 4:30pm-6:30pm, certain heavily trafficked arteries will have one way traffic only and the beltways slow to a crawl. Driving at night is dangerous in the Southeast quadrant and beyond the Anacostia River in the Northeast quadrant.

Trains: Amtrak, Union Station, 50 Massachusetts Ave., 484-7540 or 800-USA-RAIL (800-872-7245).

Bus Service: Greyhound/Trailways Lines, 1005 First and L Sts. N.E., 289-5155.

Public Transportation: The Washington Metropolitan Area Transit Authority, 962-1234, offers bus and subway service. Metrorail subway system has 69.6 miles of track. Fares and schedules are posted in every station, and the Blue, Yellow, Orange, and Red Lines go everywhere for about $1. The subways run about every 10 minutes and operate daily until midnight. The Metrorail and Metrobus service provide a coordinated public transportation system. Metrobus offers 400 bus routes, costs about 85 cents, and also operates daily until midnight. For further information call 637-7000.

Road Service and Repairs: AAA, 222-5000; Capitol Hill Chevron Station, 543-9456; Georgetown Amoco, 337-9759
Towed? Call 727-5000. Vehicle release requires a payment of $50 if the car has been towed by the city.

International Travelers

Information Sources: International Visitors Information Services, 733 15th St. N.W., 783-6540
Foreign Currency Exchange: Deak International, 1800 K St. N.W., 872-1427
First American Bank of Washington, 740 15th St. N.W., 637-4609
Sovran Bank, Dulles International Airport, 703-661-8861
TeleTrip, Washington National Airport, 979-8383
Translation Services: Berlitz Translation Services, 1730 Rhode Island Ave. N.W., 785-7840
Dulles International Airport, ground floor
Inlingua Translation Service, 1030 15th St., 289-8666
Washington National Airport, lower level
Foreign Books and Periodicals: News Room, 1753 Connecticut Ave. N.W., 332-1489
News World, 1001 Connecticut Ave. N.W., 872-0190 or 332-1487
Periodicals Plus, Metro Market, International Square Lower Level, Farragut West Metro Station, 1825 I St., 223-2526

Business Visitor's Needs

Banking: American Security Bank, 1501 Pennsylvania Ave. N.W., 624-4000
Crestar Bank, 1445 New York Ave. N.W., 879-6000

First American Bank, N.A., 740 15th St. N.W., 637-6100
The National Bank of Washington, 619 14th St. N.W., 537-2000
The Riggs National Bank, 1503 Pennsylvania Ave. N.W., 835-6000
Secretarial Services: Dulles International Airport, ground level
House of Typing, Inc.: 360-3933
Kelly Services: 296-2424
My Other Secretary: 429-1997
Washington National Airport, lower level
Copying and Printing: Dulles International Airport, ground floor
Kinko's: 547-0421 (open 24 hours)
Minuteman Press: 466-2826
Penn Press: 331-8224
Washington National Airport, lower level
Messengers: Cheetah Express: 823-4020
Pronto: 882-0291
QMS (Quick Messenger Service): 783-3600
Telex Facilities: Western Union: 624-0100
Medical Needs: Doctor referral: Physicians Home Service: 331-3888 (house calls to hotel, office, or home)
Dental referral: Dental Referral Bureau: 723-5323
Pharmacies: Giant Food Pharmacies: 628-0577
Midtown Pharmacy: 265-6333
Rite Aid Discount Pharmacies: 332-1718
Hospitals: D.C. General Hospital: 675-5000
Georgetown University Hospital: 687-0100

Convention Center
Washington, D.C. Convention Center, 900 9th St. N.W., 789-1600. The Convention Center is quite roomy with 800,000 sq. feet of exhibition space, 40 meeting rooms, and 4 exhibit halls.

Entertainment, Sports, and Culture
Ticket Services: Ticketplace: TIC-KETS (842-5387). Half-price tickets on day of performance.
Sports: Basketball: Bullets, Capital Center, NBA-DUNK (622-3865)
Football: Redskins, Robert F. Kennedy Stadium, 546-2222
Hockey: Capitals, Capital Center, 350-3500
The Arts: Information Services: Smithsonian Dial-A-Museum: 357-2020
Ford's Theatre, 347-4833, is slated to re-open in 1990. The state-of-the-theater at the time of Lincoln's assassination has been preserved in the museum below the Theatre.
Jazz is alive on Blues Alley in Georgetown.
John F. Kennedy Center, 467-4600, is home to the National Symphony, Washington Opera, and American Film Institute.

Dining: Four Stars and Our Stars
Jean Louis, Watergate Hotel, 298-4488. Jean Louis Palladin is the renowned chef whose specialty is nouvelle cuisine. Elegant, intimate, and very expensive.

Jockey Club, 293-2100. The Jockey Club was a favorite of the Kennedys, with a 1928 clubby ambiance.
Le Leon d'Or, 296-7972. Fabulous classic French menu.
Mr. K's, 331-8868. A Chinese menu featuring giant shrimp and frog's legs. Elegant touches of jade, porcelain and tapestries keep you enthralled.
Le Pavilion, 833-3846. This restaurant is frequented by Washington society and by the after-theater crowd.

Home Away from Home: Where to Stay
Four Seasons, 2800 Pennsylvania Ave., 342-0444. Single rooms range from $175-$205 and can have views of either the Chesapeake and Ohio Canal or the park.
Hay-Adams, 1 Lafayette Square N.W., 638-6600. Singles $125-$260. Country estate ambiance. Concierge, health club, and jogging track are included.
Ritz-Carlton, 2100 Massachusetts Ave. N.W., 293-2100. Single rooms go for $160-$240. With Federal decor, this restored hotel has charisma.
The Westin Hotel, 2401 M St. N.W., 429-2400. Single rooms cost $165-$225. Lots of glass and antiques grace the Westin, but best of all is the comprehensive fitness center.
Willard Intercontinental, 1401 Pennsylvania Ave, N.W., 628-9100. Single rooms are $175-$250. In the scheme of Washington's political history, the Willard, built in 1847, was where the term lobbyist was coined.

Keeping Your Tone Away from Home
Joggers, Hikers and Bikers: Washington is a jogger's heaven. The most popular run is along the Mall past the Washington Monument, the Reflecting Pool, and the Vietnam Veterans Memorial. Also available is the C and O Canal Towpath along the Potomac, 301-739-4200.
Health Clubs: City Sports: 659-9570
Westin Fitness Center, 457-5070

Shopping
Shopping in Washington, D.C. can be a full-time job. Boutiques abound on Capitol Hill. Connecticut Ave. stores have designers like Ralph Lauren, and the Connecticut Connection Mall is comprehensive. For European fashions, try the Watergate complex which has designer boutiques. Don't miss The Shops at National Place and the Old Post Office Mall.
Georgetown Park has lovely boutiques and a classy, old-town feel. The Mazza Gallery is a stop on the Metrorail and has Lord & Taylor and Saks Fifth Avenue nearby.
Florists: Baroque Blumenhaus: 833-1987
Georgetown Park Florist: 342-9402
The Window Box Florist: 347-7865